Traditional Bows and Wild Places

A Lifetime Afield with Bow and Arrow

Copyright © 2022 E. Donnall Thomas Jr.
All rights reserved.

This book, or parts thereof, may not be reproduced in any form without permission from the author.

Thomas Jr., E. Donnall
Traditional Bows and Wild Places
1. Bowhunting
2. Wildlife
3. Adventure travel
4. Conservation

ISBN: 9798218019228

Cover and interior design by: integrativeink.com
Photography by Don and Lori Thomas
Cover art by Bob White

Printed in the United States of America
1 3 5 7 9 10

Also by E. Donnall Thomas Jr.

Longbows in the Far North
Whitefish Can't Jump
Fool Hen Blues
Longbow Country
Dream Fish and Road Trips
To All Things a Season
The Double Helix
Outside Adventure: Fly-Fishing
By Dawn's Early Light
The Life of a Lab
Labs Afield
Hunting Labs
My Kingdom for a Lab
Redfish, Bluefish, Ladyfish, Snook
How Sportsmen Saved the World
Language of Wings
Have Bow, Will Travel

Traditional Bows and Wild Places

A Lifetime Afield with Bow and Arrow

By
E. Donnall Thomas Jr.

Foreword by
T.J. Conrads

To our children: Nick, Gen, Nicole, and Scott.

Acknowledgements

While much of this material has appeared previously in magazine form, all has been re-written for this book. Original sources include *Traditional Bowhunter Magazine, Bowhunter, Alaska Magazine, Gray's Sporting Journal, Big Sky Journal, Strung,* and *Backcountry Journal.*

I appreciate the opportunity to rework these pieces for this book. I am also indebted to the many fine editors I encountered along the way, who never stopped encouraging me and made me a better writer. I am especially grateful to TJ and Robin Conrads at *Traditional Bowhunter,* for letting me edit and contribute to the magazine for 30 years. Thanks as well to my valued hunting partners, many of whom are named in the following text. The "band of brothers" concept may sound like a cliché, but when you're packing out a moose or tracking a wounded bear, it quickly becomes real indeed.

Special credit goes to Bob White (bobwhitestudio.com) for the original cover art. Finally, I can't forget my wife Lori, without whose photography and editing this book would not have been possible.

Table of Contents

Preface xiii
Foreword xvii

Section I: Alaska 1
   1. Life and Death on the Tundra 3
   2. First Course: Caribou 7
   3. Ghosts of the Rain Forest 15
   4. Hunting the Food Chain 23
   5. The Animal Nobody Knows 29
   6. The Last Best Wild 35
   7. Moose John Miracle Bull 45
   8. Arctic Circle 53
   9. Bad Black Bears 61

Section II: Montana 71
   10. B-Tag Adventure 73
   11. Rattling 101 81
   12. Four Hundred Turkeys 87
   13. Nothing but a Hound Dog 97
   14. Fine Madness 109
   15. Dog Gone 117
   16. I Married a Serial Killer! 125
   17. Close Encounters 135
   18. Big Sky Pronghorns 143

 19. Smaller Bulls, Greater Satisfaction 151
 20. The Crazy Season 159

Section III: The Pacific 169
 21. Monsters from the Basalt Wall 171
 22. My Heart of Darkness 177
 23. Pick a Spot 189
 24. Getting Your Goat 197

Section IV: Around the Country 205
 25. Swamp Things 207
 26. Pigs Along the Border 215

Section V: Field Notes 225
 27. Hunting with the Bushmen 227
 28. The Art of the Ground Blind 237
 29. The Story Underfoot 245
 30. The Blue-Collar Super Slam 253
 31. The Once and Future Predator 261
 32. Heavy Bows Revisited 271
 33. Snow Never Lies 279
 34. Shooting Down 285
 35. Sterling's Arrow 293
 36. Did I Ever Tell You About the Time…? 301

About the Author 311
About the Photographer 313

Preface

As a lifelong outdoorsman, I have grown progressively more concerned about the state of modern big game hunting and the writing—not to mention television and other media—that describes it. As a model of the first-person hunting story, I have always looked to the work of Col. James Corbett. Although he wrote about hunting man-eating tigers and leopards in India, Corbett always kept his own courage and accomplishments in the background while he gave center stage to the wildness of the jungle where he hunted, the bravery of the native people in the Indian highlands, and above all the great cats themselves.

Nowadays, however, such considerations all too often seem forgotten as the writer or videographer rushes to promote products, sponsors, and himself. Even the conduct of the hunt seems to have grown irrelevant in the quest for the more and bigger "trophies" that have become the de facto measure of success in the field. These developments leave me saddened and offended on so many levels that I can't do the subject justice in this short space.

However, these concerns do explain the choice of material that follows. I have enjoyed my share of success with the bow, and the reader will indeed encounter some dead animals on the way to this collection's finish. As I look back over my decades in the field, many of these episodes remain personal favorites for a variety of reasons: the challenging nature of the hunt, the wildness of the terrain, the fascinating people I met along the way. These factors explain their inclusion in this volume, which was never intended to be a record of personal accomplishment.

If the previous three paragraphs sound familiar, that's because they are—*verbatim*. When I sat down to write a brief description of the rationale for the text that follows, I realized that I'd already said much of what I had to say on the subject before, in the preface to my last bowhunting book, *Have Bow, Will Travel*.

I have always felt that writing about hunting should include material accessible to non-hunters. Wildlife and wild places need all the help they can get now, and friction between its hunting and nonhunting advocates is counterproductive and unnecessary Accordingly, I have included material that any reasonable member of the second group should be able to read. In roughly half of the following chapters, nobody kills anything, not because I haven't done so (I have) but because I also wanted to address such topics as wildlife observations, wilderness advocacy, non-lethal outdoor skills such as tracking and archery, and other cultures I've encountered during my travels. I hope these might be of interest to non-hunting friends and family, and that they might help create a different image of hunters. Avid hunters should not regard these choices as dereliction of duty. Hunting is just about so much more.

There are practical reasons why this volume contains previously published material, including time I'd like to spend in the field or with my family and the scant monetary returns writing about the outdoors produces. I have deliberately chosen work from magazines that do not deal with bowhunting specifically so that readers of *Traditional Bowhunter*, for example, will have access to plenty of material new to them.

Many outdoor magazines emphasize instructional ("how-to") pieces. I've generally avoided that genre for several reasons. It would require me to pose as an expert when the only aspect of bowhunting I'm really good at is enjoying the wild. Over the years, I haven't learned all that much by reading. "How-to" doesn't really invite the kind of writing I enjoy. Nonetheless, anyone who does something enthusiastically for long enough will learn some things worthy of being passed along. Several chapters reflect this conclusion.

Don Thomas
Lewistown, MT

Foreword

I felt humbled when Don Thomas asked me if I would pen a foreword to the first book he has written in several years. As one of the most prolific authors in the so-called hook-and-bullet world today, Don is well-known—and well-read—by outdoorsmen and women from all walks of life, all over the world. He has an innate ability not only to entertain readers through his unique gift of the written word, but he also has a special talent of teaching through his stories. He has that ability to draw the reader into the story, taking him or her with him on his travels. That is a rarity in much outdoor writing today, and this book is filled with such adventures!

I first met Don over 33 years ago, just after I launched my publication *Traditional Bowhunter*® Magazine (*TBM*). I was a fan of his writing through several other outdoor publications I read, including *Gray's Sporting Journal, Outdoor Life, Field and Stream*, and several fly-fishing magazines when a submission from him hit my desk for the first time. That article, *Ashes to Ashes*, which appeared in the *Fall 1990* issue of *TBM*, was the beginning of a personal and professional relationship between us that has lasted to this day.

Don served as my Co-Editor for over 20 years before stepping back recently to spend more time traveling and writing. Don was instrumental at *TBM*, working with all our writers while simultaneously penning over a hundred articles and editorials over the years. He not only took a huge load of work off my shoulders, but he also built lasting, working relationships with all our writers and contributors, and he continues to produce excellent material for *TBM*.

Over the last three decades, Don and I have shared many hunting and fishing trips together, from Alaska, across dozens of states in North America, to South Africa and Zimbabwe, and a few other places around the world. He has been not only a partner in business, but a good friend who has shared may adventures with me. He has made me a better writer as well. For that, I am eternally grateful.

In this book, *Traditional Bows and Wild Places*, Don takes us all over North America, the Pacific, and Africa in search of game and wild experiences. After over 60 years of traveling, Don has a unique cache of experiences while hunting and fishing from all over the world. His ability to effortlessly weave a captivating story has earned him a loyal following from readers all over the world as well.

Across this wide spectrum of some 36 chapters, the reader will be exposed not only to stories of the chase, but also about the little things that make any outdoor experience memorable. After all, not all hunting or fishing trips end with an animal on the ground, or fish in the creel; the true outdoorsman and outdoorswoman sees beauty in all things wild. Don has a special talent to do just that in this collection of essays about many of his most memorable experiences during a well-lived life in the great outdoors.

There is much to learn in this book, another collection of great stories from one of our best outdoor writers today.

T.J. Conrads
Danskin Mountains, Idaho

Section I

Alaska

1.

Life and Death on the Tundra

"There's nothing in Alaska cuter than a baby moose," my nearest (and only) neighbor told me shortly after I moved north 40-odd years ago. He was a crusty old-timer, and the thought of him labeling anything "cute" practically defied belief. But then one day the following spring I got my first good look at a newborn moose calf, and I understood. The little guy was a living cartoon, all nose and ears and fuzzy fur, balanced improbably on a quartet of long, spindly legs that made each step look like a miracle. I'd seen plenty of whitetail fawns and elk calves, but nothing that could rival this for what could indeed only be described as cuteness.

The wilderness of the upper Alaska Peninsula where I used to guide bear hunters doesn't hold a lot of moose, but when you spend 18 straight hours every long spring day studying the landscape through binoculars and spotting scope, you see those that are there. My old front yard on the Kenai Peninsula offered better moose viewing than that whole valley, but we still saw moose every other day or so. We were always glad to spot them, for they provided a source of interest for the hunters, many of whom had never seen a moose before, and welcome relief from the monotony of studying alders, barren tundra, and old snow.

One pleasant day in May, a flicker of brown in the scrub across the valley caught my eye. We hadn't seen a bear since our hunters arrived days earlier. They were growing impatient, even though my partners and I knew it was only a matter of time until the bears began to descend along the valley floor from their denning sites high in the mountains. My initial excitement waned quickly when the movement turned into a moose rather than a bear, but at least it gave us something to look at and talk about.

We'd watched the cow pick her way slowly across the hillside for nearly an hour when she suddenly lay down and treated us to a remarkable spectacle. By the time we realized we were watching a live birth in progress, a soaking wet calf was tottering beside its mother in an awkward effort to keep its center of gravity atop its shaky legs. After a tentative step or two, the newborn followed its mother's lead into a nearby clump of brush, and the pair disappeared for the remainder of the day.

The following morning, I headed up the hill early to glass while the rest of the crew enjoyed pancakes and bacon back in the wall tent. I'd logged several hours of nothing by the time they joined me, but then the new day suddenly grew interesting when a large brown bear appeared across the valley. The first indication of anything out of the ordinary derived from the bear's direction of travel: back up the valley instead of down it, as most bears move after emerging from their dens. The bear walked with a deliberate gait, but every so often it would halt, point its nose up, and then tack back and forth across the hillside like a bird dog trailing a running pheasant. We quickly realized that although the bear was a mile downwind of the spot where we'd last seen the moose cow and calf, it was using its nose to stalk them.

Although we weren't sure where the moose were, we'd marked the patch of brush they'd disappeared into, and that's where the bear wound up. When the cow moose jumped from the cover and staggered awkwardly downhill in front of the bear, I realized we were watching a large-scale version of a mother bird's classical broken wing act, meant to lure a predator away from her nest. The cow deserved an Oscar as she led the bear down the hill, staying barely ahead of its claws.

Finally, the bear seemed to realize it was being had. Breaking off its pursuit of the cow, it headed back uphill toward the brush with the cow right behind. When the cow realized it couldn't lure the bear away a second time, it did the most courageous thing I've ever observed in the wild. Front hooves flailing like a windmill, she attacked the bear head-on. Brave as these efforts were, the moose was no match for the bear, and soon her shoulders were red with blood even though she somehow kept the bear far enough away to keep it from killing her.

For the second time, the bear indicated that the cow wasn't its prime objective and headed back up the slope, where it dived straight into the brush. Moments later the calf appeared, tossed above the alders like a mouse being toyed with by a house cat. However, the object was no longer a moose calf but a brown rag doll—bloody, lifeless, and broken.

The cow quickly recognized that she had lost the battle for her calf. Courage yielded to resignation as she turned away and walked downhill to do the best thing she could to contribute to the propagation of her species—recover from her wounds and hope she could breed successfully again that coming fall.

What's to make of this remarkable drama played out upon the tundra? This account, although rendered honestly, contains some inevitable anthropomorphism. What appears to us as courage is really just maternal instinct, complex innate behavior selected for over generations by virtue of its ability to produce more moose. But does that make it any less remarkable?

Many readers likely found themselves cheering for the moose to triumph over the odds and somehow save her calf, as did we. But the qualities we ascribe to the participants—bravery, viciousness—are just our own projections. Does a moose calf really have any more right to survival than a brown bear? At the end of the day, moose aren't brave, and bears aren't vicious. They're just moose and bears… and we're just humans trying to learn what nature has to teach us.

Back in the day I could pack a caribou out of almost anywhere. I'm older now.

2.

First Course: Caribou

A strenuous four-hour hike had taken me from the banks of the Mulchatna River to a ridge top overlooking a hidden basin that probably hadn't seen human footprints in years. As the late August sun finally began to burn away the last of the valley fog, I took a break and sat down to glass. When a brown bear sow with two cubs in tow appeared at the head of the basin, I carefully noted her position and direction of travel, not because I was hunting bears but because I didn't want her hunting me. Then as my binoculars swept the opposite hillside, I noticed an unusual cluster of barren brush protruding above a strip of scrub willow. Careful study finally convinced me that I was looking at a bedded bull caribou's sweeping antlers.

I spent nearly an hour studying the terrain before I set off on the stalk, memorizing landmarks, ensuring that the bull was alone and above all monitoring the progress of the sow. Finally, I shouldered my pack and set off on an approach calculated to bring me over the far ridge on top of the bull with the wind in my face. Since I was hunting with a longbow, I didn't want to see the caribou again until he was less than 20 yards away.

A lot of things had to go right for this ambitious plan to work, but the wind held steady, the bull remained in bed, and the bears continued out of harm's way over the top of the basin. An hour later, I rose slowly to my knees and identified the velvet tops of the caribou's antlers right where I expected them.

Despite our proximity, the bull didn't offer much of a target. With an arrow in place on my bowstring, I waited patiently for him to rise and savored the irony of the situation. Often, caribou seem to be in a constant state of motion, but I'd found one that didn't want to move at all. Finally, the biting flies exceeded his tolerance, just as they were about to exceed my own. When the animal lurched to his feet, I came to full draw and sent a cedar arrow whistling through his chest. Moments later I watched him fold into the tundra as gracefully as a dying swan.

Field dressing chores completed, I glassed the basin again for bears and set off for a pre-arranged rendezvous with my hunting partner. Meeting him on schedule, I gave him the good news and the bad news, which happened to be one and the same: the bull was big, and he was dead. A hard day's work lay ahead of us. No matter: this was what we had come for, and as events unfolded, I had an opportunity to repay him for his effort by helping him pack out a bull of his own a few days later. Majestic antlers, delicious steaks, breathtaking terrain, and memorable companionship—all essential elements of a good caribou hunt, one of Alaska's signature outdoors experiences.

Circumpolar in distribution, caribou range from Labrador to Alaska in the New World, from Siberia to Norway in the Old. Despite considerable variation in size and appearance, all belong to a single species: *Rangifer tarandus*. In North America, sporting organizations recognize five subspecies as distinct for the purpose of classification and record keeping: woodland caribou in Newfoundland, Quebec-Labrador caribou in the rest of eastern Canada, central barren ground caribou in the Northwest Territories, mountain caribou in the Canadian Rockies and the barren ground caribou of Alaska and the Yukon. Distinctions blur along the borders of these ranges and some mountain caribou may inhabit Alaska along the

Canadian border. Practically, it's safe to assume that Alaska caribou belong to the barren ground subspecies.

A Barren Ground bull on the tundra in autumn.

Caribou demonstrate several distinct biologic traits. Caribou cows are the only female deer that develop antlers. Cows have smaller antlers than mature bulls, but hunters still need to exercise caution in areas where harvest is legally restricted to one sex. Highly aquatic, caribou routinely swim lakes and rivers while migrating and readily take to the water to evade wolves, their principal predators. Splendidly adapted to the arctic environment, their splayed, convex hoofs provide sure footing in boggy tundra and snow.

Those hoofs are responsible for a topic of frequent debate. Caribou make a distinctive clicking sound as they walk, which sometimes provides a useful clue to their presence. The source of the sound remains controversial, as some observers argue that it arises from hoofs while others attribute it to tendons in the lower leg. Hunting in Africa, I was surprised to hear an identical sound coming from eland as they walked and to listen to the same argument regarding its origin. Photographing game from a pit blind gave me an opportunity to observe walking eland with my eyes at ground level. The characteristic clicks clearly arose when the splayed lobes of each hoof struck each other as the animals raised their feet from the sand. I feel confident that the same mechanism applies to caribou. Let that longstanding North country debate come to rest!

Compared to the moose that frequently occupy the same area caribou may look small, but size is always relative and all North American land mammals looks small compared to a moose. Mature barren ground bulls weigh 400-500 pounds and will yield around 200 pounds of boned meat, making a challenging but manageable load when it comes time to pack one out. Even though many Alaskans prefer moose on the table, caribou venison is delicious.

Caribou antlers are the most complex of any deer. While their basic structure—shovels, bez points, rear points or "backscratchers", sweeping main beams and long top tines—remains more or less constant among mature bulls, no two look exactly alike. True "double shovels" occur rarely. Bulls begin to shed their velvet mid-August. By the time the rut begins in late September, mature bulls look their most dramatic, with polished, mahogany horns and flowing white throatlatches.

With the possible exception of the black bear, the caribou is Alaska's most widely distributed big game animal. Alaska caribou occur in relatively distinct populations ranging in size from hundreds of animals on the Kenai Peninsula to hundreds of thousands in the Western Arctic herd. Almost all of Alaska's Game Management Units have some caribou season except those in Southeast. Seasons and limits are usually more restrictive in road accessible areas, where drawing or registration permits may be required. Favorite caribou hunting areas include remote parts of southwestern Alaska, the Alaska Range, and the Brooks Range. The Porcupine herd's annual summer migration from Alaska's Arctic Coastal Plain eastward into Canada is one of the continent's most spectacular wildlife events, although logistics make the area difficult to hunt. (See Chapter 6.)

As always, expending more effort to reach a wilderness area generally results in a more satisfying hunting experience.

Seasons and limits vary considerably by GMU, but generosity can be deceptive. While some seasons open in July, hunters will face meat care problems and see bulls with incompletely developed horns that early in the year. Hunting caribou after mid-October may mean facing highly demanding weather conditions in the field. August and September are prime months in most areas. As always, consult Alaska's complex game regulations well before taking to the field.

Because they receive so little hunting pressure, wilderness caribou are relatively easy to stalk even in the open terrain they prefer. Their sight and hearing are fair at best, but they have good noses, so wind direction is always the prime consideration when planning a stalk. While caribou herds often appear at great distances on open tundra, a careful approach will often bring the skilled hunter into surprisingly close range.

Despite their size, caribou are thin-skinned and light-boned and aren't particularly tenacious. Any archery tackle adequate for deer should suffice for caribou, although the nearly universal presence of brown/grizzly bears in caribou country justifies erring on the heavy side.

Visiting hunters familiar with the highly migratory Quebec-Labrador herd often ask me where the caribou will be in a given area at a specific time of year, often because they've had a bad experience and "missed the migration" in Quebec. I seldom know the answer, and that's because the caribou themselves seldom know. While Alaska caribou do migrate, their movement patterns in some herds are often unpredictable. Fortunately, good caribou country almost always holds some animals, nullifying the "feast or famine" phenomenon common in eastern Canada. It's best to rely on current local knowledge from a resident or air charter service to get you into an area with animals and hunt hard once you arrive. There may follow days when you see ten caribou and days when you see ten thousand, but you should see game—and it only takes one to end a hunt.

How does one choose a starting point for a first Alaska caribou hunt? Options abound, but after years of experience with caribou across the state, here's how I would go about it. I'd hunt late August-mid September, when meat care in the field is easier than it is earlier, and bulls have largely shed their velvet. Instead of worrying about locating large concentrations of animals, I'd cover a lot of ground and glass the ridge tops for isolated mature bulls trying to escape heat and flies. When I located the right caribou, I'd take my time, study the wind and terrain, and move in. Alaska offers countless variations on the theme, but that version has always worked for me.

Now back to our original thesis: why caribou make an ideal quarry for novice Alaska hunters, even among a wealth of challenging big game species.

Consider legal considerations first. Non-resident hunters after sheep, goat, and brown/grizzly bear must hunt with a registered guide. Financial considerations and the appeal of hunting on your own eliminate those possibilities for many. Furthermore, experienced resident hunters know how much time one can spend pursuing those animals without ever taking a representative of the species.

Black bear and Sitka blacktail are at least locally abundant and both can be challenging to hunt. But deer and black bear can be hunted elsewhere, an important consideration for visitors interested in a unique Alaska experience.

Moose are an obvious potential quarry for a first Alaska hunt, and I've certainly enjoyed my share of time hunting them. But because of their low population density and habitat preferences, moose can be difficult to locate even under the best conditions. Moose populations fluctuate, and antler restrictions apply in many areas. Furthermore, as experienced Alaskans know, the best way to ruin a good moose hunt is to shoot a moose. The physical demands of packing out a thousand pounds of moose meat inevitably limits where you can hunt and what you can shoot. I fare better in the Bush on a longer leash.

Caribou, on the other hand, are impossible to hunt in other parts of the country. With some exceptions, Alaska caribou populations are stable, and seasons remain generous. With a fit hunting partner or two, you can pack a big bull out of just about anywhere in one trip, leaving you free to roam the tundra at will. In good caribou country, you should see game, possibly in staggering numbers.

The satisfaction of a successful caribou hunt derives from more than venison and antlers. True icons of the Far North, caribou define Alaska hunting in intangible ways no other game species can rival. The sight of a caribou herd grazing freely across the tundra has a unique capacity to fix the setting in the deepest reaches of the memory. Win, lose or draw in the stalk that follows, you'll always know that you've hunted Alaska.

3.

Ghosts of the Rain Forest

High in southeast Alaska's sub-alpine muskeg, the vegetation underfoot formed an intricate floral mosaic of color and texture. At another time, the naturalist in me might have yielded to the temptation to stop, explore, and analyze. But after catching a glimpse of brown hide in the stunted evergreens between the muskeg and the towering forest below, I'd made a sudden transition from observer to predator. Easing gently back and forth into the wind, I finally reestablished visual contact with my quarry, a Sitka blacktail buck feeding along the edge of the trees.

The deer was only fifty yards away, a range that would have marked the end of the hunt had I been carrying a rifle. But as always, I was hunting with my bow, and I still needed to cut that distance in half. Gauging the vectors of wind and terrain, I plotted an approach to a tree that looked like an ideal spot to intercept the buck.

Steeped in caution by the area's robust wolf population, local blacktails usually found a way to avoid the proximity that bow and arrow demand. But this stalk, like a well-conceived gambit on a chessboard, worked to perfection. Just as I reached the tree, the buck wandered back into view less than 20 yards away, his red summer coat glowing in the midday sun. At that range, I could count his eyelashes and listen to the sound of his teeth grinding as he browsed. Despite the enormity of the wild terrain surrounding us, I felt as if the buck and I were sharing a room together.

But my hunt still wasn't over. Discipline is paramount to the bowhunter, and with the deer quartering slightly toward me, I needed him to turn and expose his ribs without interference from his shoulder. This needed to happen before the fickle mountain wind swirled and betrayed my presence to that keen nose, but there was nothing I could do but wait. While the middle three fingers of my right hand played nervously against the bowstring and the buck continued to feed, I took advantage of our impasse to consider what a remarkable and under-appreciated game animal the Sitka blacktail deer can be.

Back when I first moved to Alaska, I promptly fell under the spell of the north's signature big game animals and had difficulty imagining why anyone would want to travel to wet, windy places to hunt a miniature version of the West's familiar mule deer. Common to new arrivals, that attitude reflects ignorance about the Sitka blacktail and the lure of the wild places this unique little deer calls home.

While caribou, moose, wolves, and grizzlies typify Alaska wildlife in the common imagination, all are newcomers to the area themselves, at least according to the time frame of biological history. These species are all descendants of Eurasian animals that crossed the Bering Sea land bridge as recently as 10,000 years ago, along with human immigrants. On the other hand, fossil records indicate that deer have inhabited North America for some four million years, developing from common ancestors into whitetails in the east and blacktails on the Pacific coast, eventually producing the hybrid mule deer.

Today's Sitka blacktail, Columbian blacktail, and mule deer are all members of the species *Odocoileus hemionus*, but the first has changed least of all over time, as reflected by certain anatomic and behavioral features. Sitka blacktails run with a peculiar, splay-legged gait reminiscent of caribou, likely an adaptation to the slick footing in the damp climate familiar to both. In contrast to the whitetail, which relies on speed, and the mule deer, which uses its bounding gait to outdistance pursuit in rough terrain, the Sitka blacktail primarily depends on stealth to elude predators in thick coastal forests. Both structurally and functionally, the Sitka blacktail is anything but a pint-sized version of the continent's other deer.

In fact, they aren't even that small. Mature bucks generally weigh 120-140 pounds, but weights of 200 pounds have been recorded. (Believe me, by the time you've packed one out through several miles of typical coastal habitat, an average buck can feel even heavier.) And every pound of that venison should be cause for celebration. Many experienced Alaskan hunters regard blacktail meat as the best of the best, surpassing even sheep and moose on the table.

Sitka blacktail antlers lack the dimensions of their cousins' farther south, but they display a special character of their own: compact yet heavy, often stained a deep mahogany through rubbing on undergrowth. Besides, if you share my conviction that the true measure of a trophy lies in the effort expended in its pursuit, few deer in the world can rival Alaska's.

Whether motivated by a desire for antlers, prime table fare, or both, increasing numbers of hunters are heading to the field for deer in Alaska each fall. For out-of-state visitors and residents of Alaska's south-central population centers, that usually means a trip to Kodiak, which offers abundant game and relatively open terrain conducive to spot-and-stalk hunting. While I've enjoyed many memorable weeks chasing blacktails on Kodiak, I've spent more time hunting them in Alaska's southeastern panhandle, for a variety of reasons in addition to the fact that I once lived there.

That's where Sitka blacktail deer *belong*, and I'm the kind of hunter who appreciates such nuances. Blacktails have now inhabited Kodiak and the Prince William Sound area for so long it's easy to forget that these deer are the result of planned introductions decades ago. In fact, the Sitka blacktail is native only to Alaska's panhandle, the northern coast of British Columbia, and adjacent islands. This coastal terrain constitutes the world's largest temperate rain forest, and even after all the time I've spent there, the scenery and proximity to the sea are still enough to take my breath away when game proves scarce.

As an added bonus, it's possible to hunt deer in parts of Southeast without worrying about brown bears, which, in that area, inhabit only the mainland and so-called ABC islands (Admiralty, Baranof, and Chichagof). I enjoy calling blacktails as discussed below, but I learned years ago that deer aren't the only animals that respond to fawn bleats on Kodiak. Since I dislike lugging around a firearm for bear protection, in brown bear country I get nervous hiking through thick brush in the dark with a load of meat in my pack. Hunting the numerous islands in southeast that contain deer but no brown bears obviates those concerns.

Harvest statistics confirm the wisdom of choosing Southeast as a blacktail destination for purely practical reasons. Game Management Unit 4 (the ABC islands) produces more deer than any other in the state and the harvest in GMU 2 (Prince of Wales and adjoining islands) rivals Kodiak's.

Deer season in southeast generally begins in early August. At that time of year, mature bucks concentrate in bachelor groups at high elevation. Coastal alpine provides superb stalking conditions as well as stunning scenery, with open terrain that allows glassing but enough contour to allow stalking into archery ranges. Early season bucks will likely still be in velvet. In many ways, August hunting offers the most predictable opportunity to locate big deer, provided you can reach them. Accessing the alpine often requires hours of steep climbing through thick brush at lower elevations, although flying in to a high mountain lake can reduce the workload considerably.

Bucks begin to filter out of the alpine to join does at lower elevations mid-September, although weather can affect these seasonal movement patterns. For the next month or so, finding deer in thick cover at intermediate elevations can optimistically be described as a challenge.

Fortunately for frustrated deer hunters, the onset of the rut in late October initiates a surge in deer activity. Bucks move constantly in search of does and can be found anywhere they are present. Nonetheless, deer can still be hard to locate because of thick cover, which makes them much more difficult to spot than in more open terrain like Kodiak's.

But the rut also provides an opportunity to employ an exciting Alaska deer hunting technique: calling. Over the course of a long career in the field, I've enjoyed calling everything from turkeys to moose into bow range but have seldom seen any animal respond to a call quite like a Sitka blacktail doe. Under certain conditions, their determined response to a fawn bleat can be amazing. A few seasons back, an experienced hunting partner had a doe knock him over when he made one bleat too many.

Unlike most animals, blacktail does responding to calls will often remain in the vicinity for some time even when they have the hunter in sight. While solitary bucks are less likely to respond to calling, during the rut they will sometimes follow does in to close range. Bucks will respond to calls on their own too, although they tend to approach much more slowly and cautiously. Over the years, I've coaxed does in to touching distance with a wide variety of deer and predator calls, although those with a higher pitch produce the most consistent results. Whatever the choice of calls, this method offers a unique opportunity to get close to elusive bucks during the rut. But if you are hunting in brown bear country, remember to be prepared for an unpleasant surprise every time you blow a deer call. On one Kodiak Island hunt, my two hunting partners—one of whom had drawn a bear tag for that area—decided to see if they could attract a brown bear with a deer call. The harrowing success they enjoyed on their first attempt consigned that plan to the "seemed like a good idea at the time" pile.

Alaska's generous deer seasons run through December in many areas, and heavy late season snows can push blacktails all the way down to the beach. Short days and harsh weather can make hunting difficult, but relatively easy access by boat still allows a significant harvest then.

Because of better security cover, blacktails in southeast Alaska generally avoid the large fluctuations in population numbers that harsh winters sometimes produce on Kodiak. Nonetheless, good resource stewardship remains an obligation for every hunter. Because wolves arrived in North America recently in biological terms, blacktails are poorly adapted to defense against them, and wolves prey significantly on deer throughout many parts of Southeast. However, population studies show that deer generally select habitat with good cover and high wolf numbers over areas with poor cover and few wolves, reflecting the importance of good winter habitat to their survival. Old growth forest, with trees at varying stages of development, provides that kind of habitat. Unpopular as this opinion may be in certain circles, the bulk of scientific evidence suggests that clear-cut logging practices ultimately cost Alaskans deer, a factor to consider in future resource management.

Back on that lonely mountainside, all this lore and natural history was about to reach a conclusion of its own. After what felt like an interminable wait on my part, the buck turned broadside before the wind betrayed me. Rising slowly from a crouch, I mentally isolated a spot on his side, drew my bow and released, sending a heavy cedar arrow through the center of his chest. He never knew what hit him, and moments later I watched him fold to the ground for good.

Sadness on my part? Sure—there always has to be a little. But I'd taken this deer from a distance at which a wolf would have been lethal, too. At the end of the day, I was just a descendant of another predatory species that crossed the land bridge 10,000 years ago trying to find something good to eat in the brave new world on the other side.

Fortunately, Alaska still has room for us all.

4.

Hunting the Food Chain

Few colors in nature resemble the coat of a prime fall black bear. That's technically a misstatement since black represents the absence of color on the visual spectrum. But save for ravens and an African sable's hide, I can't think of anything natural that looks remotely as black as *Ursus americanus*, especially when light rain and warm autumn light have combined to emphasize a good hide's glossy highlights. Throughout much of their range farther south, black bears come in a variety of shades ranging from cinnamon to blonde, but color-phase black bears are extremely rare in Alaska, and a glimpse of true jet-black hide through the binoculars usually means nothing else.

Hence my immediate interest when I spotted the distinct black dot on the open tundra a mile away across the valley. I didn't need my glasses to tell me I was looking at a bear, but I pulled them out of my daypack anyway and spent some time studying the opposite hillside, assessing the bear's size, confirming the absence of cubs, and noting landmarks for the upcoming stalk. Although nominally hunting caribou, black bear season was in progress, and I seldom pass up an opportunity to try stalking within bow range of a good boar.

With my quarry confirmed as such and details of the terrain committed to memory, I finally set off on a long, circular approach that left me a hundred yards above and downwind of the bear. Although their eyesight is relatively poor, bears have good ears, and their noses are the keenest of any game animal in the north. Experienced hunters quickly learn that wind is everything when stalking bears, especially at the intimate distances the bow demands.

From my new position, I had the wind but little else. A soaking belly-crawl down a low line of brush allowed me to cut the distance nearly in half, but at that point I ran out of cover while still out of range. Taking up position behind a clump of alders, I settled in to do what predators of many species have done for ages: wait.

One of the incidental pleasures of hunting with the bow is the amount of time its limitations obligate the hunter to spend in the company of wild animals. It's no coincidence that most of the best amateur naturalists I know are bowhunters (and most of the best bowhunters I know are amateur naturalists). Often denied the ability to make things happen in the field, we perforce spend countless hours every season observing game animals at close range, animals that rifle hunters often would already have dressed and packed back to camp. No disrespect intended toward those who hunt with firearms, but bowhunters' limited "success" by conventional standards does have its compensations.

For the next hour or so, the bear provided me with plenty. The time was late September, and the bear had already felt the stir of the changing seasons. Instinctively aware of an upcoming date with his winter den, the boar circled aimlessly through the lush carpet of berries underfoot in a driven effort to consume as many calories as possible and convert them into fat prior to hibernation. I sensed that given enough time, the bear would eventually wander into bow range unless the breeze switched and betrayed my presence first.

Insulated from the elements by his thick autumn coat, the bear looked a lot more comfortable than I felt, especially after I'd spent an hour motionless in the cold, gray drizzle. Every few minutes, I'd rise to one knee to check on the bear's location before curling back up into a ball at the base of the alders. Over the course of many seasons, I'd learned plenty about the fine art of patience, but I also recognized that at some point I would have to disengage and begin the long hike back to camp unless I wanted to spend the night on the tundra.

But the bear never let it come to that. The next time I rose to monitor his position, the berry patch looked empty. Unable to understand how the animal had disappeared, I rose a little further and saw a line of black hair on the other side of the alders barely a bow's length away. Quickly calculating the bear's route, I nocked an arrow and turned into position for a shot as he came around the brush. Suddenly we were face to face, and when he stopped to shake his wet coat like a dog, the water that flew from his hide anointed me. Frontal shots are anathema to bowhunters because arrows penetrate bone poorly, but by the time I started to draw the bear had already stepped by without seeing me, offering a perfect broadside. Even at point blank range, the hunting archer must have the discipline to pick an imaginary spot for a target rather than shooting at the whole animal, and I did. The arrow passed through the bear's chest as if he were made of feathers, and moments later he collapsed without ever realizing what had happened, which was probably fortunate for me. I later measured the range of the shot at four feet.

Bowhunters often neglect to base practical calculations on the possibility of success. Far from camp in deteriorating weather, I realized that I'd committed myself to a miserable slog back to the tent in the dark. But as I set to work detaching the hide and boning out the backstraps, I told myself that the hours of labor ahead were nothing but the price of admission to the show.

And what a show it had been.

With the exception of caribou, black bears are the most numerous and widely distributed big game animals in Alaska, with generous seasons and limits in almost every part of the state except Kodiak, the Alaska Peninsula and the North Slope. I've targeted them specifically from the southeastern panhandle to the heart of the interior and pursued them as targets of opportunity while hunting everything from blacktail deer to moose. But Alaska is a huge place with plenty of thick cover in which animals as cunning as bears can easily disappear. Finding them, as usual, depends above all else on an intimate knowledge of the quarry.

Bears – black and brown – are true omnivores, a surprisingly rare trait in the animal kingdom shared with only a few other species including our own. Bears don't just eat everything; they eat a *lot* of everything, a biological necessity for animals that spend almost half of every year living off fat stores accumulated during the other half. Bottom line: find the food and you will have found the bears.

During the spring season, preferred ursine food sources usually consist of emerging forbs and grasses, supplemented by winter-killed carrion. While I've spent countless memorable days stalking spring bears along coastal beaches and the interior's receding snowline, there's a special magic to hunting bears during the fall.

Why fall bears? From late August until mid-October, bear habitat from high alpine along the coast to interior tundra comes alive with color, offering the most spectacular scenery of the year. With hunting seasons open for other species, black bears offer additional opportunities for hunters after other game, and hunters targeting salmon streams can enjoy great fishing right along with the bears. While many experienced hunters think the very best hides come from spring bears, hides are certainly more consistent in the fall, when rubbing is not a problem.

Hunting fall food sources basically means one of two things: berry patches or salmon streams.

Anadromous fish play a unique role in Alaska's biologic life cycles. Despite its natural splendor, the far north would be a remarkably sterile ecosystem if it weren't for the huge infusion of organic nutrients that arrives every summer courtesy of salmon fighting their way upstream to spawn and die. Distasteful as it may be for salmon anglers to think of their favorite quarry as fertilizer, that's the biologic reality. The fish drive the food chain, all the way from aquatic plants and insects at the bottom to eagles and human beings at the top, and no species appreciates this natural bounty more keenly than bears.

Nothing concentrates bears as intensely as heavy salmon runs, although in areas with lots of streams to choose from they may not be distributed randomly. It's generally easy to tell when you're on the right stream. If you're not seeing lots of fresh tracks and fish carcasses marked by tooth and claw, look somewhere else. While bears can be found on streams at any time of day, they're most active at last light. I generally try to set up hunts so that I have a favorable wind while carefully still-hunting likely areas just before dark. Distracted by fish (as I am myself when carrying a fly rod), salmon stream bears often allow careful hunters a relatively easy approach to close range, an obvious advantage for bowhunters.

But there are two important drawbacks to hunting black bears along salmon streams. In areas that support both black and brown bears, hunters need to be alert to the possibility of an unexpected close-range encounter with an aggressive grizzly, and salmon stream bears are virtually inedible.

Over the years, I've dined enthusiastically on all manner of wild game ranging from alligator to mountain lion. Spring black bear meat is quite good (although it should always be cooked thoroughly to avoid the possibility of trichinosis). So is meat from fall bears taken in the high country. Bears that have been feeding regularly on salmon, however, produce the worst tasting game meat I've ever encountered. The state of Alaska acknowledged as much when it enacted its meat salvage law for black bears a few years ago (a principle I heartily endorse). Hunters are now required to pack out black bear meat in the spring but not during the fall (consult regulations for details). Fair enough, but I still prefer to salvage all my wild game for consumption, a good argument for hunting fall bears in another of their favorite dining areas: berry patches.

In the mountain west, hunting berry-eating bears in high bush shrubs like chokecherry and serviceberry can be difficult because of the thickness of the cover. In Alaska though, many choice berry species grow on open tundra where feeding bears are visible from long distances, a perfect recipe for classic spot and stalk hunting. Despite the open terrain, scattered brush and rolling contour often provide surprisingly good cover, and soft, damp tundra offers the quietest footing imaginable. Factor in stunning autumn colors and the opportunity to enjoy eating some fresh berries myself and it's easy to understand my enthusiasm for stalking fall bears in the high country.

Over the years, I've enjoyed particularly good berry patch bear hunting on the Kenai Peninsula and Game Management Units 17 and 19 west of the Alaska Range, although similar opportunities abound throughout the interior. Even in coastal areas, bears often seem to prefer berries to fish, although in any given year their distribution will depend on the relative strength of the berry crop and local salmon runs. Furthermore, tagging studies have shown that individual black bears rarely spend more than two weeks eating fish, so fall bears may make good table fare even in areas with salmon streams nearby. The key to finding them is studying the sign, since bears leave a lot of it. If you're not seeing it on the salmon streams, it's time to head to the hills.

Often overlooked by hunters intent on more glamorous game, fall black bears provide an excellent opportunity to enjoy hunting Alaska's wilderness, whether the goal is a 7-foot hide from the coast or a winter's worth of stew meat from the interior. Because of their voracious appetites during the fall, black bears are seldom hard to find once you've learned what they're eating. From then on, they're there to enjoy, whether you choose to do so with a bow, rifle, camera, or simply a set of binoculars and an appreciation of wildlife.

5.

The Animal Nobody Knows

One September day I was sitting atop a ridge in the foothills of the Alaska Range glassing for caribou when I noticed a small, dark form scampering across the tundra several hundred yards away. My first impression registered as "bear cub" even though it clearly wasn't. My "What the…?" moment proved brief as I quickly realized I was watching the first wolverine I'd ever seen. That encounter took place over 30 years ago, and I haven't seen one since.

The physical aspects of wolverine biology are well established. Like many of Alaska's large mammals the wolverine enjoys a circumpolar distribution, with substantial populations in Northern Europe and Russia as well as Alaska and Canada. Despite a superficial resemblance to bears, the wolverine is actually the largest member of the mustelid (weasel) family. Most adults weigh 20 to 40 pounds, with males roughly twice the size of females. Wolverines have a short, muscular frame. Their broad, splayed feet are well adapted to travel over snow, and their powerful jaws can crunch through bones and frozen animal carcasses. Potent scent glands enable wolverines to mark their territory, a habit responsible for their inaccurate nickname "skunk bear."

But animal behavior can be harder to describe than the animal, a problem compounded in this case by the wolverine's natural low population density and a huge body of misleading folklore.

A common figure in arctic legend, the wolverine's reputation for strength and ferocity has made it a popular mascot for sports teams (including my own high school's) and provided inspiration for a popular fictional movie hero. Is the wolverine truly the "devil bear" and "demon of the taiga" as lore surrounding the species suggests? Finding out requires the study of one of the North's most elusive animals.

Although wolverines occupy a lot of Alaska—they're just about everywhere except some of the state's islands—there aren't a lot of them anywhere. That's simply the nature of the beast. Largely solitary and highly territorial, wolverines just don't tolerate each other well. Most population estimates derive from aerial surveys conducted over fresh snow, a technique prone to underestimate the actual number of wolverines in the area. Using this method, biologists with Alaska's Department of Fish and Game estimated a density of 1.3 wolverines per 100 square miles in a portion of the Chugach Mountains.

Studies conducted with radio tracking collars and GPS technology have confirmed the wolverine's reputation as a nomad. Males typically have a home range of around 200 square miles, while females are less prone to travel. In the Chugach study, one male covered over 30 miles in a 24-hour period, through deep snow and rugged terrain. In an ongoing study conducted in the Berner's Bay area north of Juneau, a team of ADF&G biologists led by Steve Lewis "lost" a collared wolverine in 2008. A trapper eventually accounted for the animal on the Canadian side of the border in the Stikine drainage over 200 miles away.

Other purported aspects of wolverine behavior are more difficult to confirm. The species' scientific name, *Gula gula*, derives from the Latin root for "gluttony," as does the wolverine's common name in several Eurasian languages. (The origin of the name "wolverine" is a matter of dispute.) Old trappers' tales describe wolverines destroying cabins and killing and devouring large animals in traps (which they certainly did.) But they also include accounts of wolverines routinely attacking wolves and grizzly bears and chewing large steel traps to pieces (which seems less likely.) Scientists of the day weren't very helpful. One 19th century zoologist described wolverines killing caribou by attracting them with bits of fodder, leaping down on them from trees, and sucking blood from their bodies until they collapsed.

But reliable observers confirm the ability of wolverines to kill caribou, Dall sheep, and even moose, a remarkable feat for a 40-pound animal. Wolverines remain abundant in Scandinavia, where they prey so frequently on domestic reindeer and sheep that the governments of Sweden and Norway have established a formal program to compensate herdsmen for their losses. A recent study in the Western Arctic that analyzed the stomach contents of wolverines taken by hunters and trappers showed that caribou made up most of the animals' diet, followed by moose and a variety of odds and ends in small quantities including rodents, hares, and other wolverines. However, the proportion of caribou was highest when caribou mortality was highest, not when caribou were most abundant. This observation supports the generally accepted view that despite their remarkable ability to kill large animals, wolverines are more efficient scavengers than predators.

Verified accounts of wolverines attacking bears and wolves prove scarce. Relationships among such high-end predators are certainly complex. Biologist Kevin White and his colleagues describe two "crime scene investigations" demonstrating that wolves kill wolverines. However, because wolverines are such efficient scavengers, they also feed frequently on carcasses of animals killed by other predators. Consequently, wolverines potentially both benefit and suffer from proximity to wolves.

Wolverine hides have long played an important role in traditional arctic apparel. Wolverine fur is hydrophobic—it repels moisture and resists frost formation. These qualities make it uniquely suited to lining parkas in areas where human breath can condense and freeze. In Alaska, wolverines are managed as both game animals and furbearers, with seasons and limits established to prevent overharvest.

In February 2013, the United States Fish and Wildlife Service proposed listing the wolverine as a threatened species across its limited range in the Lower 48 states, where small wolverine populations persist in the North Cascades and Northern Rockies. Wolverine population dynamics there differ considerably from Alaska's. Wolverines have rigid habitat requirements, including limited contact with human development and a reliable abundance of snow that persists through their late spring denning and birthing season. This has led to geographic isolation across their southern range, with a subsequent lack of genetic diversity. If Alaska continues to provide vast tracts of contiguous wilderness habitat, its wolverine population should remain viable.

I consider myself lucky to have lived in not one but two states with wolverine populations. While there aren't many of them here, Montana is one of the wolverine's last bastions in the Lower-48. Bob Inman, Carnivore and Furbearer Coordinator for the Montana Department of Fish, Wildlife, and Parks, confirmed the difficulty of surveying a species as secretive and sparsely distributed as the wolverine but offered an informed estimate of 2-300 individuals living in Montana.

In addition to Montana, three other states in the Lower-48—Idaho, Washington, and Wyoming—have wolverines. Several years ago, Inman participated in a cooperative study to survey the species across this range. Since they couldn't count wolverines from the air, the biologists divided areas of suitable habitat into grids and installed trail cameras that could at least establish the presence of a wolverine in the area under study. Every segment of the Montana grid in the Greater Yellowstone and Northern Rockies ecosystems recorded at least one wolverine. While the Montana population estimate previously cited may not sound like a lot of individual animals, it exceeds that of any other state with the possible exception of Idaho. It seems fair to call Montana the last stronghold of the wolverine south of Canada.

Wolverine management in Montana has enjoyed a checkered past. By the early 1900s they had probably been extirpated from the state, although they slowly began to re-populate naturally. Prior to the mid-1970s they were treated as varmints, with no regulation on their take. Between 1973 and 2011 they were classified as furbearers with an annual quota of five animals divided among different areas in western Montana, with harvest in isolated island mountain ranges prohibited. While some observers criticized even this limited take as a step backward for the species, it at least allowed for management of their harvest in a regulated manner. No wolverine trapping (or hunting) has been allowed since 2011.

Following their elimination from the Lower-48 states, wolverines began their comeback on their own, with no efforts at re-introduction. Recently, isolated but credible evidence of wolverines has been reported from Colorado and California for the first time in a century. It is possible that Montana wolverines might someday be transplanted to these areas to aid in their repopulation.

Despite all the anecdotal tales of wolverines behaving badly in the Far North, I never heard a reliable report of cabin destruction or similar misdeeds when I lived in Alaska. Inman reports a similar track record in Montana. While he remembers one wolverine being shot in a chicken coop in northeastern Montana (not typical wolverine habitat) and another being removed from Billings, he knows of no instances of property destruction or livestock predation by wolverines here. He attributes this record of good behavior to an abundance of marmots and other favored food sources.

What does the future hold for Montana's wolverines? Currently, no hard science exists to document whether their numbers are stable, decreasing, or increasing, although their recent appearance in places they have not inhabited for years provides grounds for optimism. We'll know a lot more when biologists conduct a five-year follow-up to the population survey described earlier. Certainly, the continued presence of large undisturbed tracts of suitable forest habitat will remain crucial to the wolverine, not just in Montana but across its wide boreal range.

Subject to scrutiny, much of the folklore surrounding the wolverine appears to be just that. However, it is still a remarkable animal capable of amazing feats of strength and endurance, not to mention the ability to survive in some of the world's harshest environments. So, keep your eyes open for tracks, sign, and perhaps the elusive animal itself. You might become one of the lucky few to enjoy a wildlife encounter like the one I experienced long ago on the Alaska tundra.

6.

The Last Best Wild

*"Here still survives one of Planet Earth's own
works of art. This one symbolizes freedom."*
—Lowell Sumner, National Park Service Biologist, 1953

As was our tradition, we spent the first night at the Char Hole. Four miles upstream from the gravel bar landing strip, it made a perfect place to end our first-day shakedown hike, during which we adjusted the straps on our heavy backpacks, checked our feet for hot spots, and found the rhythm we'd need to maintain during the 20 challenging miles ahead to our sheep hunting base camp.

After gratefully slipping out of my pack and letting it drop onto the streamside gravel, I climbed a boulder and studied the pool below the waterfall. My eyes required some time to adjust to the optical illusions the current created, but then I saw them: a dozen undulating shapes, each representing a char nearly two feet long. I flashed a thumbs-up sign downstream to my hunting partners, confident that we'd soon be enjoying the best evening meal of the next two weeks, unless one of us actually killed a sheep.

Scrambling back down the boulder, I located my backpack fly rod and dug through pockets for my minimalist collection of wilderness flies. I didn't really care which one of us caught the fish or who cooked them. It was enough to be camping north of the Arctic circle again.

Newcomers to the Great North should think of Alaska more as a subcontinent than a state—it's that huge and complicated. The Southeastern Panhandle and the heart of the Interior differ more from population centers around Anchorage than do many foreign countries. Trying to pick a favorite outdoor venue from this smorgasbord of possibilities is probably a fool's errand, but even though I've been lucky enough to spend time in almost every part of Alaska one location somehow stands out as more majestic than all the rest: the North Slope of the Brooks Range and the adjacent Arctic Coastal Plain. A surreal world of endless summer days and delicious loneliness, the landscape seems constructed by magic rather than the usual factors of weather and geology. Now, however, it stands threatened by human forces.

The Arctic National Wildlife Refuge (ANWR, or "the Arctic Refuge") lies tucked up against Canada to the east and the Arctic Ocean to the north. Today it is impossible to appreciate this remarkable wilderness and the challenges it faces without understanding its recent history.

Many of us know that our National Wildlife Refuge (NWR) system began with Theodore Roosevelt (and wouldn't we all love to see TR back in the White House again!) With the stroke of a pen in 1903, Roosevelt created the Pelican Island NWR in Florida, to protect its vulnerable birdlife from exploitation by commercial plume hunters. NWRs have played a vital role in the preservation of American wildlife (and hunting and fishing opportunity) ever since.

Remote even by Alaska standards, the Arctic Refuge is not a place one visits casually. Save for a scattered indigenous Native population, no one knew much about the area prior to Alaska statehood. In the early 1950s, National Park Service planner George Collins and biologist Lowell Sumner explored the area and drew attention to it with a study titled "Northeast Alaska: The Last Great Wilderness." In 1956, Wilderness Society President Olaus Murie and his wife, Margaret, made an extended expedition into the Sheenjek River valley on the south side of the Brooks Range, accompanied by Supreme Court Justice William O. Douglas and several young biologists including the later world-renowned George Schaller. Upon their return, this group lobbied Congress for permanent protection of the area. In 1960, President Dwight Eisenhower created the Arctic National Wildlife Range there, including nearly nine million acres of designated wilderness, the federal Government's highest level of habitat protection.

To address longstanding Alaska Native land claims and allot land management responsibilities among state and federal agencies, Congress passed the Alaska National Interest Land Conservation Act (ANILCA) in 1980. None of the stakeholders got everything they wanted, but the Eisenhower era Wildlife Range was folded into the newly created 19 million-acre ANWR. While most of the additional land did not receive wilderness designation, ANILCA specifically required formal Congressional approval prior to any oil and gas development within ANWR.

The North Slope of the Brooks Range.

No one shot a ram the year Doug Borland and I went on our marathon pursuit of the big arctic grizzly.

Weather had haunted that trip right from the start, delaying the last leg of our flight to the gravel bar beside the river and obscuring the peaks in fog and snow every day we hunted from our upstream base camp. We had only seen one borderline legal ram in ten days of hunting, and the best to be said about the long hike back to the airstrip was that our packs were lighter, and it was downhill all the way. We were still exhausted when we finally reached the gravel bar, but the bears hadn't found the extra food we'd cached there, and the six-pack of beer we'd left in the creek proved every bit as cold and delicious as I'd imagined.

We were out of sheep country by then, but I wasn't quite ready to stop hunting yet. As Doug started a coffee-boiling fire out of willow twigs the following morning, I walked down the bar to glass for a bear. I hadn't even sat down before I saw a large blonde grizzly digging pikas out of a rock pile on the opposite riverbank.

Thirty minutes later, we were cautiously paddling our tiny inflatable raft across the current. Although Doug was way ahead of me in the Dall sheep column, he had never killed a grizzly with his bow (as I had by then). That made him the designated hitter that morning, so he sat up front clutching his longbow while I paddled and wondered how, absent a firearm, I'd back him up if it came to that.

The bear had disappeared by the time we beached the raft, but after climbing the bank we relocated him easily as he ambled across the open tundra a quarter of a mile ahead of us. Although arctic grizzlies and coastal brown bears are members of the same species—*Ursus arctos*—they are very different animals. While brown bears are living the good life and gorging on salmon, their Brooks Range counterparts have to spend their brief arctic summers extracting a whole year's worth of nutrition from painfully lean habitat. The bear we were following had already entered the period of pre-hibernation hyperphagia, and he wasn't going to stop walking until he found something to eat.

His pace may have appeared casual, but it was all we could do to keep up with him and we certainly weren't gaining any ground. We needed him to find another pika colony, a berry patch, a dead caribou calf, or *something*… but he never did. We followed him for miles before we finally gave up and turned back.

Perhaps that was just as well. When last I saw the bear, the breeze was puffing his backlit fur into a golden halo that made him look like a creature in a Renaissance painting. I tipped my hat to him and wished him the best for the winter ahead.

An interior grizzly on the tundra.

By the time ANWR was created, it was common knowledge that the coastal plain adjacent to the Arctic Ocean contained substantial oil reserves. To the west, the Prudhoe Bay oil field had been actively producing since 1977. The terms of ANILCA identified a 1.5-million-acre parcel of the Arctic Coastal Plain within ANWR boundaries as the "1002 area" and designated it as suitable for oil and gas exploration, although Congressional approval would still be required prior to further development.

Over the next four decades, the issue of drilling (or not) on the coastal plain became a prototypical political football. The details rapidly grow monotonous, so I'll stick to the highlights. In 1986, as chair of the House Interior Committee, Morris Udall successfully acted to kill a bill that would have authorized drilling. In 1989, a similar bill was making its way through the Senate when the Exxon Mobil disaster in Prince William Sound made support for drilling toxic. In 1996, President Bill Clinton vetoed a bill that would have authorized exploratory drilling in the Refuge. In 2000 and 2002, the House and Senate took turns passing drilling authorizations that were rejected by the other Congressional body. In 2005, the House added a clause to an Energy Bill that would have cleared the way for drilling, but it was removed during the reconciliation conference with the Senate. That same year, Alaska Senator Ted Stevens added a similar clause to the Defense bill, but it died by filibuster. A 2015 Obama administration effort to grant permanent wilderness level protection to most of the Refuge went nowhere. *Whew.*

Proponents of drilling invariably cited the potential to create new jobs and the country's need for oil independence, the latter consideration despite studies showing that even if all the known oil in the 1002 Area could be extracted and delivered to market, it would barely satisfy U.S. energy needs for a year.

Drilling opponents cited the intrinsic value of the country's largest remaining true wilderness as championed by the Muries a generation earlier. They also emphasized the biological value of the arctic coastal plain as a nesting area for nearly 200 species of birds that migrate throughout the country, and as critical habitat for recently endangered species such as polar bears. Then there is the complex matter of the Porcupine caribou herd, in which Canadians just across the border also have a vested interest.

By the time I made my second trip to ANWR, I had learned that one of the surest ways to ruin a good sheep hunt was to shoot something bigger than a sheep. The obligation to care responsibly for the meat from a big bull caribou or a moose meant the end of most sheep hunts. However, when I saw a band of caribou bedded on a rocky ridge a thousand feet above the valley floor, I had a variation on the usual theme in mind.

I'd already killed a number of big bulls with my bow and didn't need more antlers on my wall. I could plan on losing a pound per day on our usual sheep hunting menu of freeze-dried backpack food, hopefully supplemented by occasional char and ptarmigan. What I wanted was a caribou calf small enough so I could cut it all up and get it back to camp that night but large enough to feed four of us for the next week. Since the wind direction excluded the possibility of a direct approach, I circled around to the back side of the ridge, re-checked a few landmarks, and started to climb.

Numbering around 200,000 animals, the Porcupine caribou herd is one of the continent's largest. For millennia, gravid cows have delivered their calves during late spring on the Arctic Coastal Plain, in the heart of the contested 1002 Area. From there, they begin a two-thousand-mile clockwise circle by traveling east into Canada before moving south and west again to winter in the southern part of the Arctic Refuge before returning to the point of beginning. Along the way, they nourish an entire population of predators and scavengers ranging from bears and wolves to raptors and wolverines. The indigenous Gwich'in people, who inhabit much of ANWR south of the Brooks Range crest, depend on caribou as a source of food and hides as heavily as our Plains tribes once depended on bison.

Since most of the herd has already passed into Canada by the time sheep season opens in Alaska, I have never personally witnessed the peak of the migration. Friends who have assure me that the event is as spectacular as anything seen on Africa's Serengeti. Perhaps it's just capricious fate that placed all that oil beneath the most crucial habitat the Porcupine herd crosses during its travels. Most knowledgeable observers agree that disruption of the coastal plain would be a disaster for the caribou, the Gwich'in, and ultimately the whole arctic ecosystem.

Fortunately for the Gwich'in, they must be better caribou hunters than I am. After picking my way up through the rocks for nearly an hour, I peeked over the top and saw all the caribou grazing back down on the valley floor, right where I had started.

In 2017, the House and Senate included authorization to begin selling oil leases in the refuge in President Trump's new tax bill. In August 2020, Interior Secretary David Bernhardt announced that the department would begin accepting bids for oil leases on the Refuge and predicted lease sales by the end of the year despite a world oversupply of oil and limited interest from big oil companies. (A former oil industry lobbyist, Bernhardt and his department have faced multiple accusations of ethics violations during his tenure.) Within the month, a consortium including the Gwich'in, National Wildlife Federation, the Canadian Parks and Wildlife Society, and the Wilderness Society had filed suit against Bernhardt and the Bureau of Land Management, charging them with violating the terms of ANILCA, the National Environmental Policy Act, National Wildlife Refuge System Act, and Endangered Species Act.

In announcing the suit, Bernadette Demientieff, executive director of the Gwich'in Steering Committee, said: "BLM's decision to violate lands sacred to my people and essential to the health of the Porcupine caribou herd is an attack on our rights, our culture, and our way of life. We have lived and thrived in the Arctic for thousands of years. We have listened to and learned from our elders, and we know that we must stand united to protect future generations, the caribou herd, and sacred lands."

The final chapters of this complex story—if there ever are any—remain to be written.

Despite its size, the Arctic Refuge is one of the country's least visited. Friend, neighbor, Fish and Wildlife Service veteran, and frequent hunting partner Glenn Elison served as director of ANWR for ten years beginning in 1983. During that time, he estimates that fewer than 1200 people visited the refuge annually. Chalk that up to logistics. There are no roads to or within the refuge, save for the immediate area around scattered Native villages. Getting there requires a bush flight, usually from Barter Island or Arctic Village. The area's inaccessibility reflects the essential paradox of wilderness. If ANWR received tourists like Yellowstone National Park, it would no longer be wilderness.

Why bother going to all that trouble, or even caring about ANWR's future? I spent some time considering that question the evening before we were due to fly out on my last trip to the Refuge. Despite the amount of time I've spent far from the nearest road all over Alaska, the country, and the world, ANWR affects me in a qualitatively different way. Earlier during that trip, for example, I'd started to reach for my bear spray cannister when I spotted a brown, furry hump approaching me above the top of the streamside willows. I stood pat and soon found myself surrounded by a herd of musk ox, one of the few North American big game animals I'd never encountered in the wild.

These primitive Ice Age relics co-exist poorly with humans, which is why their U.S. population is limited to the North Slope of the Brooks Range and a few remote islands in the Bering Sea. Yet there they were, standing before me like characters in a dream.

In the future, I'd like to be able to share that dream with family and friends. That will mean leaving the Arctic Refuge the way it is and always has been.

7.

Moose John Miracle Bull

A strong Arctic high-pressure system had driven the scud from the sky and left the air as crisp and clean as the current in Alaska's legendary Moose John River. The equinox still lay a week away, but the autumn foliage had already exploded in a stunning display of color. Migrating cranes turned in aimless vortices overhead and we could practically feel the moose beginning to stir with imperatives of the rut. Although it was our first night on the river, no one felt much like loafing in camp. It was time to go moose hunting.

Especially for me. Over the course of the previous two weeks, I'd killed a Sitka blacktail buck near our second home in southeast Alaska, tested my fly rod against countless silver salmon, and spent several enjoyable days stalking bears from the base camp upriver. I'd almost managed to forget the bow season I'd left behind in Montana and finally felt ready to do what we'd come to do.

With our gravel bar campsite secure, Alaska veteran Doug Borland and Montana bowhunter Chad Sivertsen vanished into the brush in opposite directions while Ernie Holland and I forded the river to explore a series of beaver ponds on the other side. The river nearly tricked me, as the current ran so clear that water appearing no more than ankle deep threatened to overflow my hip waders. But by prime calling time, we'd reached a slough overlooking a long beaver pond shrouded with willows: textbook moose habitat.

Ernie began with a series of soft bull grunts, but the freshening breeze tossed them right back in our faces. Intent on reaching more territory, he finally raised his freshly made birch bark call, threw back his head and offered a truly inspired rendition of a lovesick cow's haunting moan. Then we settled back against the soft carpet of moss to wait.

Fifteen minutes passed and I felt myself sinking into a trance. Then I cast my eyes back toward the river and almost choked. "Bull moose!" I whispered, amazed as ever by the ability of anything so large to appear so silently. With soft evening light playing across his muscular outline, he seemed posed for a cover photo. Yet I couldn't help feeling a pang of disappointment, for we didn't need binoculars to see that he fell well short of the area's 50-inch or four brow-tine minimum for non-residents, which I was at the time. As an Alaska resident Ernie could have shot the bull, but we'd already decided that we couldn't float two moose out in our raft. Since I was now a visitor, Ernie had graciously left the shooting honors to me.

"Should I go ahead and call him in?" Ernie whispered.

"I think you already have!" I replied.

And sure enough. A moose's ability to pinpoint sound from great distances practically defies belief. In fact, sound amplification and localization are the principal functions of a bull moose's palmated antlers. Without another cue from us, the bull slogged across the pond and slowly turned, giving me an excellent opportunity to complete the mental exercise of picking an imaginary spot on his side. Then he lumbered up the bank beside us, paused again barely three bow-lengths away, and eased off into the brush. Even without a shot opportunity, it was hard to deny that our long float was off to an exciting start.

Halfway down the Moose John with five days left to go.

Over two decades have passed since Doug, Jay Massey, and Dick Hamilton pioneered bowhunting opportunities in this remote corner of Alaska's vast interior. When Jay created Moose John Outfitters and began taking other hunters down the river, the Moose John rapidly acquired a reputation as one of the most exciting bowhunting opportunities in the North. After Jay's untimely death, mutual friend and registered guide Ernie Holland took over the operation. Despite increasingly difficult moose hunting conditions throughout interior Alaska due to an odd combination of politics and predators, Ernie's bowhunters had come off the river with five large bulls the previous year.

Now it was our turn to get the new season off to the right start.

When we told our story around the campfire that night, Doug listened with particular attention. As a resident, he wasn't limited by the 50-inch minimum, and with a basement full of moose horns already he was more interested in moose meat than another set of antlers. Ernie and I felt confident that the young bull hadn't spooked despite our close encounter, and early the following morning Doug set off across the river to kill him while the rest of us dispersed behind camp.

Ernie and I returned mid-morning to find Doug brooding unhappily over a cup of re-warmed coffee. Although I've hunted with Doug all over the world under some of the most demanding conditions imaginable, I couldn't remember ever seeing him so despondent. When we asked how his morning had gone, he gestured toward his quiver, which contained two broken arrows. Each had snapped right behind the broadhead, and neither showed more than a few inches of blood on the shaft. As Ernie and I reached for the coffeepot, he began to tell his story.

He'd set up near the spot where Ernie and I had called in the bull the night before. His first soft grunt produced an immediate reply, followed by the unmistakable crack of antlers on wood somewhere in the willows. One more grunt was all it took. A bull appeared out of the brush so quickly that Doug knew he had him. After slogging across the slough, the bull climbed the bank five yards from the water, offering Doug the same chip shot I'd envisioned the night before.

"Was it the same bull?" I interrupted, unable to contain my curiosity. "Thirty-six inches or so?"

"Afraid not," Doug replied ruefully. "This was a dandy, mid-50's at least. I wish you'd been there to kill him." As a matter of fact, I did too, but that was academic at this point.

Doug has killed too many moose with his bow to let a close-range encounter rattle him. He picked a spot, drew, and hit the tuft of hair he was aiming at, admittedly no great archery challenge when the target is a broadside bull moose at five yards. To his dismay, even though he felt he was safely behind the shoulder, the arrow struck with a loud *crack*, apparently producing limited penetration. As the bull trotted off, Doug took another shot, one that he never would have taken under different circumstances, and felt he struck the shoulder blade with his second arrow.

After waiting an hour, he tentatively started on the trail just to assess the quality of the sign. This provided the morning's only grounds for hope, as he found frothy blood that looked as if it might have come from a lung. However, he recovered both arrows, neither of which showed evidence of much penetration. With that, he backed off and returned to camp to give the trail some time and wait for help.

We decided to assume that he might have hit one lung and waited a full four hours after the shot before taking up the trail. Despite their size, moose are not particularly tough and will often bed down quickly after a marginal hit that would make an elk run for miles. Finally, we crossed the slough, planning to track very cautiously in hope of getting another shot at what we felt was at best a wounded animal. As we retraced the first part of the track, however, I noted aerated clots of blood floating on the surface of the pond, confirming the suggestion of a broadhead in the chest cavity despite the shaky appearance of Doug's two arrows.

When we reached the spot where Doug had abandoned the trail earlier, we stopped to rest and prepare ourselves mentally for the task ahead. As Doug double-checked his tackle, Ernie and I glanced casually into the brush and simultaneously felt a surge of elation and disbelief. The big bull lay piled up less than fifteen yards away.

Nothing can convert despair into elation like the sight of a dead moose… at least for a little while. Those who have known the joy of butchering and packing out a big Alaska bull will understand. Fortunately, the stricken bull – which only traveled a hundred yards after Doug's first shot – had wandered back toward the riverbank, leaving us with a packing job about as easy as a big, dead bull moose ever offers, not that any of them are really easy.

What did the autopsy have to tell us about what those two shots really did? The chest cavity was full of blood and both lungs were down. We found one broadhead floating free in the thorax and never located the second. Doug's first shot had been spot-on, hitting a rib squarely but still penetrating the chest. His second shot had been perfectly placed as well. He hadn't really been in position to assess the second arrow, and I suspect the apparent lack of penetration by the first was simply an optical illusion caused by the arrow backing out instantly when the animal brought his near front leg back. I've almost been fooled that way a time or two myself. Moral: assume every hit is lethal until proven otherwise.

While Doug and Chad began the butchering work, Ernie and I searched for a good route through the brush and blowdowns that would lead us to the river and the raft. That's when I experienced a moment of inspiration that should have occurred to me years before. After removing the oars from the raft, I laid two backpack frames across them at right angles and lashed them down with the tie-down straps that should be part of every moose hunting expedition. This created a stretcher with which the two of us could easily maneuver a whole moose quarter through the brush and back to the raft. This allowed us to leave the hide in place to protect the meat from bugs, dirt, and rain, which we felt certain would catch up with us somewhere in the long river miles ahead.

"It's a miracle moose," Doug said at the campfire that evening as we prepared to grill some liver. I politely disagreed and expressed my opinion that either shot would have killed the bull by itself. Doug felt that either shot alone would have hit just one lung, leading to a far more difficult recovery or perhaps no recovery at all. I didn't argue the point too strongly, since Doug now owed me owe me a moose-packing job and I doubted I'd ever earn such a debt as easily.

Besides, the Moose John has always been famous for producing miracles. Now we had one more to add to the list.

Doug Borland glassing for sheep north of the Arctic Circle.

8.

Arctic Circle

I had been here before and thought I knew what lay ahead, but as the peaks of the Brooks Range consumed the sound of the departing Helio Courier, I experienced an overwhelming sense of doubt. When I stared across the gravel bar where we'd landed and up the drainage that marked our route, I couldn't even see our destination 22 miles away. Perhaps I hadn't trained hard enough. Perhaps the 60-pound pack was too heavy and perhaps it wasn't heavy enough, given that its contents would have to shelter and sustain me for the next two weeks. Perhaps I really was too old now to do what I'd first done 30 years earlier and last done a decade ago. Plenty of people seemed to think so. The decision to go not gently into the night was mine alone.

We were over 200 miles north of the Arctic Circle, just inland from the frigid Beaufort Sea. The tree line lay far behind us, and no vegetation other than stunted willows along the waterways rose above the level of the tundra. It was the first week of August, and although the Northern Hemisphere's longest day lay weeks behind us, there would still be no true nightfall during our stay. Even as an Alaska resident again, I'd forgotten how different the Arctic environment can be. With a laugh, I dug out my headlamp and tossed it in the tote containing the supplies we planned to leave behind on the airstrip. My pack had no room for useless weight.

The last big game animal I killed with a rifle was a Dall sheep taken from the Wrangell Mountains in 1981. By the first time I headed to the Brooks Range a few years later I was committed to the bow, but on each of my two previous visits an unseasonable August blizzard quickly turned my sheep hunt into a survival exercise. I had never come close to a ram. It's not that I thought the Arctic owed me a sheep, but I looked forward to an opportunity for an honest try. I planned to ask nicely.

Whatever reservations I felt about myself, I enjoyed full confidence in my companions. My gracefully aging contemporary Doug Borland had pioneered this area nearly four decades earlier. The year before, while hunting this same drainage with his wife Olga, he had taken a 40-inch ram with his longbow, a sheep that would no doubt earn a lofty spot in the record book if Doug cared about records. Dick Robertson and his son Yote completed our party. Dick is one of the country's premier custom bowyers (I carried one of his takedown recurves) and Yote provided enough youthful endurance and energy to inspire us all. Among the three of them, they had taken seven full curl rams here with traditional longbows. It could be done, and I could imagine no convincing excuse for my own failure to get it done.

Base camp wasn't getting any closer. We spent several minutes subtracting a few more questionably essential items from our packs and adding them to the tote. Then we blessed our little cache against attention from marauding grizzlies, groaned our way into our packs, and set off up the creek we would follow into the rugged country ahead.

We only meant to make a few miles that first afternoon, to shake down our packs, test our legs, and enjoy a good night's rest before tackling the one truly nasty piece of terrain between the airstrip and base camp: Heaven's Gate once it's behind you, Hell's Gate when it still lies ahead. Here the steep walls of the canyon converge in a tight jumble of boulders covered in brush that makes it difficult or impossible to see where your feet are going as you try to negotiate the talus while balancing a heavy pack. It's a great place to break a leg.

The route through the tight spot may be intimidating, but its downstream edge offers a great apology for what awaits: the Char Hole. North Slope drainages lie beyond the home range of the salmon and trout that define angling elsewhere in Alaska, but they compensate in other ways. In August, big sea-run char (actually Dolly Vardens, which are members of the char family) surge upriver on the way to their headwater spawning grounds. The cataract that marks the stream's exodus from Hell's Gate empties into a deep pool, where char often congregate while awaiting ideal water conditions to leap the falls and proceed upstream. We'd found them there before, and if they were there now, we could look forward to something better than dehydrated hash browns for dinner.

Doug and I rigged our fly rods and approached the pool as cautiously as if we were stalking sheep. And there they lay, brilliantly colored char from six to ten pounds, stacked up in the tail-out of the pool. An hour later a willow fire was smoking in front of our tents, slabs of char were waiting their turn in our lone frying pan, and it was almost possible to forget about Hell's Gate and the 20 miles of climbing and river crossings beyond it.

After breaking camp in a cool, grey drizzle the following morning, we cursed and fought our way through the boulders and brush, breathed a sigh of relief at the open terrain beyond, and ran into the first bears of the trip. Arctic grizzlies may be less than half the size of the coastal brown bears we all knew well from innumerable encounters farther south. Denied the luxury of salmon runs as a food source and forced by circumstance to pack on a year's worth of nutrition in a few short months, they can be more aggressive, and we treat them with great respect. Grizzly season was open, but all of us except Doug had killed grizzlies with our bows and didn't really want to do so again unless we had to. Fortunately, the sow and her twin cubs passed harmlessly by on the opposite side of the creek.

Then it was time to struggle back beneath our loads and tackle the rough footing and frequent stream crossings that lay ahead.

Four days later I lay sprawled across the tundra beneath clear blue skies enjoying weather reminiscent of Hawaii. Our tents lay two thousand feet below on a willow studded gravel bar that seemed pleasantly familiar after a ten-year absence. After the long, wet slog up the creek beneath the burden of a fully loaded pack, the climb up the mountain to the outlet of the basin that morning felt positively enjoyable. All I had to do for the rest of the afternoon was lie there and glass.

When writers describe shadows crawling up hillsides they usually speak in metaphor, but not in the Arctic. Here the sun never ascends far above the horizon during the endless summer day, and since the upper rim of the Brooks Range consists of one craggy peak after another the result is an ongoing series of sunrises and sunsets, with complex shadows bursting up and down the opposing mountainsides like time lapse photographs of flowers erupting in bloom. The effect was mesmerizing, and I admit that I was paying more attention to the light show than the sheep habitat.

Then my binoculars made another slow, methodical sweep across the terrain above me, and I realized that the number of sheep-sized white rocks some mischievous force has scattered about the North Slope had magically increased by one at the head of the hanging valley. Since the sheep was solitary and situated as high above the valley floor as possible it was almost certainly a mature ram, as a backlit golden glow atop its head soon confirmed. But at that distance I could not positively identify the full curl sweep of horn needed to make the animal legal game. Since I'd left my spotting scope at home as a concession to weight there was nothing left for it but to gird up my loins and start picking my way across the jumble of scree between us.

An hour later I had confirmed a definite probable, with an important asterisk. The ram was feeding casually high on a nearly vertical face amidst some of the nastiest terrain I'd ever seen a Dall sheep occupy. A safe approach would have required technical climbing gear. I knew that 30 years earlier I would have tried the stalk anyway, but that was then, and this was now. I waited in vain through two more false sunsets in hope that the ram might descend, and then I reluctantly headed back downhill toward camp. Did this decision reflect the infirmity of age or wisdom? I could only wonder.

Over the course of the next week my hunting partners and I encountered multiple versions of the same theme. The weather was sweltering, the bugs were out in force, wolf tracks covered the valley floor, and some combination of these factors had pushed the rams higher and farther back than any of us had ever seen them. Younger and tougher than the rest of us, Yote made two ridiculously challenging stalks that resulted in clean misses, a development he accepted with laudable stoicism. By this time, I had come to terms with my limitations and realized that I wasn't going to stalk a ram unless one came down into more reasonable terrain.

Perhaps I really had grown too old to be backpack sheep hunting with a bow.

I set out several mornings later in deliberate search of just such low-lying fruit and found it literally, in the form of blueberries.

Serious backpack hunting involves a grim nutritional accounting. I figure that a typical day of sheep hunting can require four or five thousand calories worth of fuel, and a serious stalk will demand even more. But you can only carry so much food on your back, and on an extended hunt like this, demand almost always exceeds supply. A dead sheep would have solved the problem, but now we needed to pursue other possibilities, of which the North Slope potentially offers several.

We had continued to take advantage of the char, smaller versions of which occupied the little stream beside our camp, but you can only eat so much fish. The great Porcupine caribou herd calves each spring on the nearby Arctic Coastal Plain, and every summer hundreds of thousands of these nomadic deer travel eastward from there toward the Yukon. Caribou season was open and a calf for camp meat would have been manna from heaven, but this year we couldn't even find a straggler. On previous trips to the area, I'd packed enough arrows to produce several ptarmigan dinners, but this year I hadn't seen a single bird. Mushrooms don't pack a lot of nutritional punch, but a pan of sautéed boletes can turn a bland packet of rice into a mouth-watering main course. Thanks to the brutally hot weather, mushrooms were as scarce as caribou. No wonder that bag full of blueberries made me a hero when I returned to camp that night.

For we hadn't neglected to pack in one of the two culinary necessities for any sheep hunting trip: Krusteaz pancake mix. Soon after we crawled out of our tents the next morning willow smoke was drifting down the gravel bar, and then blueberry pancakes began to slide one at a time from our frying pan onto our plates. That breakfast would have put IHOP to shame.

Thus fortified, we held a reluctant council of war. Our pickup was due in three days. We were nearly out of food. We could have stayed where we were and hunted for another day, but if someone killed a sheep, recovering it and getting the meat and our camp back downstream in time to meet our airplane would require round the clock travel. Yote voted to stay, and I admired him for his determination, but age prevailed in the end. We old men offered him our apologies, which he accepted graciously.

Two days later, rain had started to fall again by the time we broke for lunch before tackling Hell's Gate. Dick had flipped one of the two inflatable pack rafts we'd used to line our camp downstream, and a lot of our gear was soaked. Since we didn't know whether our cache had survived two weeks in bear country we stopped at the Char Hole, where the fish were even bigger and more plentiful than before. But the sign made it obvious that a grizzly had discovered this bounty as well, and with visibility limited by willows, we didn't linger once we'd taken a few fish for dinner.

Back at the strip on the main river a few hours later, we made a delightful discovery. The bears had found our fishing hole, but they hadn't found our cache, which contained, among other things, a bottle of fine Australian red wine and two cans of Alaska's second backcountry gourmet essential: Spam!

I don't know what is in a can of Spam, and I don't want to. But next to Hawaiians, Alaskans enjoy the highest per capita Spam consumption rate of any state in the nation. When you are hungry, wet, and exhausted nothing promises to enliven the spirit more than slices of Spam singed to a crisp over an open fire, especially when washed down with wine from a tin cup.

The next morning, I said goodbye to the Arctic for what I knew would likely be the last time.

The circle provides an ideal geometric metaphor for this narrative. A circle separates the Arctic from the rest of the world, right there on the map, defined for once by geographical certainty rather than some political power's arbitrary whim: the southernmost point at which the sun doesn't set on the summer solstice. A circle also defines the languid course the northern summer sun follows around the horizon, playing peek-a-boo through the peaks as it treats the observer to a dozen dawns per day. A circle also represents the course I've taken over all these decades in the outdoors, as I realized after nearly three weeks in the wildest wild our continent still has left to offer. I had come back to the point of beginning, and thanks to lessons learned in the Arctic, I had accepted the terms of my own unexpected return.

I began as most of us did, as a kid with a fiberglass rod, a beat-up shotgun, and a disobedient dog, perfectly content with whatever a day afield might provide. Then I began to push myself against terrain, weather, and the inherent challenge of hunting big game in the most difficult manner possible. While I remained an observant hunter and an enthusiastic student of natural history, the final motivation to do much of what I did outdoors depended upon the possibility of killing a large animal with my bow. While I never cared about trophies (whatever that word means), I gladly went through all kinds of exertion, deprivation, and risk in order to experience the almost indescribable excitement of taking big game from close range with simple sticks and strings. The mere possibility often proved sufficiently intoxicating to make me abandon my common sense. And "intoxicating" may be just the right word. I wanted it the way I've heard recovering alcoholics tell me they once wanted their next drink.

I don't need to do that anymore. The Arctic taught me this simple lesson. It's not because I'm too old—this trip reassured me on that score. It's because watching sheep can be as gratifying as stalking them, because a char can be as important as a ram, a blueberry as important as a char. I understand all this now and feel at peace with this conclusion.

This hunt took place with an asterisk I have not yet mentioned. While training for the trip, a fall led to a severe rotator cuff injury in my right shoulder. Although I carried my bow, I hadn't shot it in two months. Even if I had been able to stalk within twenty-five yards of a ram, I probably wouldn't have been able to shoot, and I knew it. (The shoulder underwent surgery not long after I returned.) I now have the Arctic to thank for inviting me to look ahead to whatever remains in a gentler, more thoughtful fashion, with my fly rod, shotgun, and bird dogs once again, and most importantly, with friends.

9.

Bad Black Bears

We had spent a long week on the legendary Moose John River's headwaters. Ordinarily that open tundra terrain is teeming with black bears in early September, but the berry crop was poor that year and bears proved scarce. However, the weather had treated us civilly, at least by Alaska standards, and the country was beautiful as ever, so I'd enjoyed the opportunity to get back into hunting shape and let the demands of civilization recede gently into the distant recesses of my memory.

I was hunting with Kevin Low, one of New Zealand's finest bowhunters. After enjoying a high-country hunt for free-range tahr with Kevin the previous year, I'd invited him to join me stateside to hunt the quarry of his choice, and he'd picked Alaska black bears. Since he is a not a U.S. citizen, Alaska law required him to hunt with a guide, in which capacity I was happy to serve. That meant that I couldn't do any personal hunting on our trip, and I hadn't even packed a bow into camp. I didn't really care. I've taken my share of bears, and helping Kevin enjoy his first experience in the Alaska Bush provided all the reward I needed.

During the week after old friend Ernie Holland shuttled us in to the strip, we'd seen one or two bears daily while covering a lot of miles through the high tundra, a fraction of what I expected. Most were either too small to shoot or too far away to stalk. Kevin had spent one interesting morning playing cat-and-mouse with a nice mature boar only to pass up a shot just under 30 yards because he thought he might be able to get closer. As our hunt drew to a close, he was beginning to second-guess that decision. I couldn't blame him—Kevin is an excellent shot—but I'll never criticize a bowhunter for exercising restraint in shot selection.

On our last evening in camp, by the time we'd settled in to rest our legs and turn the last of our supplies into dinner, Kevin had broken down his three-piece longbow and stowed it away in anticipation of flying out the following morning. We'd pitched our tents near an abandoned mining camp next to the area's rough little airstrip. To keep food away from our sleeping quarters—always a good idea in bear country—200 yards down the hill from the strip we'd stretched a tarp and some scavenged Visqueen sheeting over an old frame structure about 20 feet square to provide some shelter from the wind and rain while we were cooking and eating. I was turned away from the little shelter's "door" and starting to work on dinner when I suddenly saw Kevin's eyes grow wide. I sensed what was happening even before he cried, "Don, there's a bear!"

I turned around just in time to see a black ursine rump disappearing *back* through the shelter's entrance. The animal had to have been close enough to bite me in the butt moments earlier. Although the bear quickly disappeared into the thick brush just beyond the cook tent, that brief glimpse left me convinced of two things: the bear was a mature boar, and we hadn't seen the last of him. "We need your bow right now!" I told Kevin, and then we sprinted uphill to our tents. While Kevin began to fumble frantically with his broken-down longbow, I retrieved the only firearm in camp: a .44 handgun Ernie had insisted I take prior to his departure. While I consider myself competent with rifles and shotguns, I rarely shoot handguns and knew I would be lucky to hit my own tent with this one if I were sitting inside it.

I reached the cook tent well ahead of Kevin, who was still up on the hill assembling his archery tackle. I wanted to turn the bear's aggressive behavior into an archery opportunity for Kevin, but I also realized that we were going to have to deal with this animal one way or the other, and I wanted to do so during daylight. A camp-raiding bear in the middle of the night can spell trouble under any circumstances.

Accordingly, I decided to do exactly what I'd been doing in the first place, which was making dinner. At the time of the bear's first appearance, I'd just taken a package of bacon out of the metal barrel where we'd stored it, and I decided to go ahead and cook it as originally planned. Trouble was, when I went to reach for the bacon, it was gone. The bear had already revisited the cook tent during the few minutes I'd been up the hill.

Moments later, Kevin arrived carrying his longbow. "Nock and arrow and get ready," I whispered. "No way this bear isn't coming back, and we need to take care of him before dark."

Then we sat down and waited.

Whenever the discussion turns to dangerous bears in the Far North, the brown/grizzly bear usually dominates the conversation. (As pointed out earlier, brown bears and the grizzlies are one and the same species—*Ursus arctos*—with variations in appearance, habits, and distribution. In this chapter I'll employ standard Alaskan usage and refer to them as brown bears.) My thesis here is that it's a mistake to ignore the smaller, sneakier, and more familiar black bear's capacity to cause trouble.

Over the years I've spent a lot of time up close and personal with brown bears, as a wilderness fly-fisherman, wildlife photographer, brown bear hunting guide, and, occasionally, bowhunter. These experiences have left me with tremendous respect for the brown bear's strength, speed, cunning, and occasional unpredictable aggressiveness. Even though I've dealt with hundreds of them at close range without ever having to shoot one in self-defense, they still make my subconscious tingle with a primitive fight-or-flight response unrivaled by any other animal on the continent.

I've also dealt with hundreds of black bears at close range, frequently while stalking them with a bow. During the vast majority of those encounters the bears acted more like wary whitetails than dangerous game, bolting away at the first sight, sound, or smell that strikes them as remotely out of place. My fight-or-flight response seldom engages even at point blank range from black bears, and I don't carry a backup firearm when I'm hunting them.

Here's the ultimate irony: I have experienced far more aggressive, threatening behavior from black bears than brown bears even though, in contrast to most bowhunters, I've had roughly the same amount of experience with both species.

Some years back, I was engaged in a combination bowhunting and flyfishing writing assignment in Northern Labrador. After several days spent chasing caribou around the tundra without finding a bull I wanted to shoot, I decided to accept my host's invitation to join a group of anglers on a fly-out expedition in search of arctic char.

After we landed the Beaver on a remote lake near its outlet stream, the rest of the party—a half dozen anglers and the pilot/guide—elected to remain near the airplane and fish the lake while I struck out downstream in search of char and solitude, not necessarily in that order. When I climbed back out of the canyon several hours later (having found the solitude, but not the fish) I was surprised to see everyone else huddled together on a point in the lake as far from the shoreline as possible, all in an obvious state of agitation. "What's up?" I called out as I walked up the shore.

"There's a bear!" several voices shouted back at once.

Since we were a long way from grizzly country, I wasn't particularly worried, and I continued along the lake shore to a constant chorus of warning cries. "Where's this bear?" I finally asked as I drew closer to the group.

"Right up there!" someone shouted back. After studying the terrain above us for a moment, I finally identified the source of the panic: a mature black bear on the tundra ridge several hundred yards away, casually eating berries. After suppressing an all but overwhelming urge to laugh, I reassured everyone that the bear was not a threat and suggested that we keep fishing.

About that time the bear's head shot up, probably in response to the racket. But instead of loping away across the tundra, he began to march directly down the hill in our direction.

As it happens, the black bear season was open in Labrador and my host had kindly provided me with a bear tag. Unfortunately, my bow was a hundred miles away back in base camp. Nonetheless, I recognized an impending photo opportunity and began to fumble through my pack for my camera while everyone else discussed the feasibility of a group dash back down the beach to the airplane.

Shortly thereafter the bear popped out of the brush 30 yards away, and I snapped off a couple of pictures before pausing to take a good look at the animal. I can read bear body language well, and I frankly didn't care for what I saw: a large, mature boar whose attitude suggested aggression more than curiosity.

The rest of the party—wisely, in retrospect—had already ignored my request to allow the bear to approach for photographic purposes and had started to yell all the stupid things people yell when they are trying to scare off a bear. To no avail, in the event; the bear continued its methodical advance.

Fortunately, the beach was made up of baseball-sized stones ideal for throwing. When I dropped my camera and launched one the idea caught on quickly, and the bear, which had closed within 15 yards, was soon standing amidst a hail of rocks, which had no apparent effect. Finally, someone—I'd like to claim credit, but I can't with certainty—ripped off a high, inside fastball that caught the bear right on the tip of its snout. That shot aroused an impressive bluff charge, followed at last by a retreat that even I was glad to see.

What caused that bear's unusual behavior? Habituation to humans as a possible food source is one obvious explanation, but there was absolutely no one else in the area and the nearest Native village was over a hundred miles away. We were almost certainly the first people that bear had ever encountered, and he simply decided to investigate with an attitude. Had the object of his investigation been a lone, unarmed angler instead of a party of eight, the encounter could have ended as a wilderness tragedy.

When we finally regrouped, retreated to the airplane, and lifted off the water, I couldn't help but reflect upon the number of times I've *tried* to get 15 yards from a black bear only to be undone by a tiny sound or an errant puff of breeze. I also had to chide myself for violating one of my old friend John Roseland's cardinal rules of bowhunting: Never go anywhere during hunting season without your bow!

Despite all those deliberate close range black bear encounters that ended with the bear tearing off into the brush unscathed, not all my black bear stalks concluded that way. On two occasions, I have had to kill (with my bow) black bears that continued to advance upon me even after they had clearly recognized that I was a human hunter. Both of those encounters with belligerent bears took place on Alaska tide flats.

The first involved a large, mature boar that initially spooked back into the brush after a wind switch when I was some 30 yards away on final approach for a shot. Instead of vanishing according to script, he reappeared and continued to advance even after he had clearly seen and smelled me. The bear was 10 yards away when he finally turned enough to allow me to deliver a lethal arrow.

The second was a younger bear that wound-up right on top of me not once but twice. By the time he made his second approach, I knew that he had both seen and smelled me the first time around and had to know what I was. Crouched down in a tidal gut, I felt justified in taking a frontal shot when he reappeared over the bank right above me. The arrow hit the soft spot at the juncture of his neck and thorax before passing completely through the bear and exiting through a ham. He dropped in plain sight after running only 20 yards. After reconstructing the shot, I estimated that the bear was only three feet away when I delivered the arrow that killed him.

What accounted for the anomalous behavior these two bears demonstrated? The first one had clearly been involved in a fight with another bear, leaving his face and head covered with infected wounds. Perhaps he was just looking for something or someone smaller than his original adversary in order to even the score. Youth and inexperience could have explained the second bear's belligerence, but at age four (according to dental analysis) he should have been old enough to know better.

Expert consensus, for whatever it's worth, holds that most brown bear attacks are basically defensive or territorial: a sow protecting cubs, for example, or a bear guarding a food source such as a dead moose. Obviously, travelers in bear country should take all possible care to avoid either situation. Black bear attacks, on the other hand, usually take place because the bear is looking for food: your own dinner, as with the bear Kevin and I faced that night, or you. This theory explains why brown bear attacks are more likely to result in injury than death despite the size and strength of the bear, while black bear attacks are relatively more likely to result in human fatality.

Ernie Holland with a nice black bear taken on an Alaska beach in the spring.

Even though I was well-aware of that last statistic as Kevin and I waited for our unwelcome dinner guest to return, my own fight-or-flight responses remained in the *off* position, which certainly would not have been the case had we been dealing with a brown bear. This discrepancy simply shows how one's emotional response to the two species can stand at odds with the facts even when an experienced observer should know better. Fact is, I was more concerned with Kevin being able to take this bear with his bow than with saving our camp, or our lives.

I felt certain the bear would return shortly, and I was right. Kevin had barely settled in and checked the shooting lanes through the tattered plastic on the back of the old frame structure by the time a glossy black shadow appeared in the alders 20 yards away. Since we were going to have to shoot him one way or another, I was pleased to note that the bear was a solid 6-foot-plus boar… just the kind of bear Kevin had traveled across the Pacific to find. I really hoped I didn't have to ruin this opportunity by shooting the bear with a firearm, but I also hoped that if it came to that I could hit it with my unfamiliar weapon.

Although the bear was within bow range the moment he stepped from the brush, he was quartering sharply toward us. I knew Kevin would have the discipline to pass up the shot at this angle, as indeed he did. The next five minutes proved extremely interesting as the bear growled, slapped his paws on the ground, bluff-charged, and otherwise tried to drive us away from what he clearly regarded as "his" kitchen, all without turning sidewise enough to show us some ribs.

Then the bear was actually inside the old frame structure with us. I admit that I was trying to remember whatever little I ever knew about shooting handguns and thanking my lucky stars that we weren't dealing with a brown bear. When he finally backed out amidst a chorus of growls, the moment of truth arrived when he turned sideways.

I hope that reporting what happened next won't embarrass Kevin, who is one of the best longbow hunters I know. Perhaps it was the unusual shot angle (from his knees, Kevin was actually shooting *up* at the bear.) Perhaps it was the distraction of the maze of wooden slats and perhaps he'd just had too long to think about the shot. Perhaps some "bear fever" was involved. At any rate, Kevin sent his broadhead whistling through the gristle on top of the bear's withers, above the spine and well removed from anything the animal couldn't live without, as we proved by tracking it halfway down the mountain without finding any evidence of a consequential hit.

Despite that disappointment, we *had* accomplished our primary mission, for we never saw the troublesome bear again. Furthermore, we hadn't had to waste a perfectly good bowhunting quarry by shooting it with a firearm, and we'd taught a problem bear a valuable lesson at low cost to the animal. Hopefully, if he ever catches another whiff of human scent he'll turn around and head in the other direction.

Then again, maybe he won't. You just never know about black bears.

Section II

Montana

10.

B-Tag Adventure

The thermometer outside the kitchen window registered an even zero when I started the coffee pot, not an unreasonable temperature for November on the high plains of Montana. As I hiked down the coulee, the dead calm wind and crystalline stars overhead suggested that I'd enjoy a pleasant morning even if I never saw a deer.

Fortunately, by the time shooting light spilled over the hills to the east I already knew it wouldn't come to that. I'd caught a glimpse of a deer's silhouette moving against the pines' snowy background, and the crunch of hoofs on crusted snow soon confirmed that an animal was approaching along a trail that led from our lower pasture to the bedding area behind me. As I oozed to my feet and began to shift into shooting position, I realized that for the first time since I'd filled my elk tag five weeks earlier, I really felt like killing an animal with my bow.

But it still had to be the right animal, and a fold in the hillside terrain kept me from enjoying a definitive look at the deer even though I could plainly track its progress with my ears. The measured pace of its approach suggested that the deer was browsing its way back to the bedding cover. Since its appetite could draw the process out for a long time, I shifted my recurve under my arm so I could keep my hands warm in my pockets during the wait.

Although I do plenty of cold weather hunting, I admit that I'd started to shiver by the time the deer crested the rise, walking steadily in my direction. My first good look at its head showed me all that I needed to see, and by the time it entered the clearing below me I was at full draw. The flight of a perfect arrow toward a big game animal is always a joy to behold, and as the fletching disappeared behind the deer's shoulder, I wished I could have beheld it a little longer. Then the woods exploded in a flurry of hoofs and snow, only to fall silent a few seconds later.

Although I didn't see the deer go down, I felt certain of my shot, and good tracking snow covered the ground. Consequently, I didn't force myself to wait any proscribed amount of time before taking up the trail. I had valid reasons for breaking the rules. My fingers were numb after remaining exposed to the cold prior to the shot, I wanted to dress out the deer before it turned into a block of ice, and I'd heard coyotes howling in the coulee the night before.

The trail proved easy, as anticipated. A hundred yards down the hill, I walked up to the fallen deer and experienced the flush of satisfaction that always accompanies the conclusion of a job well done. This was the moment when I should have run my hands along the antlers and appreciated all the nuances that distinguish one set from all the rest. And I would have, except that there weren't any antlers.

The object of my morning's adventure was a doe.

B-TAG ADVENTURE

A whitetail doe in the summer.

While I've made no secret of my concerns about the preoccupation with trophy antlers increasingly apparent among bowhunters, this isn't a tirade against trophy hunting (however that's defined). Instead, I'm going to present a reasoned argument why bowhunters should look forward to filling antlerless tags each season and treat the process with the respect it deserves.

From a herd management standpoint, antlerless tags (which I'll refer to as B-tags, just because that's what we call them in Montana) play a vital role. You can't manage game populations by shooting bucks (or bulls) alone. However, the heart of my argument isn't biological. I simply feel that hunting does is a valuable part of the bowhunting experience, and we ought to approach it with more enthusiasm.

Practical considerations first. I really enjoy eating venison, and my family lives on it. Even though our kids are grown and gone now, they all keep cycling back through the house with empty coolers during hunting season, so we go through a lot of deer, especially if I haven't killed an elk that year. Despite an over-abundance of whitetails, Montana residents only get one buck tag each season, and one for Lori and one for me doesn't get the job done. While these details vary from state to state, antlerless tags are a great way to fill the freezer in most jurisdictions.

They also provide the best way I know to learn how to bowhunt big game. The same factors that make some hunters gravitate to bows and arrows often make them selective about what they shoot. That's fine, except that when a novice bowhunter who spends three seasons waiting for an opportunity at a trophy buck finally has one in range, chances are good he'll make one of the vast number of mistakes we all had to work our way through while we were starting. There's no substitute for experience in the path to successful bowhunting, and the best way to obtain it is to make some venison. Hang onto that buck tag if you want, but you'll be a better bowhunter (and a better fed one) if you've filled some B-tags by the time that big chance arrives.

Notoriously inaccurate conventional wisdom holds that big whitetail bucks are the smartest animals in the woods, and that killing a doe is so easy in comparison that it doesn't offer much challenge, even with a bow. File that one away under M for Myth. Of course, big bucks are tough, but that's mostly because: A) There aren't very many of them, and B) They are largely nocturnal most of the year. When it comes down to the skill level required to put a bow-range deer on the ground cleanly, there isn't much difference between a big buck and a wise old doe. (In fact, the former may be the *easier* quarry in November.)

One reason big bucks seem smarter than their antlerless counterparts is that their headgear allows us to keep track of them as individuals, whereas most does look pretty much the same, at least to the casual eye. Give a mature doe that has survived several hunting seasons a comparable distinguishing characteristic and you might be amazed by her acuity.

Years ago, a wise old doe haunted the coulee behind my house. Frostbite during the brutal winter of her second year had left her ears distinctively notched. It didn't bother me that she evaded me for two long seasons, for there were plenty of other B-tag candidates around the place. But the notch-eared doe had an uncanny ability to detect me in a tree stand, and whenever she did, she would back off a hundred yards and snort non-stop until darkness fell, or I went away. I have no idea how many big bucks' lives she saved before she made a rare mistake in front of my hunting partner one day. He gave those notched ears a position of honor in the forest of mounted antlers hanging from his living room walls, and she deserved it.

I've focused this discussion on antlerless whitetails simply because they're a species everyone understands, and because the combination of the Montana deer season structure and my family's appetite for venison has provided me plenty of experience with them. But these principles apply broadly, and over the years I've enjoyed memorable hunting for female antelope, mule deer, and elk as well. I really regret that I never put in for a bighorn ewe tag here (a near certain draw if you apply for several seasons) rather than wasting nearly 40 years trying unsuccessfully to draw a pie-in-the-sky ram tag.

While I could have killed a record book cougar almost every year if I didn't prefer to give most of those opportunities to others, I did shoot a female lion a few years back. We hit the track on a truly miserable January day, with howling winds and an ambient temperature below zero. The dogs did a heroic job of staying on the track across six or eight miles of rugged backcountry, which we covered on foot. When we finally reached the tree after all that effort, it just seemed right for someone to kill the cat, so I did. The experience reminded me that female lions usually have nicer hides than toms. They make better eating, too.

All of which serves to illustrate this essay's point. There are many legitimate reasons to hunt, of which horns and antlers are merely one. The judicious harvest of female big game animals is a biologically appropriate practice that will put wild game on the table and develop the hunter's skills while providing vastly expanded opportunities to do what we all love to do: bowhunt.

What's not to like about that?

Flash alert! Just as I was completing work on this book, we learned that Lori drew a ewe bighorn tag for the Missouri River Breaks. Well acquainted with the area, I know we'll see plenty of sheep and have a great time. Sure, a lot of those sheep will be big rams, but I'll be happy just to watch them and shoot them with my camera. If Lori's arrow flies true, I'll also enjoy an opportunity to solve a mystery that has perplexed me for years. Friends who have been luckier in the drawings than I have consistently complain about the poor quality of the meat from their trophy rams. After eating plenty of delicious sheep in Alaska, I find this hard to believe. Most Alaska sheep hunting occurs well before the rut. I've never been a believer in the theory that old males of any species taken during the rut provide inferior venison, just because I've eaten so many bulls and bucks taken then that produced wonderful venison.

Do rutting bighorn rams really produce poor quality meat, or is it just that Montanans don't like mutton? Hopefully, I'll have more ideas on the subject by the end of the upcoming season.

11.

Rattling 101

It was the last hour of a bitterly cold November afternoon, and I hadn't seen a buck all day. I was sitting at the corner of two fencerows overlooking a vast alfalfa field when I finally spotted movement on the snow a half-mile away. My binoculars revealed the silhouette of a full-racked buck. After observing the whitetail for several minutes, I concluded that he wasn't coming anywhere near me without some encouragement. With nothing to lose, I reached for my trusty rattling antlers.

The response could not have been more dramatic. At the first crash, the buck spun in my direction and started across the field at a dead run. I then made a cardinal error: eager to hold the buck's attention, I continued to grind the bases of my horns together while forgetting how fast a motivated buck can cover ground. Moments later, the buck was standing 15 yards away while I stood armed with nothing but shed antlers.

I didn't try to force the issue by reaching for my bow while the buck was staring at me. Eventually, the buck drifted off down the fence line and gave me a chance to pick up my bow undetected. A backhanded tinkle from my horn tips brought him right back on the run, and as he stared down into the thick brush behind me looking for the fight, I sent a cedar arrow through his ribs.

I'd had plenty of opportunity to study the buck's antlers during this sequence of events and I didn't need to run my hands along them to know he carried six points on a side. His headgear wasn't the issue though. It was the dramatic conduct of the hunt that burned that chilly afternoon's events into my memory—and illustrates why I don't go deer hunting during the rut without a set of rattling antlers in my daypack.

Whitetails have probably generated more discussion and theories than all other species of big game combined. Scrapes, rubs, scents, calls, moon phases: good grief! I decided years ago to concentrate on what I observed myself in the field. I learned that most whitetail theory is just that, with two important exceptions: scrape hunting and rattling.

One caveat: with the sole exception of cougars, whitetails are the New World's most widely distributed big game animal and their behavior varies by location. While I've hunted them from Mexico to Alberta, most of my own observations took place near my home in the Mountain West. Many of my conclusions can be generalized to whitetails elsewhere but some differences need to be considered in other locations, particularly regarding rut timing.

I'm always surprised by the number of experienced bowhunters who seldom rattle at all. Explanations generally run along the following lines: "I bet I rattled a dozen times last season and never saw a deer." Or more discouraging yet, "I saw a big buck coming down the fence line and when I rattled he turned and ran away." But as my father told me years ago: "When you're hunting big game, whatever you're doing only has to work once."

Whether the quarry is ducks or moose, most calling instructions begin with elaborate descriptions of the sounds you're supposed to make. Helpful hint: it doesn't much matter. Whatever you're calling, the most important variable is the mood of the animal, over which you have no control. The next most important factors are when you call and how you set up. The actual sounds you make rank a distant third. Tinkle the top tines together, grind the bases, and you'll be rattling whitetails.

At what point in the whitetail season should you rattle? Conventional wisdom holds that rattling is most effective just before the rut since that's when bucks are establishing dominance. However, while hunting elk early one September years ago, I heard the distinct clash of antlers ahead of me in the aspens. Assuming I'd located sparring bulls, I eased forward into the wind only to find two mature whitetails tussling in the middle of a meadow with two smaller bucks observing them. As I watched, two more bucks materialized from different directions to watch the show. That was one of the finest examples of natural rattling attracting bucks I've ever seen, and it took place weeks before it should have.

I've personally experienced my best rattling during peak rut, the last two weeks of November where I live. Bucks may be busy chasing does then, but all that testosterone makes them bold and aggressive, and that's exactly the mindset that produces aggressive rattling responses.

I've rattled bucks in at all hours of the day. During the rut, I usually stay quiet right after daylight to avoid disrupting the does' natural movement patterns. At that time of year there's nothing better than unsuspecting does filing by, and rattling isn't going to help that cause. Mid-morning through noon is my favorite time to rattle, followed by mid-to late afternoon. I usually tone it down again an hour before dark.

I divide the way bucks respond to rattling into two categories: aggressive and tentative. The six-point described earlier typifies the aggressive response: direct and immediate, with caution thrown to the wind. Bucks don't always respond that way, but when they do you will witness one of the most dramatic moments in bowhunting. Some bucks respond much more cautiously however, as if their instincts tell them to investigate before committing to a fight. That behavior illustrates the tentative response alluded to earlier. These bucks may be younger and smaller, but not always. They're also more likely to circle downwind, and they may require a bit more encouragement to bring them into bow range.

Some seasons back, Lori and I were sitting in stands several hundred yards apart in a timbered coulee below our rural home when I heard her start to rattle. Immediately, a 4x4 appeared in front of me and began to walk slowly in her direction. Because of the terrain, I knew that she couldn't see the deer. As soon as she stopped rattling, the buck halted but continued to stare in her direction, only to resume his measured approach when she started to rattle again ten minutes later. "Keep rattling, Lori!" I wanted to scream as this continued for nearly an hour. Darkness fell before she could lure the buck into bow range, and she never even saw the deer. Moral: be patient, and when conditions are right, keep rattling.

Sometimes, silence is golden. We've already talked about the need to avoid spooking does. Should you rattle as soon as you see a buck you want to shoot?

The answer is an emphatic *no*... at least initially. The first thing I do in this situation is observe the deer. If there seems to be any chance that he will do what I need him to do on his own, I remain silent. Calling any game animal represents an exchange of information between offense and defense that can hurt either side. If it's apparent that the buck isn't headed my way, I'll rattle, usually waiting until the deer is out of sight to minimize the chance that he'll see me move. I've watched too many bucks come in from great distances to worry about letting one get out of rattling range.

The Girl Scouts advise us to *Be Prepared* and no one has said it better. A buck responding tentatively may allow plenty of time to get ready for the shot, but my own rule is: Never rattle unless you're ready for an immediate, aggressive response.

A whitetail buck's ability to localize sound from a distance is uncanny. An aggressive response doesn't just mean having a deer appear in sight; it may well mean having a deer within a few yards of you *right now*. Exchanging rattling antlers for bow sounds simple enough, until you've tried it with a buck staring at you from point blank range. An admission from a hunter who's been caught off-guard? You bet. I learned years ago that you can't kill a buck while you're holding rattling antlers.

Before you rattle, make sure you can exchange antlers for bow quickly. This is especially important in tree stands. Your bow should be hanging from a hook or a branch where you can reach it with minimum movement, and you should have a similar arrangement ready for your rattling antlers. (I always join mine with a leather thong threaded through holes drilled in the bases so I can hang them up quickly.) If you're hunting from the ground, nock an arrow and hang your bow from a branch where you can reach it easily. On cold, still mornings when I love to rattle, I make my first sequence short and immediately exchange antlers for bow. If a buck is going to respond aggressively, he'll usually do so at once.

I'm old fashioned and still prefer to use naturally shed antlers. The "rattle bags" available on the market now make rattling easier, since they're less awkward and require little movement to produce effective sounds. Lori loves hers; perhaps she'll convert me someday.

As usual, attitude may be the most important element of technique. Calling any game animal into bow range requires confidence in the method, but for bowhunters accustomed to silence there's something counterintuitive about making noise to attract a wary animal. Developing that confidence usually requires either a positive experience or a leap of faith. But as anyone who has called a spring gobbler into range or bugled in an elk knows, there's no more rewarding hunting experience than learning to speak the quarry's language and talking one into a fatal mistake.

12.

Four Hundred Turkeys

"I ran into Bill Edgars at the feed store the other day," Lori's ex-husband said over coffee in our kitchen the morning before the opening day of spring turkey season. "Says he had four hundred turkeys in his pasture out on the divide the other day."

As it happens, I was in the process of organizing my turkey hunting pack for a pre-dawn departure the following morning, although I had not yet decided upon a destination. Like many local Montanans I have lost access to a lot of the property I used to hunt, but I still had four great places to pursue turkeys, which is all I've ever needed. Three of those are foothills ranches owned by old friends, and one of those three lies immediately adjacent to Bill Edgar's pasture.

"How many did you say?" I asked Pete as my head turned away from the pile of diaphragms, slates, and box calls I'd spread across the counter prior to testing each of them for tone after what had been a long absence from the game.

"Four hundred," he repeated. There has never been any animosity among Pete, Lori, and me following a rearrangement of marriages two decades earlier. The three of us hunt and fish together all the time, and I had no reason to suspect deliberate inaccuracy in his reporting. Nonetheless, that was an awful lot of turkeys. As my brain began to process this intelligence, numbers zipped across the computer screen in my cerebral cortex like a scene from the *Matrix* movies. First, I cut the original number in half on general principles, because all hunters are deliberate liars, subconsciously prone to exaggeration, or both. Two hundred turkeys. Then I halved it again, because the information came third hand. One hundred turkeys.

That's still a lot of birds, but the number was not implausible. Although wild turkeys have thrived in Montana since their initial introduction in the 1950s (I can see the site of the first release from my house), they are not native to the state. They couldn't survive during long periods of deep snow on the high plains until ranchers brought them the gift of feedlots. During the winter now, it's not unusual to see large congregations of turkeys picking through cow turds for food when the landscape lies blanketed in white, an image best suppressed when preparing a spring gobbler for the table. Those big flocks usually disperse rapidly and head for the hills once the snow starts to melt, and it had been an early spring. Still, I could believe a hundred turkeys right across the fence from my friend's property, which would ensure a target rich environment for whatever calls I chose from the pile on the counter.

Unable to resist this unsolicited lead, I'd made up my mind about my opening day destination by the time I started to grill a backstrap from the previous year's whitetail that night. Lori and I had only been back in Montana for a few days after several months of travel, and I'd had no opportunity to do any scouting on my own. Furthermore, I'd missed the last three spring turkey seasons completely while chasing steelhead near our Alaska home. I was rusty, and my turkey intelligence was badly outdated. Four hundred turkeys sounded too good to ignore, no matter what effect reality had upon the actual number.

It was a pleasant spring evening, and I suggested that we move the venison, the salad, and our plates onto the deck overlooking the coulee on the west side of our property. In truth, I had an ulterior motive for this decision beyond the appealing weather. The last on my list of four great places to hunt turkeys is my own backyard, and

I couldn't think of a more enjoyable way to scout than by sitting down and listening while holding a glass of Malbec.

Lori and I took our time with the meal. Cooked rare and sliced thin, the backstrap offered supporting evidence for my contrary position in the "big old bucks taste terrible" debate. The deck sits within sight of the kennel, and the Labs and wirehairs were already lined up competing to see who could offer the most heart-rending appeal for the leftovers. Lori was reflecting upon our busy winter when I rudely interrupted her with a loud *Shhh!* and an upheld hand. She knew what I was up to and did not protest my bad manners.

"Where?" she whispered quietly in her best hunting voice. I pointed silently toward the southern end of the coulee. Years of shotguns and aircraft engines have taken their toll upon my ears. Lori can hear bugling elk and buzzing rattlesnakes better than I can, yet I have retained an ability to hear gobbling turkeys, as if that elusive, mercurial sound somehow bypasses the usual route from the real world to my brain. Even so, I could not yet confirm what I'd heard or exactly where I'd heard it.

But the next gobble left me with a reasonable estimate of range and bearing, and that was all I needed. Dusk was rapidly enveloping the landscape, and the gobbler had to be near his roost tree.

"What are you going to do in the morning?" Lori asked. She was still whispering even though the bird was a long way away—a reflection of the great habits she has acquired during our marriage. I simply pointed south up the coulee. "What about the four hundred turkeys?" she asked.

"Don't leave birds to find birds," I replied, subconsciously whispering myself. Then I scraped the leftovers onto a plate and headed to the kennel to pick the winner of the hungry dog contest.

I hunt spring turkeys with my ears. The increased level of attention and concentration demanded during a turkey hunt opens the hunter up to a whole new audial world of wildlife activity at sunrise. As I set off up the coulee the following morning, the beginning of an eventual chorus of awakening robins told me when to start listening seriously, for I seldom hear a gobble from a roost tree until the robins have started to sing. There followed the eerie quavering of a courting snipe high overhead, a distant coyote's howl, and a *bronk* from one of the geese nesting on the creek nearly two miles away—a testimonial to the acoustics of crisp, still morning air. Then a pair of ravens started to quarrel at the head of the coulee, bringing me to an abrupt halt mid-stride. Experience has taught me that a raven's call will often elicit a shock-gobble from a roosted tom, and sure enough. The bird was a little farther away than I'd estimated the night before, but now I knew where I had to be. Like a vampire scurrying back to his coffin before sunrise, I broke into a trot so I could set up under the cover of darkness while the bird was still in the tree.

And I made it—barely. Deciding when to keep moving on a roosted tom and when to stop and prepare an ambush evokes an adage from William Blake's *Marriage of Heaven and Hell*: "You never know what is enough unless you know what is more than enough." *More than enough* means blundering into the bird, spooking him, and ending the hunt before it starts. Decades of experience in the spring woods have left me all too familiar with the problem. *Enough* means getting sufficiently close to the bird to attract its interest during the brief chaos that ensues when a flock of turkeys flies to the ground at first light. However, the greater the distance from the roost tree you set up, the tougher the calling will be. Getting it just right is like calling for another hit at the blackjack table. Since even a little *not quite enough* works better than any amount of *more than enough*, I stopped a conservative distance away, stretched a strip of netting around the branches of a fallen pine, and set three decoys up ten yards in front of me.

My decision three decades prior to hunt turkeys exclusively with traditional bows and arrows is central to this narrative. The difference in degree of difficulty between firearms and archery tackle is greater with turkeys than any other quarry I know, up to and including grizzly bears. I've taken my share of turkeys with a bow during those years, less because I'm an exceptional turkey hunter than because I live near a lot of turkeys that don't face the amount and sophistication of the hunting pressure their cohorts deal with in other parts of the country. Even so, I've worked for every one of those two-dozen birds.

Bowhunting for turkeys underwent a revolution of sorts some years back with the development of the pop-up blind, which allows the hunter a mobile means of total concealment. It's hard to understand how birds that can see you blink from a hundred yards away can totally ignore an artificial blind four feet in diameter when they're practically on top of it, but they do. The difficulty of killing a turkey with a bow derives from the motion needed to come to full draw with the bird at close range. The pop-up blind largely eliminates that problem. Since the essence of turkey hunting derives from calling a wary gobbler into range no matter how you're hunting, I justified killing a few birds from pop-ups but never felt quite right about it. On those occasions I left the woods feeling as if I'd caught a trout on a worm during a PMD hatch. Now I've gone back to my old ways, relying on nothing but a bit of netting, natural cover, and good timing to let me get away with drawing my bow and delivering a lethal arrow.

After completing my hasty set-up, I settled into place on a log and offered a soft tree yelp just to let the gobbler know I was there. After receiving an immediate reply, I shut up and waited for my ears to tell me when the bird had left the tree. My hope was that the tom was a lone gobbler preparing to spend the morning looking for a receptive hen.

But that was not to be. After a quick flurry of spontaneous gobbles convinced me that the bird was on the ground, I began to yelp vigorously. While over-calling is a fault to be avoided in the attempt to lure anything from turkeys to moose into range, I like to call like a fool right after fly-down to take advantage of the inevitable confusion. For several minutes I thought I was about to enjoy a short turkey season. I didn't hear any hens, the gobbler was answering all my calls immediately, and he sounded as if he were headed straight toward me.

The moment of first visual contact with a calling gobbler always arouses excitement as your eyes confirm what your ears have been telling you. Suddenly, the white semi-circle of a tom Merriam's fanned tail feathers appeared over the lip of a little rise just up the hill from me, and hubris allowed me a silent "Gotcha!" That's when my plans fell apart. First, I heard a hen yelp. Then dark figures were swarming over the hill beside the gobbler like ants. Finally, the slutiest sounding hen I've ever heard began to yelp like an actress in an X-rated movie for turkeys.

I just couldn't compete with the real thing. The gobbler followed the hen past me 40 yards away. Since a turkey is a difficult target for a bow at half that range, discipline overcame the temptation to launch a Hail Mary. The birds disappeared in the direction of my house. I remained crouched amidst the branches of the fallen tree, calling intermittently and hoping the tom had ended the tryst one way or the other.

I gave it two hours, and then I picked up and walked home for breakfast.

That evening found Lori and me back on the deck with a slab of the previous summer's king salmon on a platter between us and the wirehairs reminding us that the Labs had received the treats the night before. "Where are you going tomorrow?" Lori asked.

"Guess I shouldn't ignore those four hundred turkeys out on the divide," I replied.

Then we both heard it, too loud for anyone to ignore—a loud, thunderous gobble just over the rim of the coulee that couldn't have been more than a hundred yards away. The dogs barked, and the turkey gobbled back at them.

"Get your bow and go shoot him!" Lori exclaimed.

"It's not like that," I said. "You hunt spring turkeys in the morning, not at night."

"Why?" she asked, not unreasonably.

"I don't know. For the same reason you don't shoot turkeys out of trees or cast blindly to bonefish when you can't see them anymore." Although an accomplished bowhunter in her own right, Lori has never been able to wrap her brain around turkeys. That's probably because her brain is larger than mine.

"So, what are you going to do in the morning?"

"You don't leave birds…"

"I know," she said. "Eat the last of that salmon."

I remained on the deck until color had drained from the landscape, confident that my ears had accurately pinpointed the gobbler's roost tree 200 yards behind the kennel.

The dogs sounded off when I tried to sneak past them in the dark the following morning, but I reasoned that the birds had to be used to them. Certain that I was dealing with the same tom and likely the same company of hens, I tested the limits of *more than enough* by creeping within 50 yards of the spot I thought they had roosted. By the time robins started to chirp, I felt securely hidden and happy with the position of my decoys.

I felt even happier when the bird began to sound off practically overhead. Spooked turkeys don't talk like that, and I was close enough to be within the likely perimeter of his landing zone when he left the tree. And I was—in fact, at fly-down several hens practically landed on top of me, although none appeared aware of my presence. But the gobbler wasn't interested in *those* hens. He only had eyes for another shameless hussy as he strutted past me at 30 yards—close, but still not close enough. By the time I stopped calling and headed up the hill to feed the dogs, I was thinking about the last turkey I'd killed with a shotgun. Nothing about that memory seemed regrettable.

"Here we go again," Lori said when the bird sounded off that night as we were eating the last two mallards from the freezer. "Sure you don't want to go look for the four hundred turkeys out on the divide?"

"I'm sure," I replied tersely. "This has become personal."

"How can anything become personal with a *bird*?"

"You'd have to be there to understand. Matter of fact, why don't you come with me in the morning?"

"Because I'm smarter than you are."

To which I had no reply. The following morning, I set up on the gobbler again. This time I called sparingly, offering just a single yelp when he left the tree. Once again, I watched him follow his hens off into the distance without offering me a shot. This time, I stuck it out until noon, but I never saw the bird again that day.

Not this year.

In fact, I never saw that bird again at all. Shortly after that last futile encounter, we left for our old Alaska hometown to chase steelhead for two weeks. A few days of legal spring turkey hunting awaited us upon our return, but I never made contact of any kind with the gobbler in our west coulee. He may have left the area and he may have bred all those hens and shut up for the year, but in either case our chess match was over. Perhaps I'll run into him when I'm hunting deer nearby this fall, but I doubt I'll take a shot at him if I do. We had established the rules of engagement during the month of April, and to kill him during a chance encounter in November would feel like a disappointment no matter how good the bird tasted on the table, smothered in the morels we'd gathered and frozen upon our return from Alaska.

What of the 400 turkeys on the divide? They turned into the season's ultimate McGuffin. I never even went out to look for them. Was that wise? Obviously not, at least if you measure the success of a hunting experience by the quantity of game in the bag at its conclusion. It is impossible to kill fewer turkeys than I did hunting behind my own barn that spring season, and I will not pretend that I don't enjoy killing big, mature gobblers with my bow.

However, I have reached an age at which I'm willing to sacrifice results for intensity, and I find something indescribably intense about devoting my energy to the pursuit of one specific quarry, be it a bull, a buck, or, as in this case, a bird. That tom threw down a gauntlet when he gobbled at me from my own backyard, and for better or worse I picked it up. I may have lost the duel, but I wouldn't have missed the fight for anything—not even for a morning surrounded by 400 turkeys.

If they really were out on the divide that spring, some of them would be back next April. Perhaps I will be, too.

13.

Nothing but a Hound Dog

Fresh snow always has a tale to tell. After a winter storm, the only way an animal can avoid leaving a record of its activities is to fly or sit still. The wildlife has been active overnight, and after two hours studying the dots and dashes flowing past the headlights, the sudden appearance of the track we are seeking feels like the discovery of a gold nugget at the bottom of a pan. As we slide to a stop, coffee cups and Pop Tarts – the official Breakfast of Lion Hunters – scatter everywhere. After tumbling from the truck, the cold morning air feels like after shave lotion slapped across my cheeks. It is wonderful to be outside at last.

To many, the track would be nothing but another disturbance in the snow, but experience has taught us better. The prints look round as saucers and their measured stride suggests confidence and purpose. Out here in the open, the deep powder makes it difficult to evaluate their size. Flashlights in hand, Rosy and I follow them down into the trees along the creek where the snow is more compact and revealing. Even there the verdict is equivocal. The lion might be a tom, but it might be a female. What the hell; the dogs need the exercise, and so do we.

Back at the truck, we load our packs and discuss strategy. This morning, we are an eclectic crew. If lion hunting had an equivalent of the esteemed (and, according to most indications, soon to be extinct) British MFH, John "Rosy" Roseland would be one. He was hunting cougars in these hills before the idea even occurred to anyone else. On the other end of the spectrum, Anne Williams has never seen a mountain lion. She is here this morning because of curiosity and friendship and, I suspect, because she has decided that running up and down mountains benefits you as much as running up and down StairMasters, with the advantage of superior scenery. After a decade of hounds and lions, my level of experience falls somewhere on Rosy's side of the midline.

Tucked away in the back of the truck, the more experienced dogs have already figured out what's up, and an excited clamor greets us as we throw down the tail gate. I snap a leash on Drive and walk him to the track while Rosy follows suit with Charlie. Both hounds like what they smell. Turning Drive loose feels like launching a warm-blooded cruise missile. Back at the truck, Anne has instructions to hang onto the rest of the dogs, but that is too much to ask of anyone and as Drive and Charlie charge down the slope and across the creek, the young dogs escape her grasp and tumble along behind.

Ignoring the urge to shoulder my pack and get on with things, I stand in the snow and listen. Lion hunts are long distance affairs guided for the most part by nothing more dramatic than tracks in the snow, interrupted by occasional opportunities to follow a chase with one's ears. I don't get to listen to my hounds as much as I would like except at the beginning and the end. Somewhere out there in the gloom, Drive's mellow baritone marks the leading edge of the chase. Because I have raised him from a puppy, I close my eyes and follow his progress with pride even though there is no way anyone but God could take credit for that incredible nose. Charlie's bawl sounds steady and competent as always. Somewhere behind them, Axle, Rosey's second black and tan, chimes in with his distinctive high-pitched bleat. I like to imagine that Pete, my young dog, is adding his voice somewhere to the chorus, although if pressed I would admit that might be wishful thinking.

Finally, they are out of earshot, their lovely voices lost to the mountain wind. High overhead, the dark peak looms, eclipsing the first warm glow of the sunrise. The sweet part is over. As we collect our gear, we debate the need for snowshoes. No one wants to bother with them, but I elect to hedge my bets by strapping mine behind my pack. Then there is nothing left to do but begin the long, uncertain climb uphill into the darkness.

Forget—at least temporarily—retrievers, pointers, and setters. Historically, the essential relationship between man and hunting dogs is best defined by hounds.

Ever since some distant human ancestor first stood on two legs and picked up a stick, *Homo sapiens* has enjoyed only two advantages over the rest of the competition in the food chain: a prehensile thumb and a brain (only one of which works consistently). On the other hand, the animals our forebears longed to eat (and the animals that longed to eat them) were their overwhelming superiors in sight, hearing, smell, speed, and strength. The logical remedy was to enlist some assistance. *Voila*: hounds.

Edward Steichen's spectacular photographic collection *The Family of Man* contains an arresting image of a Kalahari tribesman about to plunge a spear into the chest of a gemsbok his dogs have brought to bay. The composition is fraught with tension: the hunter looks pitifully small next to the gemsbok, and it is hard to avoid the feeling that all hell is about to break loose. *This says it all*, I thought as soon as I saw that picture. *A hungry hunter. A dangerous quarry. Some damn good dogs.* No doubt a victim of my own instincts, the rest of the collection scarcely seemed to matter.

By the time of the American revolution, hound hunting in the British Isles had already undergone a paradoxical transition from the realm of the hunter-gatherer to a defining pastime of the upper classes. In fact, it is precisely that element of snobbery that underlies the modern drive to ban hound hunting in England, a movement that has less to do with foxes and hounds than with class resentment and the marginalization of rural values in an increasingly urban society. Outdoorsmen on this side of the Atlantic should take note. The more any activity becomes the exclusive province of the privileged, the harder it is to defend in an egalitarian society.

Of course, early Americans saw things differently. In my own revisionist view of history, I sometimes suspect that the American revolution had more to do with hunting rights than unfair taxes. At any rate, hounds were an integral part of America's outdoor heritage from the beginning, especially in the south, where the gentry raised hounds to hunt bears for sport and sharecroppers used them to put possum pie on the table.

Regional biases were an important factor in hound hunting's eventual fall from cultural grace. The end of the Civil War marked a period of general disenchantment with southern cultural values during which it was all too easy for outside arbiters of taste to associate hound hunting with evils as diverse as chewing tobacco and Jim Crow racism. Remember how the press once pilloried Lyndon Johnson for having the bad judgement to tug on a beagle's ears in front of a camera? The ruckus wasn't as much about the hound as it was about Johnson's refusal to check his down-home cultural values at the door when he moved into the White House.

These attitudes laid the foundation for the current assault on hound hunting by animal rights activists. Give the devil his due. Today's organized opponents of hunting know how to play the media like a fiddle, and they have convinced a remarkable number of naïve and misinformed voters that hound hunting is a barbaric cultural relic that should be banned as we move forward towards a vegan Brave New World. An outdoor columnist with whom I have butted heads over this matter in print once labeled hunters' concerns over such loss of rights hysterical. Hysteria is an unreasonable fear. Try explaining this alleged unreasonableness to houndsmen in California, Oregon, and Washington, where political correctness has turned good lion dogs into pot-lickers forever.

The traditional anti-hunting elements of modern society aren't the only ones to question the propriety of hunting cougars with dogs, an activity that occasionally raises eyebrows among hunters themselves. Because of my own deep commitment to traditional bowhunting—arguably the most demanding and nuance-laden hunting method of all—I've listened to my share of criticism from skilled bowhunters who think lion hunting with hounds consists of nothing more than following a pack of dogs to a tree in order to shoot a helpless cat. In fact, while lion hunting can certainly be reduced to a charade by overuse of machines and gadgets, in its purest form it demands as much skill and physical effort as any outdoor activity I know.

At least skeptics in this group can usually be educated. I have far less patience with objections to lion hunting that come from young, affluent, non-hunting outdoors enthusiasts who think that owning a pair of hiking boots and subscribing to a few trendy magazines makes them authorities on wildlife. (I once accused a capable and well-known wildlife writer of harboring such biases. As I've reported elsewhere, we eventually worked out our differences over a mountain lion dinner.) To many members of this set, the idea of shooting a mountain lion under any circumstances evokes the kind of revulsion most societies reserve for matters of religious heresy. Many cite biology as the basis of their convictions. Never mind that these individuals and the institutions they support think nothing of patronizing destination ski resorts carved from winter habitat critical to the survival of deer, elk, and cougars. I think the real offense stems from the failure of most lion hunters to acknowledge the most important principle in the yuppie canon of ethics: the necessity of looking *great* in the latest fashionable outdoor wear.

All of which helps explain why I'm not just going hunting when I load my pack and start up the mountain after the dogs this morning. Like any other disenfranchised member of society, I am defending my own cultural values and way of life.

It has already been a long winter and several cycles of freezing and thawing have left a treacherous layer of ice beneath the new snow, which makes the long climb up the mountain a classical exercise in the *two steps forward, one step back* means of locomotion. The rocks are treacherous, and at times we are reduced to traveling on hands and knees. Pete has lost the chase and doubled back, adding additional confusion to the jumble of tracks weaving back and forth across the mountainside. But every time the trail seems uncertain, we spread out and study the sign, and somewhere in the riot of dog tracks we always manage to find the cat's. Despite the silence up ahead, the chase is still on.

There are ways to make this process easier. You can outfit the lead dogs with radio collars and use snow machines to shorten the track, all of which makes chasing lions a lot more like a video game and a lot less like hunting. As someone once said: *include me out*. The dignity of lion hunting is inseparable from its difficulty. Take away the woodsmanship, the tracking skills, and the burning legs, and the hunt is soon reduced to an execution. Some cats have eluded us over the years because of our stubborn adherence to this principle, but I don't need to kill anything badly enough to justify its compromise. It's a wonder that anyone does.

As we finally begin to close upon the ridge line, the sun breaks through the trees and the breeze starts to freshen. Although the morning has become quite pleasant, wind and rising temperature mean difficult scenting conditions for the dogs. To make matters worse, the exposed ridge is almost bare of tracking snow. We follow the track to a barren cliff where it finally disappears in the rocks. Our ears tell us nothing. The dogs are out there somewhere, but the mountains seem impossibly vast and indifferent. *Hell.* There is just no better way to describe the situation, not after the long climb and the realization that our dogs are missing in action.

After a brief strategy discussion, I set off around the cliffs to see if the track has gone over the ridge while Rosy and Anne skirt the side hill below. Within minutes, we are out of vocal contact. If all goes well, one of us will find the track and the chase intact, and we can get on with the business of trying to tree the lion. If all does not go well, we may spend the next week combing the mountains for the dogs.

Critics may call lion hunting many things, but I defy them to accuse it of being easy.

In some parts of the country, folks tend to go on and on about their hounds like soccer moms going on about their children. While I genuinely like my hounds, I'm perfectly willing to be realistic about their limitations. Perhaps I've just spent too much time with Labrador retrievers, but from stink to stupidity, the list of generic hound faults sometimes seems overwhelming. A good hound can only expect to have five entries in its CV: four legs and a nose. Additional positive qualities usually exist only in the imagination of the handler. As Elvis once reminded us in "You Ain't Nothin' but a Hound Dog" (actually first recorded by Willie Mae Thornton), it's hard to beat a hound as an icon for slouching opportunism.

I came by my affection for hounds the old-fashioned way: I inherited it. As a kid, my father chased all manner of game around north Texas river bottoms with his dogs before he went on to other things, including, eventually, the Nobel Prize in Medicine. (So much for the houndsman's conventional bubba stereotype.) I got to listen to those stories around the fireplace when I was a kid, and the reading matter my family shared around the same fireplace was as likely to include *The Voice of Bugle Ann* as Shakespeare. Enthusiasm for hounds has always depended upon just the kind of tradition that is best handed down through generations. The odd thing is how strongly our multicultural society has endorsed the validity of some cultural traditions at the expense of others.

In contrast to most contemporary sporting breeds, hounds hunt with us rather than for us, an attitude that tends to alienate bird dog handlers accustomed to subservience in the field. In their defense, I can only describe the performance of good hounds on a track as a miracle. As members of a species that has somehow outgrown its own sense of smell, we should view with awe a hound's ability to stick its nose into a day-old lion track and follow the smell into the next county. The sensory cues that define such a performance are immeasurable, and all the king's horses of the modern computer age remain incapable of reproducing it, no small reassurance to those troubled by the notion that technology has rendered instinct obsolete. Anyone who shares my own discomfort with cyberspace should be able to regard a determined hound running a track as a cause for celebration.

Following a lion chase on foot is essentially an exercise in logic. Circling through the snow on the far side of the blown-out ridge reveals no sign of a track, and if the dogs had the cat treed nearby, I would hear them. Ergo, they must have gone below.

After picking my way back down through the rocks, I angle across the slope until I can confirm the hypothesis. The first canine print is circling aimlessly through the pines, and I suspect that it belongs to Pete, who hasn't quite got the hang of this yet. A hundred yards farther across the hill, his track joins a jumble of others and I pause to sort them out in the snow. They belong to three more dogs, the cat, Anne, and Rosy. When I stop and listen hard above the sound of the wind in the trees, I can finally hear the crisp, staccato chop of the dogs at the tree. Somewhere down in the dark reaches of the canyon below, the chase is over.

Slipping and sliding down the fall line, I arrive at the base of a towering ponderosa to find Anne and Rosy staring into the branches overhead. At the base of the tree, Axle and Charlie are doing their best to become airborne. Drive, whose strength has always been on the track rather than at the tree, is yapping away indifferently while Pete trots in circles looking for faces to lick. The best I can hope for the pup today is that he has learned something.

And then there is the cat. No matter how many times I stare up into an evergreen canopy and see a mountain lion, I doubt that I will ever become accustomed to the experience, and I hope I never do. Tawny and graceful, the cat looks as if it belongs on another continent, if not another planet. Remarkably indifferent to the ruckus at ground level, it is studying us coldly, as if it knows it could bound down out of the tree and kill us all at will, which, since we are unarmed except for longbows, is probably true.

So why is the cougar sitting passively overhead? It turns out that the familiar animosity between dogs and cats long preceded their domestication. Recent field studies suggest that in areas where their ranges overlap, wolves drive cougars away from over half their kills and claim them for themselves. While a grown cougar can hold its own against anything in the woods, lions are solitary animals that never emulated the canine instinct for hunting in packs. Cougars evolved in the New World prior to the arrival of humans, which meant that climbing trees effectively removed them from the reaches of all their naturally occurring predators. Our cat is simply doing what its instincts have told it to do.

The chase may be over, but the hunt is not. The kill may come as something of an anticlimax at the end of a long, uncertain trail, but it is still an integral part of the event that must be dealt with, like the final act of a play or the sword at the end of a bullfight. However, there is still one important issue to resolve, for we are not yet certain of the cat's gender (although after studying several miles of tracks, I'm practically certain that it's a large female). That can be a difficult determination to make, especially when the anatomically correct object of scrutiny is tucked away high in the branches of a pine tree. Rosy finally shinnies part way up the tree and confirms my assumption.

The female quota in this district is still open, and there are many reasons for one of us to string a bow and shoot it. The cat is as big a female as Rosy and I have ever seen. Killing her would provide the dogs with a welcome conclusion to the hunt, and after the long chase, there is no doubt that they have earned one. Female lions often have nicer hides than males, and they taste better on the table. I don't know a single local rancher who wouldn't be delighted to have one less cougar in the hills. The problem is that I just don't want to kill a female and neither does Rosy. After an appropriate period of discussion, we dig the leashes out of our packs and begin the process of dragging the disappointed hounds away from the tree. In contrast to the dogs, Anne is plainly relieved by our decision.

Personally, I'm satisfied to write off the long morning as just another day of catch and release lion hunting.

Don and Sadie after a long, cold chase.

The best thing to be said for the long walk off the mountain is that it's all downhill. With melting snow creating a slick patina of water on top of the ice, the footing is even worse than it was during the climb. The dogs seem to think their leashes were meant to let them amuse themselves by hog-tying their handlers. By the time we reach the truck, we are all bruised and battered, and I have enough snow and pine needles down the back of my jacket to make my skin crawl. Without a lion hide or hindquarters in my pack, it's hard not to wonder if it's all been worth it.

Pleasantly exhausted, the hounds seem happy to return to the security of their familiar dog box. Back inside the truck, we round up enough leftover junk food to replenish a few of the calories we burned on our way up the mountain. Even the cold coffee tastes good. Although no one has enough energy left to express it, we share a feeling of satisfaction appropriate for a job well done even though we didn't kill the cat. As we turn the truck around to face the long road home, each of us seems to understand that we have witnessed something special and timeless.

I'm glad the lion is still up there somewhere.

14.

Fine Madness

April in Montana is a time of unrequited seasonal yearning. No matter how badly the outdoors enthusiast longs to believe that spring has arrived, on any given day unpredictable weather can refute all hope. When my southern friends talk about turkey hunting, their stories sound idyllic and pastoral. Here on the high plains, the opening day of turkey season is more likely to mean wool coats and snow shovels than crocuses and bluebirds.

Which explains why I was shivering as I listened to a splendid rendition of the most compelling chorus in the world: the crescendo gobbling of tom turkeys about to leave the roost tree at first light. In classical fashion, I had put the birds to bed the night before, and my knowledge of their location allowed an approach to close range under the cover of darkness. Eighty yards up the ridge from the roosted birds, I had cobbled together a makeshift blind behind a fallen tree. A trio of silhouette decoys turned slowly in the breeze 15 yards from my hiding place. Enthusiastic gobbling from the nearby pines confirmed that I had managed all this undetected. This morning's hunt, I told myself with more confidence than decades of experience had any right to suggest, had all the makings of a slam dunk.

Licking my diaphragm call into my mouth, I offered a few soft tree yelps to suggest the presence of receptive company just up the hill. Then I shut up and waited, working my muscles against the chill and wondering why I don't get to hunt turkeys in places that smell of spring flowers. Somewhere in the distance, a coyote howled. Down on the creek, a pair of geese took noisily to the air, and the turkeys shock-gobbled in response to every honk. But until the birds decided to stir, there was nothing for me to do but hunker down and enjoy the music.

Finally, the brainless gobbling from the roost tree reached a climax and the sound of heavy wings filled the air. The only predictable moment of confusion in a tom turkey's day comes at fly-down, and experienced turkey hunters go to great lengths to exploit it. I began to call while the birds were still in the air, to make them hit the ground with my position locked into their brains before their own hens could distract them. Yelping furiously, I did my best to sound like a hen turkey that has thrown caution and virtue to the wind, and it worked.

Two jakes came first, oozing slowly up the open ridgeline with surprising discretion for youngsters. The lead bird offered a standing shot at 20 yards, and I seriously considered taking it. Then a loud gobble sounded just over the edge of the hill and a real limb-hanger strutted into view. Greed—or whatever emotion makes hunters chose large representatives of the species over small—overwhelmed me, and I let the young tom pass. A soft cluck earned me a thunderous gobble in reply, and I began to visualize a perfect spot for the broadhead on the big gobbler's chest.

I timed my draw to coincide with the bird's passage behind a nearby pine, but in the rush of events, I had failed to keep track of the jakes. As soon as I began to move my bow arm, a sharp putt sounded from the middle of the decoys, breaking the spell like shattering glass. Transformed instantly from target to survivor, the big tom broke strut and streaked over the hill. I rose and turned to kill the jake that betrayed me, but he and his buddy had already melted into a bronze blur. The woods fell silent. It was over. All I could think of was the refrain from an old Hank Williams classic: *You win again!*

FINE MADNESS

Hunting wild turkeys with bow and arrow is truly a fine madness. *Meleagris gallopavo*, as Benjamin Franklin pointed out two hundred years ago, is everything a shrewd American should be: alert, suspicious, trusting nothing that hasn't been proven. Firearms hunters have respected the great bird's cunning since the era of the blunderbuss, as well they should.

Over the years, I have hunted the sharpest and toughest big game animals in the world with my bow, from wild sheep to grizzly bears, enjoying a generous measure of success. But no quarry has proven more consistently difficult than the wild turkeys in my own back yard. Licensed to perform difficult skills ranging from managing heart attacks to flying airplanes through clouds, I can assure you that none of those tasks is more difficult than killing a wild turkey with traditional archery tackle.

As an incorrigible aficionado of archery, I would argue that the bow is an ideal instrument—at least for me personally—with which to hunt all big game with one exception: the wild turkey. (And yes, I consider turkeys big game.) The essence of the turkey hunting experience is acquisition of the knowledge and calling skills needed to coax a mature tom into shotgun range, at which point it becomes entirely honorable to end the contest with the most efficient weapon possible, a 12-gauge. Like all seasoned turkey hunters, I have great admiration for those who manage to do so consistently, and yet I persist in playing the game differently.

The bowhunter's dilemma stems from a devilish Catch-22: if you are close enough to kill a turkey with an arrow, you are too close to draw a bow undetected. Chalk this paradox up to the wild turkey's incredible vision, which is capable of detecting motion within a nearly complete circle around an alert tom's head. Simply stated, it can't be done no matter what the hunter's level of skill unless the turkey makes a mistake, and mature wild turkeys don't make many mistakes.

So why bother trying? *Why* questions are always hunting's most difficult. During turkey season, I stick stubbornly to my bow for two reasons. First, the pure, personal satisfaction of accomplishing anything this difficult is immense, even if shared only with a handful of fellow fanatics. I clearly remember every turkey I have killed with a bow, and the sense of amazement felt equivalent to that which came from taking more conventional big game, from elk to kudu. Second, hunting with the bow makes turkey season last a whole lot longer, and hunting turkeys, like certain other of life's great pleasures, is best enjoyed over time. Montana only gives hunters one turkey tag each spring, and it's not a note I wish to cash quickly.

The bow guarantees that I almost never do.

The weather has let up a bit by the second week of the season, which means that I'm down to one layer of wool. Dawn light is rising over the mountains to the east as hunting partner Ray Stalmaster and I strap on our arm guards and shooting gloves outside the truck. This is new cover, but we heard birds here the previous evening and left them alone with the promise to return at first light and kill one—bold words indeed. Now we bear the onus of backing them up.

A hundred yards from the truck, the first gobbles of the day rise above the sigh of the breeze in the pines, but they come from Ray's direction, and I leave the birds to him. Twenty minutes later, patience becomes its own reward as another chorus of gobbles rises from the ridge below me, and I hurry through the last of the night to work my way into position near the birds.

I am comfortably set up by the time the turkeys leave the tree. The first bird to hit the ground is a raucous hen with whom I am unable to compete. Three mature toms strut their way across the clearing in vain pursuit, but the old girl's appeal is such that nothing in my turkey vocabulary can interest them. Yelps, cuts, clucks, purrs… all prove futile. An hour later, I watch this odd parade disappear over the hill, indifferent to my calls.

Western turkey hunting differs in many ways from the eastern version of the game, especially when it comes to covering ground. Merriam's turkeys move constantly in the spring, and I frequently hike for miles just to find them. I've made a long loop through the hills by the time I finally hear another gobble from the base of a rock face five hundred yards away across a broad meadow. My first soft yelp produces an immediate response, and the next gobble sounds significantly closer. Suddenly two large toms appear at the edge of the meadow, headed for my position like cruise missiles. Hen-less and horny, there's nothing coy about this pair. They're ready to tango, as am I.

Dropping back over the nearest rise, I quickly set out a pair of decoys, stretch an eight-foot length of camo netting across a fallen pine, and dive for cover. Because of the terrain, I can no longer see the birds. As soon as I have an arrow on the bowstring, I offer another soft yelp. There is no answering gobble, and I'm briefly worried that the birds might have spotted me as I moved back over the rise.

Then the resonant bass notes of a tom's wings drumming rise through the air. Just in time, I make a last-minute adjustment in position so that I can shoot past the edge of the netting. By the time

I'm frozen back into place, the first red head has crested the rise 12 yards away. No moment in outdoor sport conveys a more immediate sense of excitement. Jittery as a novice performer alone on a stage, I clench my teeth and wait for my carefully crafted illusion to unravel. But this time I have found the right birds in the right mood and said just the right things to them as they rushed across the field to the hen that wasn't there. They have come with one thing in mind, and for once it isn't survival.

At the first sight of the decoys, both toms fluff up and charge. Mentally calculating their pace, I draw as the lead bird passes behind a tree, and when he emerges from the other side, I pick a spot and release the arrow. Anatomically, a strutting tom turkey is as deceptive as an image in a fun house mirror. Most of what you see is feathers, through which I have sent more than one arrow whistling harmlessly. But not this time. The broadhead passes cleanly through the base of the tom's neck and drops him in his tracks.

Amazingly, his companion remains in full strut less than five yards away, pirouetting like a broken windup toy and banging his inflated chest against the decoys. At first it seems incredible that the mere desire to procreate can reduce something so wary to such a foolish state. Then I remember what I was like when I was a teenager. Finally, the bird turns straight away with his displayed tail eclipsing his own vision. I stand, reach over the top of the netting, and tap his tail feathers with the tip of my bow.

It is a rare occasion when a bowhunter gets to kill a big tom and count coup in the same morning.

It seldom ends this way, of course. As I walk back to the truck with the bird slung awkwardly across my shoulder, I remember some of the mornings when the turkeys won even after I called them into certain shotgun range. That list of memories proves longer than the hike, and by the time I rejoin Ray, I haven't come close to exhausting its resources. I wistfully recall defeats by big turkeys and small ones, by singles, pairs, and flocks, on morning hunts and evening hunts, courtesy of mental errors, misses, and plain bad luck. If nothing else, this litany of humiliation helps lighten my load and sweeten the story I get to share.

The decision to hunt spring gobblers—already one of the most challenging quarries in the woods—with bow and arrow represents a celebration of process at the expense of result. It's not that I don't enjoy killing turkeys; I'm simply willing to defer that part of the hunt, in no small measure because that deference affords me so much additional time in the woods. This realization produces a sinking feeling as I heave the bird over the tailgate to begin the trip down the mountain toward home. My tag is validated, the day's date notched along one edge with a sharp broadhead from my quiver. My spring turkey season has ended.

But as we rattle along down the hill, we're already deciding when and where we'll cook the bird, and the thought of moist slices of wild turkey smothered in morel mushrooms is enough to cancel all kinds of regret. Besides, the big mountains to the south are showing us a new layer of fresh tracking snow, and bear season has just opened.

Stalking bears with the bow; now *there's* another story…

15.

Dog Gone

The day-old skiff of fresh snow stretched out ahead of us in the headlights' beam like a welcome invitation, beckoning us onward into the mountains ahead of dawn's advance. But the best tracking conditions in the world amount to nothing absent a track, and by the time we drew near our customary turnaround spot at the top of the pass I was beginning to feel disappointed. It was the first weekend of the Montana mountain lion season, and all three of us felt eager for a chase.

So did the assortment of dogs in the back of the truck. A year ago that spring, I'd selected Belle as the pick of a promising bluetick litter. I liked the puppy so much I talked my young friend Mark Schwomeyer into selecting Belle's sister, June, as his first lion hound. Both now rode in the back of the truck. Mark's brother Dave had brought along his untested young black-and-tan, Mack. The only proven lion dog in the pack was Sadie, my gracefully aging Walker.

Belle and June made an interesting pair. I may have enjoyed first pick, but it looked as if Mark had drawn the ace from the bottom of the deck. Whereas Belle hadn't shown much interest in raccoons that summer, June was treeing them like a seasoned veteran. I honestly couldn't blame the difference in the two littermates' performance on luck. Mark had spent a lot more time working his young dog than I had spent on mine, and his effort was earning its just reward.

I'd grown lazy. Once you've taught a young hound to come when you call it and broken it from chasing deer, the best way to develop it into a finished product is to turn it loose on a lot of tracks with older dogs that know how to hunt. Although she was accumulating a lot of miles on her odometer, Sadie was still capable of playing that role, and we expected to spend the winter watching her teach her three novice companions how to be lion dogs.

We were discussing our Plan B for the morning when I spotted something out of place in a jumble of deer and coyote tracks just short of our turnaround. As I backed the truck down on the track, closer inspection confirmed my first impression. "Anyone want to chase a bobcat?" I asked.

The question was unnecessary. Over 30 years my juniors, Mark and Dave were full of energy and eager to get their young dogs on a cat. The track headed into some nasty terrain I knew all too well from previous chases, and it was a couple of hours older than I would have liked. Nonetheless, there was no restraining my hunting partners' enthusiasm. We parked the truck, drank coffee, and told stories for half an hour until legal hunting light arrived, and then we introduced the dogs to the track.

I didn't expect any of them to smoke it, and they didn't. After a minute or two of snuffling around in the snow June and Sadie took it, with Mack and Belle flopping along behind them. A bobcat in rugged, rocky terrain is a challenge under the best of conditions and I didn't feel particularly optimistic, but with the lead dogs sounding intense there wasn't anything to do but shoulder our packs and set off along the record in the snow.

Four hours later, I was trudging back up the hill toward the road with Belle on a leash. The chase had gone south on us as I'd suspected it might. According to the tracks and our ears, June had bayed the cat up in a hole in the rocks, but in typical bobcat fashion the little weasel had squirted out the back and eluded her. Mack and Belle had done nothing but track up the snow, making accurate reading of the sign impossible. I couldn't find Sadie, but I expected her to be waiting for me back at the truck.

She wasn't, but I didn't really feel worried. Gifted with a remarkable amount of sense for a hound, she had been through numerous versions of this scenario before, always returning to the road in due course. We waited, called, and honked the horn. When she didn't appear, we drove the road looking for hound tracks. With no sign of the dog by dark, I left a blanket, a dog box, and dog food at the start of the chase and headed for home.

I fully expected to find Sadie lying on the blanket when we returned in the dark early the following morning. When she wasn't, I finally started to worry. She had my name and contact information on her collar, but I still visited all the ranch houses farther down the valley and asked the occupants to watch for her. I drove the roads all day looking for dog tracks to no avail. I was scheduled to work at an Indian Health Service clinic out of town that week, and in fairness to the patients I couldn't cancel the commitment. Mark and Dave promised to continue the search however, and I knew I could rely on them.

No phone call came, either from my hunting partners or a rancher with a strange dog in his yard. Mark and I contacted all the local lion hunters and asked them to keep their eyes open. When I returned to town from the clinic, I made one last ritual trip up and down the road she disappeared from without seeing any sign of a lost dog. I told myself I still might receive a phone call, but she'd been missing for a week, and I felt she almost certain she was either dead or tucked away in some unscrupulous lion hunter's kennel.

Lori and I were scheduled to leave for a trip to Texas. Convinced that there was nothing more I could do at that point, we proceeded as planned. I felt despondent as we headed down the road, toward friends in Texas and away from the best hound I've ever had.

Some hounds amount to little more than a nose mounted on four legs, but a few have real personalities. Sadie was one of the latter.

Operating on the assumption that no one ever parts willingly with a good dog, I almost always choose my hunting dogs as puppies straight from the whelping box. Sadie was a rare exception. She was two years old when she came my way after her original owner took a new job out of town and couldn't take her with him. Beauty was obviously not one of her strong points. A heat lamp had left a scar on her head as a puppy, and she had somehow managed to get her tail tangled up in a lawnmower. She eventually acquired a battle scar on one ear from a lion's claw that just missed something important. More than one observer declared her the ugliest hound they'd ever seen. I never bothered to argue.

Sadie had never run a lion track before she arrived at our house, but her first summer of training on raccoons left me optimistic. That winter she didn't disappoint me, and by the end of our first season together I knew I had a dog to rely upon. That level of confidence is crucial. When you put your pack on your back and head off into tough terrain at 10-below, you need to know you've got a dog that can put a cat up a tree and keep it there.

Like all hunting dogs of any breed or purpose, Sadie had her strengths and weaknesses. Her nose was good but not great. She was steady at the tree but not as tenacious as some. And she certainly wasn't any speed demon.

I recognize that so far this report card doesn't sound all that promising. Sadie had two qualities that more than compensated for her shortcomings: brains and determination. For a variety of reasons, dogs can become totally mixed up during an otherwise promising chase. The cat may do something tricky, the scenting conditions can deteriorate, and the chase may enter terrain so rugged the dogs have trouble staying on the track. More times than I can count, we'd find all the other dogs running around hopelessly in circles at some such point only to pick up the cat's track again after considerable searching, with Sadie's track right on top of it. She may have been slow, but her ability to work out difficult tracks often got her to the tree ahead of faster dogs. When the scenting conditions deteriorated, she was always the last dog to lose the track. There were times when I wished she had given up a little sooner. More than once I walked out of the woods in the dark with Sadie on a leash long after we'd collected all the other dogs after an unsuccessful chase.

But what I remembered most about Sadie was her personality, something many hounds lack. An incorrigible escape artist, she always seemed to find a way to get out of her kennel no matter how much time I spent securing it. When she went missing around the house, it was usually only a matter of time until some neighbor called to report that she had treed their house cat. Whenever I let her into the house—something I seldom did with other hounds—she would search out all the bones and chewies the Labs and bird dogs had hidden, pile them up underneath my desk, and gnaw on them noisily while I worked. Even Lori had to admit—grudgingly—that she made good company around the house.

Oddly enough, I never personally killed a mountain lion over Sadie, although we treed plenty of them that were taken by friends and visitors. She developed a special relationship with Mark right from the start. There are only two people in the world I trust enough to let them take one of my hounds hunting without me, and Mark is one of them. One afternoon late in the season on a day I couldn't hunt, Mark showed up with Sadie and a big smile on his face after the two of them took Mark's first cat together right outside of town. The following season, he and Sadie repeated that performance on a big tom. I began to think that if Sadie wanted a dead cat at the end of the day (and what hound doesn't), she'd rather hunt with Mark than me.

By the time we turned out on that bobcat, eight winters had passed since I'd killed a cougar myself, and I finally felt ready again. But once Sadie was gone and I had no hound in the kennel to replace her save for the young (and thus far useless) Belle, my heart just wasn't in it anymore. Besides, much as I hated to admit it, I was getting old to be running around the mountains on foot in the winter. As we headed down the road toward Texas, I came face to face with a hard realization. My days as a lion hunter might be over.

According to an old axiom in the outdoor writing business, you should never write about dead dogs. There's a good reason for this proscription. No matter how much any of us might miss a good, loyal hunting dog, it's extremely difficult to convey that sense of loss without sounding trite, boring, or maudlin. But don't worry; I've got a trick up my sleeve that will keep us from coming to that.

Our time in Texas passed quickly even though I never nocked an arrow. I did shoot a bunch of ducks on the Gulf Coast, prove that desert mule deer are smarter than I am, and pack a javelina out of the hills after Lori anchored it with her recurve… not bad for a week's work in the company of old friends. My only regret was that we had to return to Montana, winter weather, and the shortest day of the year with nothing to look forward to in the outdoors but late season mallards.

I was outside loading the truck for an early morning departure from Texas when I heard Lori call my name. My usual "Just a minute!" produced a "You have to come here right now!" in reply. Inside the house, Lori greeted me with a big grin on her face and our cell phone in her extended hand. The call was from another local lion hunter who had found Sadie walking the road near where she'd originally disappeared. I immediately placed a call to Mark, who assured me that he would pick her up and take care of her until we returned.

After two days of hard driving, we made Mark's house our first stop when we hit town. And there was Sadie, emaciated but otherwise well and very much alive. The reunion felt like a Christmas miracle. I took her home and began to pour calories into her: meat, eggs, milk, suet. Lori raised no objection when I gave her the run of the house during her recovery. As I write, she's lying in her favorite spot beside my desk, munching happily on a bone.

Despite its happy conclusion, this story has made me think hard about our dogs and what we ask of them, whether they're lion hounds taking a track into the wilderness, Labs plunging into icy water after a duck, or pointers covering long, hard miles in search of birds. It would be easy to call these job descriptions callous or even cruel, except for one point: No one can *make* a dog hunt. In each of these examples, the dogs are doing exactly what they *want* to do. Anyone who doubts this contention should see the looks on the other dogs' faces when I take one out of the kennel to go hunting and leave the rest behind.

Losing hounds is part of lion hunting. It had happened to me before (although I'd never had one stay out in the woods that long), and in every case the dog eventually wound up back where it started or wandered into someone's barnyard, sometimes at remarkable distances from where it disappeared. That's why I always have a metal nameplate with my contact information securely attached to my dogs' collars.

What about electronic tracking collars? I've always opposed them strongly as another example of modern technology intruding upon important elements of the hunting experience. Finding lost dogs may be the best justification for using a tracking collar, but it's all too easy to declare the dogs "lost" the moment they disappear on a track, at which point an honest chase that depends on woodsmanship and tracking skills suddenly becomes just another version of a video game.

This experience left a big impression on Mark, who had a lot of emotion invested in his promising young hound. He won a compound bow he didn't need or want at an archery club raffle. He decided to sell it and use the proceeds to buy a tracking collar for June. I know him well enough to know he'll use it honestly. Nonetheless, I'm sticking to my original principles and hoping my stubborn devotion to tradition doesn't cost me a good dog someday.

And if it does, that will be the price we pay. There is no such thing as adventure without risk, as I am comically reminded whenever I see an ad for an "adventure travel" experience offering to lead well-heeled yuppies around by the hand in some exotic but tame location. I frequently face risk in the outdoors, and my dogs can face it with me if they want to.

It's what we were born to do.

16.
I Married a Serial Killer!

I know, I know. The title of this chapter reads as if it belongs on an old true crime novel. However, at least from a bowhunter's perspective, this story should be more inspirational than lurid. Besides, the title was just too good to pass up.

As regular readers know, 2019 was not a good year for me. Strange symptoms eventually led to an MRI of my head, which revealed a tumor on the right side of my brain. I had it removed on Halloween, which was appropriate because I came back from the operating room looking like Frankenstein's monster. The tumor proved benign, so the long-term outlook was good. But I was still incapacitated for most of November, and nurse Lori (my wife, who I quickly renamed Nurse Ratched), was guarding me like grizzly sow defending her cub. (If you are too young to know who Nurse Ratched was, read Ken Kesey's great *One Flew Over the Cuckoo's Nest* or see the movie, with Jack Nicholson.) According to her, I was *not* going outside in zero-degree weather and walking on rough terrain. Doctors—at least the smart ones—quickly learn never to argue with nurses. And that's how I wound up on injured reserve for virtually the entire deer season. Why do these disasters always have to happen at that time of year?

I didn't miss the whitetail rut as badly as I thought I would, probably because I was full of (legal) drugs. I'd already decided that

I had plenty of antlers on the wall anyway. But one important practical consideration remained. I grew up cooking and eating wild game and doing so is a large part of who I am. Lori has felt the same way throughout our many years of marriage. When we had four kids at home, we could go through an awful lot of it—typically an elk, an antelope, and three or four deer per year, or a moose and a caribou when we lived in Alaska. Now that it was just the two of us our meat requirements were more modest, but the thought of facing the New Year with no venison in the freezer still felt grim. Since I was out of commission, there was just one person who could solve that problem. Fortunately, Lori tackled the matter with the enthusiasm she always brings to bear on any challenge.

By mid-November, the whitetails were doing what they always do at that time of year. The picture window in our living room affords a splendid view downhill to our lower pasture and east coulee. The ponderosas in the draw hold two of our favorite spots to ambush deer—the Thanksgiving Stand and the Spring Stand. Although I couldn't see them through the trees, I sure could see the deer as bucks chased does back and forth across the pasture, heads lowered, necks swollen, busily posturing. During the 40 years I had owned the property this had always been my favorite season, but now all I could do was watch. Wistful? Sure. Sad or angry? No. As one matures, one grows more philosophical and willing to accept one's fate, but I still wanted some venison. I shrugged my shoulders, walked downstairs to our spacious kitchen, and began to marinate a slab of king salmon we'd brought back from a visit to our old friends Doug and Olga Borland in Sitka that summer. At least the freezer wasn't totally empty.

"I'm going to go shoot a deer," Lori announced as she emerged from the mud room clad head to toe in the Sitka Gear clothing that has allowed her to hunt in cold weather that she once would have found intolerable. She was already wearing her safety harness and carrying a favorite recurve in her hand. Somewhere in her hunting pack lay one either-sex deer tag and one doe tag.

"The best two weeks of the season are still to come," I reminded her. "Are you going to be selective?"

"Of course," she replied. "I'm going to select one that's *brown*." That's one reason I've always enjoyed hunting with my wife. While I was holding out for a big buck that probably didn't exist, her shot requirements were nothing more than a valid tag in her pocket and a mature deer within bow range. My hunting partners and I have always been able to count on Lori to make things happen. Although she has killed some nice bucks over the years, she has always been a meat hunter at heart, and meat was what we needed.

"Do you have your rattling antlers?" I asked. "It's that time of year."

"Of course," she replied, and then she was off and out the door, leaving me with Rosy, my intensely loyal old female Lab.

Watching salmon marinate was about all I was good for, but when the feeble winter sun finally began to sink below the western horizon, I decided I couldn't do it properly without a glass of wine in my hand. Then I heard noise in the mud room, and Rosy trotted over to investigate. Lori walked into the kitchen carrying her bow in one hand and the broken-off fletched end of an arrow in the other. "Looks like we have a project," I observed. "Tell me about the hit."

"It was a bit high," she began. "But I was shooting down at a steep angle."

"Below the spine?" I asked.

"Definitely," she replied. "I think." I didn't bother to point out the contradiction between these two opinions.

"Penetration?" She just held up her broken arrow. There was more than enough missing to kill a deer. "Paunch"? I asked, concluding the interrogation. She walked over to the shoulder mount of a kudu that we have used to illustrate the answer to this question for years and put her finger right in the shoulder crease. "So far," I went on, "you haven't told me anything *wrong* with this shot."

"I know," she replied. "But you know how nervous I always get."

This pessimism has always been characteristic of Lori's hit analysis, and I was used to it. Like most of us, I have friends who always return from a hunt describing a perfect double-lung shot and predicting recovery within 50 yards. It's hard to keep that optimism in mind when you are one mile and three hours into a terrible trail and cut to ribbons by thorny brush. I'd rather set off uncertain and receive a pleasant surprise.

The temperature was well below freezing and a light skiff of tracking snow covered the ground. There was no weather in the forecast. I could think of a lot of reasons to hold off on the track, prime among them the possibility of bumping up a live deer that wasn't hit quite the way Lori described it. Save for the threat of coyotes, I couldn't think of any reason not to wait. But it was her deer, and she'd had more than enough experience to make the decision without input from me. She chose to wait.

At first light the following morning, we set off with the bird dogs barking their encouragement from the kennel behind us. The snow largely disappeared once the track went under the canopy, but I could identify running deer tracks left behind in the pine needle duff. Blood was scant—no surprise, since I doubted there was an exit wound. When I started to have trouble with the track, we split up to start a grid search of the steep west coulee. Then I heard a shout from Lori up the hill behind me. And there it was, a mature doe that had fallen to what proved to be as perfect a shot as one could imagine.

We still had a dead deer at the bottom of a steep hill, and after weeks of doing nothing, I was in the worst shape of my life. When I suggested that we bone the deer out on the spot so we could pack it out in manageable loads, Nurse Ratched killed that idea on the spot. "You are not handling sharp knives in cold weather while you are full of pain medication!" she informed me in no uncertain terms. "All you need now is to cut off a finger!" So, I watched as Lori field dressed the deer (a job she always insists on doing herself), and then we began to drag.

I use the pronoun "we" loosely. Thirty yards into the task, I was feeling light-headed and unsteady. Ten yards farther up the hill, I fell on my butt. "You're done!" Nurse Ratched announced.

"We could call Mark," I suggested. "Or Glenn, or Doug, or…"

"Never mind," Lori said. "I got this." And she did. Half an hour later, the deer was hanging in the barn while I was cooking breakfast and congratulating myself on my choice of wives.

Lori making venison. The deer met her trophy standards. It was brown.

"We don't have enough venison," Lori announced two days later.

"Well, thanks to you we've got…"

"That deer won't last us until spring. The kids will want some, we'll need to take some "wampum" to Alaska and Hawaii…"

"Then go shoot another one," I said, a little more gruffly than I meant to sound.

"I was just rounding up my gear," she replied.

"You've still got an either-sex tag and the best week of the season is coming up. Are you going to hold out?"

"Same answer as last time. It has to be brown. I'm not shooting a purple deer." Well, that's my wife.

When she walked into the house right after dark, she was shivering, but she was also smiling—always a good sign. "Let me guess," I began. "You shot a doe."

"That's right. A big, *brown* doe."

"And how was the hit?"

"Absolutely perfect," she replied. I wasn't sure I'd ever heard her say that before, even about hits that *were* absolutely perfect.

"Any reason to wait?"

"Not that I can think of." She was already rounding up flashlights and leading Max, our young German wirehair pointer, down to my office to keep him out of trouble while we were gone.

We'd received another shot of snow since she killed the first deer and coupled with bright arterial blood lining both sides of the track it was a snap to follow. The only hitch came when the stricken deer took us through a dense stand of doghair pines and a sharp branch hit me right in the middle of my surgical incision—ouch! Nurse Ratched ordered me out of the thicket and I obeyed, only to walk right into the dead doe. Once again, the deer had run downhill, but this time it had gone north instead of west and fallen right on the edge of one of our pastures. While Lori went to work on the carcass with her knife, I hiked back to the house for the truck. Less than an hour later, we had a second deer hanging in the barn. Three days later, Lori cut and wrapped the venison by herself.

Now we're going to fast forward into the present tense for a few final paragraphs. I'm crouched in a favorite brush blind as the season's last hours of shooting light drain from the sky. I've put a lot of thought into this blind after noting a consistent, heavy scrape line along an imposing tangle of hawthorn. A similar patch of brush 50 yards away to the south creates a natural travel route between our upper and lower pastures, where deer love to graze on the remains of the year's alfalfa crop. The location had everything but a tree, which happened to fit neatly with my earlier decision to do all my deer hunting from the ground. Those who have made a similar change in perspective know it doesn't take long to realize that shooting a deer from the ground is qualitatively harder than shooting one from a tree stand. Nonetheless, I'd killed a buck from the blind the previous year and enjoyed the challenge.

Now, I'm simply enjoying being in the woods by myself for the first time in a month. High winds and their attendant chill factor kept me indoors all afternoon, but now the air is as gentle as a baby's breath. The same storm that brought the wind on its heels also left a lovely carpet of fresh snow in its wake, and delicate flakes are now falling straight down. Despite the cold, I cannot imagine a place I'd rather be.

Some years ago, a writer—I believe it was John Mitchell, although my memory isn't as reliable as it once was—broke hunters down into four categories in which I admittedly had trouble placing myself. The first was the *trophy* hunter. Although I certainly have my share of antlers on the wall and enjoyed putting them there, they were always a low priority for me. The second was the *meat* hunter, and I have already explained the allegiance Lori and I feel to this group. The third is the *process* hunter, and I think that all traditional bowhunters belong to this group almost by definition. We are fascinated by our tackle and its history, love shooting our bows, and would prefer to come home empty-handed than find an easier way to kill game. The final group is the *nature* hunters, those who see hunting primarily as a means of understanding the great wild world around us. If you have to put me in one of these boxes, please pick this one.

Tonight, for example, in the absence of deer I'm watching magpies—shrill, sometimes aggravating birds that love to use hawthorn brush as security cover. They are all over me tonight and given this opportunity to observe so many of them at close range, I'm struck by their wariness and keen eyesight. After perching nearby, it usually takes one just a matter of seconds to zero in on my location, issue a raucous alarm call, and fly away even though I think I'm well-hidden. So, I'm thinking, what would happen if they were sitting calmly nearby instead? Might not deer interpret this as an "all clear" signal much as African plains game interprets undisturbed guinea fowl or baboons? Experienced waterfowl hunters often place coot, heron, or cormorant decoys at the edge of their duck decoy spread to create an added impression of security. Maybe next year I'll make some magpie decoys. I'll let you know how that works.

But now another season has ended and I'm trudging uphill through the snow toward home. For the first season in over 20 years, I have failed to kill a deer with my bow, an event that I am accepting with unexpected calm. Thanks to my wife's skill and determination, we'll be eating venison until the start of the season next year. Best of all, I'm alive, a state of affairs that was anything but obvious a month earlier.

Sometimes that is enough, a fact we should all learn to appreciate.

17.

Close Encounters

A tom turkey responds to a hunter's calling in one of two basic ways. The first option comes as a flat-out, aggressive charge accompanied by furious gobbling and can rapidly leave the hunter face to face with one of the most challenging quarries in the woods. A skilled and fortunate hunter may witness this phenomenon once or twice over the course of a long spring season. Or not.

The second, far more common, kind of response is a long, laborious approach conducted as if the bird were picking its way through a minefield. The tom may remain nearly silent throughout, leaving the caller attached to the hunt by nothing but a thin tether of hope. Even when the tom answers his patient clucks and yelps, the hunter may listen in despair as a flock of real hens lures the gobbler away and out of his life before he ever sees the tom. These are the times that try men's souls. They also define spring turkey hunting.

This morning, I hiked for an hour in the dark up to a mountain meadow that consistently holds turkeys by mid-April. My goal was to locate a gobbler while he was still in his roost tree, which is better done an hour too early than a minute too late. The first booming gobble of the season rolled downhill from the rimrocks above the basin just as color began to suffuse the landscape. I offered one soft tree yelp in reply just to let the tom think a hen was there. Felled by wind during a recent winter storm, a fallen pine offered ideal natural cover. Since the tom's position sounded several hundred yards away through scattered timber, I could await developments without the discomfort of remaining motionless.

The sound of heavy wings straining against air followed the bird's second gobble just as muted shafts of sunlight began to spread across the meadow. With the bird out of the roost tree and on the ground, I yelped. He answered once and then shut up. The gobbler was not going to charge me. I settled in to wait, already anticipating a long, contemplative morning of the kind Thoreau might have enjoyed at Walden Pond.

After years spent hunting turkeys in the most difficult way possible—with traditional archery tackle and usually without the aid of a blind—several elements of the experience remain hard to explain. The first is the realization that enthusiasm for hunting wild turkeys has remarkably little to do with killing wild turkeys.

This is not to say that I don't relish the satisfaction of walking up to a freshly killed gobbler, stroking its plumage, and inhaling the rich aroma of wild turkey. I haven't gone all warm and fuzzy and Save the Whales. I enjoy facing challenges in the outdoors and killing a mature gobbler is certainly that, especially when hunting with a traditional bow, an exercise in voluntary restraint that has now consumed me for several decades. Nonetheless, I do kill a turkey almost every year, a success rate that owes less to skill on my part than to residence in a rural area with lots of turkeys and not many turkey hunters. Somehow, the seasons when I end up eating tag soup prove almost as enjoyable as those in which I bring home a bird. Almost.

Geography and the calendar are largely responsible. T. S. Elliot famously begins "The Wasteland" by declaring April to be the cruelest month. He obviously never spent a winter in Montana, where desperation to roam the outdoors free of bulky winter clothing feels palpable by the end of March. Hiking the woods during our month-long turkey season allows the hunter to appreciate spring's arrival day by day. At first, I may be post-holing my way through old corn snow, but by the time it all ends mid-May the landscape will be lush, green, and welcoming. The lure of gobbling turkeys provides an ideal excuse to enjoy this transition of the seasons.

The process of spring turkey hunting can be just as rewarding as the ambience. Nothing is more central to that process than calling a wary gobbler into close range. While I've called in game ranging in size from mallards to moose, none of those experiences proved more exciting than the call-and-response dialogs established with gobbling turkeys. The importance of calling can be appreciated by contrasting spring turkey hunting, in which calling is everything, to hunting turkeys in the fall, when it matters less. I have taken turkeys during the fall and felt proud of every one of them, but few of those experiences generated the shock and awe of a spring turkey hunt. I'm not above taking a fall bird as a target of opportunity but doing so usually feels like ground-sluicing an oversized grouse. Since wild turkeys are so wary, they're always a challenge, and fall birds are delicious on the table. However, killing one then just isn't the same as hunting them in the spring.

The second great mystery of turkey hunting reflects the question of how any creature with a brain the size of a cocktail onion can be so incredibly cagey. While a mature gobbler's wariness has been legendary for as long as people have hunted them, I think this trait has little to do with "intelligence" by any generally accepted definition of the term. Two factors alone—the birds' suspicion and keen eyesight—explain most of the difficulty hunters face closing ranks with a wild turkey. Natural selection by centuries of exposure to predators ranging from coyotes and bobcats to human hunters tricked out in the latest camouflage have made turkeys what they are today. On isolated island ecosystems where wild turkeys have been introduced to habitat historically free of predators, they're dumb as barnyard chickens, which is why friends in New Zealand and elsewhere around the Pacific can't understand our passion for hunting them.

In my own case, part of that passion arises from the most basic motivation for hunting anything: delight in eating what you shoot. Regrettably, not everyone shares that opinion of wild turkey on the table, as is the case with other delicious game species ranging from bears to geese. These biases usually result from an unfortunate encounter with a badly over-cooked specimen. Cooking a wild bird the same way one would prepare a domestic turkey from the grocery store usually leads to culinary disaster. Since this isn't a cookbook, I'm not going to hold forth on the subject other than to state that a wild turkey dinner should be delightful, especially when it includes fresh morel mushrooms gathered during the hunt.

Whatever one's opinion about the wild turkey as table fare, it is hard to name a gamebird that has enjoyed a more prominent place in American lore, even though the relationship between lore and fact is sometimes tenuous.

Many Americans seldom think about turkeys except during Thanksgiving week, although there is limited evidence that the legendary event at Plymouth Colony in November 1621 actually involved eating turkey (or that the colonists called the event Thanksgiving, or that it occurred in November). Only two written accounts survive, of which Edward Winslow's reports that "Our harvest being gotten in, our Governor sent four men out fowling..." However, they could have been "fowling" for grouse, ducks, or geese as well as turkeys.

The association of the autumn event with turkey dinner arose through the efforts of a mid-19th century magazine editor named Sarah Hale, who began a concerted effort to have the occasion turned into a national holiday. (She finally succeeded during Lincoln's administration.) Hale took her cue from another colonist's records, in which William Bradford wrote, with no specific reference to the Thanksgiving feast: "And besides waterfowl there was a great store of wild turkeys, of which we took many..." Growing up, I never fretted much about Thanksgiving's historical accuracy. The tradition provided a school holiday in the middle of hunting season. Who could ask for anything more?

The popular story about Benjamin Franklin proposing that the wild turkey rather than the bald eagle become our national bird is legend as well. Granted, Franklin did admire the turkey more as expressed in a letter to his daughter, in which he described the bald eagle as a "Bird of low moral Character" and the turkey as "…a much more respectable bird and withal a true original Native of America." That, however, is as far as Franklin ever took the matter.

Historical deconstruction notwithstanding, some facts remain indisputable. The turkey is one of only two native New World birds to be successfully domesticated. (The other is the Muscovy duck.) It is the world's largest gallinaceous gamebird. The American wild turkey's population recovery from near extirpation is one of the greatest wildlife success stories of our time. That's enough hard fact for me.

Hours have passed pleasantly since first auditory contact with the gobbler, despite the absence of turkeys from the meadow. Other avian species are streaming by on their annual northbound migration—geese and cranes at altitude, warblers and robins at eye level. Somewhere in the woods behind me, a ruffed grouse has started to drum. Fresh pasque flowers dot the meadow in front of my makeshift blind, lavender pixels that seem to be erupting right before my eyes. For years I've thought of them as "turkey flowers" because their appearance seems to coincide with the elevation level the turkeys occupy as they follow the receding snowline up the mountainsides every spring. Right now, it would be nice to translate this observation into the sight of an inbound tom.

Over the course of the morning, I have heard three gobbles since the tom hit the ground, one spontaneous and two in response to my calls. While I have no reason to believe he has left the basin, the sun has climbed above the tops of the ponderosas since I last heard from him. The time has come to shake the dice.

Turkey calls come in many forms—box calls, slates, wingbones—but I prefer a mouth diaphragm because it leaves both hands free for my bow. Overly loud and frequent calling is usually unwise but having reached the point of nothing-to-lose, I cut loose with a series of excited yelps and clucks followed by a cackle. The gobbler answers immediately from the woods along the far side of the meadow. Round Two has finally begun.

To borrow a metaphor from Steven Spielberg's 1977 sci-fi cinema classic, hearing a gobbler in the woods represents a close encounter of the first kind. Repeated answers from an approaching bird represent the second, but it's the third—indisputable visual contact—that changes the whole context of the hunt. As gobbles from the newly aroused tom echo back from the rimrock at progressively shorter intervals, I train my eyes against the far edge of the trees and wait. The sound of a bugling bull elk could not demand my attention more.

Although Eastern wild turkeys have been introduced at various sites around Montana, almost all the birds I have killed here were Merriam's. Named for the noted biologist C. Hart Merriam, these western turkeys are regarded by some as the easiest of our five wild turkey subspecies to hunt. If true at all—and I remain unconvinced—their alleged naivety likely has less to do with lack of wariness than with a limited turkey hunting tradition in their native range.

However, many also consider the Merriam's our most beautiful wild turkey. I agree, and I've spent time with them all—Osceola, Rio Grande, and Gould's in addition to Eastern and Merriam's. It's the pale tips of both the outer and inner tailfeathers that demand the eyes' attention when a tom is in full strut, and those two juxtaposed white semi-circles are often the first part of the bird a hunter sees when a tom is approaching from a distance.

Such is the case this morning. My first response to the sight of the bird picking his way out of the pines and into the meadow is, as usual, a question: How can anything so small make a sound as thunderous as a gobble? The bird has arrived in full strut—tailfeathers fanned with a draftsman's precision, wingtips dragging the ground, erect body feathers doubling the size of his silhouette, naked head aglow in a fluctuating tricolor of red, white, and blue. Like most acts of courtship this one is simultaneously magnificent and ridiculous, but as always this close encounter of the third kind leaves me mesmerized.

As the tom starts across the meadow toward my position, the game becomes mine to win or lose. With the bird's radar locked onto my hen decoy, I reduce my calling to an occasional soft cluck or purr. As the gobbler approaches step by measured step my only responsibility is to hold perfectly still, which may be the most difficult part of the hunt. Then the bird is in range—longbow range, no less—but I still need him to do one more thing, and he does it. When he pivots in full strut ten yards away his extended tailfeathers eclipse his vision briefly, allowing me to draw my bow and release the arrow undetected. The stricken bird collapses in plain sight 50 yards away in the meadow, surrounded by a bouquet of purple pasque flowers.

Moments later, I'm cutting notches in my turkey tag and running my hands across tailfeathers that will eventually produce a season's worth of hopper imitations at my fly-tying bench. This is my close encounter of the fourth kind.

The only way to improve upon the morning would be to find a patch of newly erupted morels to serve with the bird after it's hung for a day or two. That's why I choose a route down the mountain that takes me through several aspen groves, while keeping my eyes trained upon the ground. The calendar may claim that Thanksgiving still lies seven months away, but I've already found one of my own.

18.

Big Sky Pronghorns

Here in central Montana, mid-September brings an embarrassment of riches. Clear weather, cool nights and warm days make being outdoors a pleasure whatever the agenda. Brown trout prowl the creeks while sharptails and Huns offer endless possibilities with the shotgun. The hills ring with the sound of bugling elk. Out on the prairie where the smell of sage fills the air and the sky seems to go on forever, the antelope rut provides a prime opportunity to explore one of bowhunting's greatest yet most accessible challenges.

The proper common name for the species *Antelocapra americana* is pronghorn, but in this chapter, I will follow regional custom and call them antelope, as Lewis and Clark did. These animals aren't really antelope at all, but on the great Voyage of Discovery both captains imagined a resemblance to African antelope, as recorded in their journals.

On one such drop-dead gorgeous morning a few seasons back, I sat nestled in a clump of sage engaged in one of my favorite occupations: observing game animals and trying to decide how to convert those observations into venison. With the rut in full swing, a pronghorn herd buck was busily defending his harem against the determined attention of three would-be rivals. Over the course of an hour, I noted that one of the three always reached the limit of the herd buck's tolerance first, and that the boss invariably walked straight down an old fence line each time he returned to his does after running the intruder off.

Over the years, I've learned that it's a lot easier to stalk the places antelope plan to be than to stalk the animals themselves. An old creek bed ran from my position to the fence line a quarter mile away, and the next time the worried herd buck took off after the irritating intruder, I dropped into the shelter of the dry wash and headed toward the fence at double time speed. Respecting my quarry's legendary vision, I never raised my head above the level of the bank to check on his location. When the fence line finally appeared 15 yards in front of my nose, I rechecked the wind and settled into a clump of brush to wait.

Ten minutes later, as if on schedule, the herd buck popped over the lip of the creek bed. Intent on securing his does before another contender could cut one from the herd, he never saw me draw my bow. At point blank range, the sight of a pronghorn buck—ordinarily little more than a puff of white in the distance—can prove unsettling, and I had to force myself to bear down and pick a spot behind his shoulder. The buck never even broke stride as the cedar arrow struck his shoulder crease. He collapsed in plain sight, and a few minutes later I knelt beside the dead buck, running my hands across the hollow-haired mane and relishing the rich smell of antelope.

And to think how many times I've been told it couldn't be done.

A Montana pronghorn buck marks his territory during the September rut.

An original product of the American Great Plains, the pronghorn has no biological relatives. As noted, the pronghorn isn't really an antelope at all, but a goat—sort of. The science may be confusing, but the species' stature as a challenging game animal has never been in doubt. Ever since William Clark killed the first accurately described specimen in September 1804 in what is now South Dakota, hunters have respected the pronghorn for its wariness and acute senses. As Clark's fellow explorer Meriwether Lewis reported following one early encounter:

> "We found the antelope extremely shy and watchful, insomuch as we had been unable to get a shot at them. When at rest they generally select the most elevated point in the neighborhood, and as they are watchful and extremely quick of sight, and their sense of smelling very acute, it is almost impossible to approach them within gunshot. In short, they

will frequently discover, and flee from you, at a distance of three miles."

Most hunters' impressions of the species haven't changed much over the two intervening centuries.

Based on many seasons of experience, I regard pronghorns as more talented than intelligent. Superbly adapted to the open spaces they inhabit, they really only do two things well: see and run. But they do both very well indeed, and anyone ambitious enough to try to take one with a bow needs to understand these abilities, as well as a few of the species' crucial weaknesses.

The pronghorn is the continent's fastest ungulate, capable of hitting speeds of 60 mph even in broken terrain. Watching rutting bucks chase does across the prairie at breakneck speed still takes my breath away no matter how many times I've observed these performances. The implications for the hunting archer are simple: once an antelope starts moving, it's no longer a target for the bow. Don't even think about it.

Understanding the pronghorn's vision is even more important to the bowhunter. Over the years, I've listened to many attempts to translate the antelope's visual acuity into optical terms hunters can readily understand, such as various powers of magnification. That's all guesswork in the end, but there's no doubt a pronghorn can detect approaching hunters at fantastic distances, an ability that would seem to make them all but impossible quarries for the bowhunter.

In fact, antelope only see two things well: motion and changes in horizon contour. Letting an antelope see you walking or popping your head over a rise to check on a buck's position usually means an end to the stalk at any range. However, understanding the weaknesses of an antelope's eyesight is just as important as appreciating its strengths. The following notes are purely the result of personal observation and have not been confirmed by objective scientific study.

Antelope don't see nearly as well in low light as they do midday, which is why I like to do my stalking at dusk and dawn. Their vision seems to demonstrate a narrow depth of field, and they are poor pattern recognizers in comparison to deer. A bowhunter hidden in a clump of brush can often get away with a surprising amount at close range, good news given the last-minute maneuvering necessary to draw and get a clean shot away. Paradoxically, I've learned it's often easier to move undetected within bow range than it is at several hundred yards.

There are three basic ways to kill a pronghorn with a bow. Optimal choice of hunting tactics depends on weather, terrain, timing of the rut, and personal preference.

No doubt, more bow-killed antelope are taken from ground blinds at water sources than by any other method. An ambush from a ground blind offers the possibility of a close, controlled shot but requires considerable patience, especially in areas with multiple sources of water. Water hole hunting is best in hot weather during the peak of the rut when bucks are highly active. Conversely, an untimely rain can effectively end hunting over water, as pronghorns will readily drink from tiny accumulations of moisture on the prairie and avoid water holes completely whenever alternatives are available—a good reason to have a backup plan in mind if you're heading west for a week of antelope hunting.

Contrary to popular opinion, elaborate blinds are unnecessary. I've killed a number of pronghorns next to water simply by sitting in a convenient bush or hiding behind a strip of camo netting. Pop-up cloth blinds are quite effective and allow greater comfort and freedom of movement during long waits for game to appear, but I find them confining and unnatural. However, antelope usually ignore these blinds completely, and it is not necessary to set them up in advance to allow the animals to grow accustomed to their presence.

Decoying – a method pioneered by several of my local bowhunting partners years ago – provides an effective alternative for hunters who don't relish the thought of sitting in a blind for long days beneath the prairie sun. At times, decoying can produce spectacular action. When I first tried decoying years ago, I had my young son operating a silhouette decoy. The first time we threw the decoy up, an aggressive herd buck literally knocked it from his hands before I could get an arrow on my bowstring.

But decoying suffers from important limitations. It is effective during a very narrow window of time during the rut. As a rule, whenever you see antelope bucks tolerating each other's presence, decoying will be a waste of time. And even when a decoy produces an aggressive response, the result is often an alert buck at a poor shot angle, even though at close range. Decoying is more effective with two hunters, one to run the decoy while the other sets up downwind of the buck's likely approach route. For reasons of safety, never use a decoy during antelope firearm season.

Stalking represents the third—and perhaps the purest—way to tackle pronghorns with a bow. The challenges should be obvious, but it can be done, and I regard all the antelope I've killed this way as honorable accomplishments no matter what the size of their horns. While stalking antelope with a bow can never be described as easy, a few simple principles will help raise the odds from hopeless to possible, with luck and skill.

1. Select appropriate terrain. Antelope on flat, barren ground are nearly impossible to approach within bow range. Look for areas with creek bottoms and ground cover. Remember that pronghorns sometimes frequent forested areas at higher elevations.
2. Stalk at first and last light, when the animals are active and their vision less acute.
3. Concentrate your efforts during the rut when bucks are distracted and on the move. Remember that it's easier to stalk their travel routes than the bucks themselves.

Last but not least—good luck. You're going to need it.

On another sweltering September day, I spent the afternoon watching a lone buck with heavy horns make his rounds across the prairie. A younger, more vigorous herd buck had evidently run him away from the does and he wasn't taking his demotion in status gracefully. For hours, he stalked the sage in wide, relentless circles, horning brush, pawing the ground, and expressing his foul mood by challenging every other outcast male that came his way. The terrain was poorly suited to stalking and the area's main water supply consisted of a large reservoir that offered no possibility for an ambush. But I wanted this buck, and I felt that if I watched him long enough from my hilltop perch, I'd notice some clue to his behavior that would allow me to approach within bow range.

And sure enough. Late that afternoon, as a fierce sun pushed the temperature into the 90's, I watched him bypass the reservoir to water in a tiny trickle of overflow beneath its earthen dam. Early the following morning, I crept up the creek bed under the cover of darkness and kicked out a hiding place in a clump of sage 20 yards downwind of the buck's secret water supply. I can't pretend that the wait proved comfortable, but determination has always been an essential part of the bowhunter's character. Shortly after noon, the buck appeared over the horizon and sauntered confidently toward my position. When he passed behind a clump of sage, I rose to one knee and drew.

The buck jumped and spun at the sound of the bowstring's *twang*, resulting in a poor hit in one hind leg. Thanks to the open terrain, I was able to track him visually for several miles before I ran out of water. Fortunately, I was able to spot the tips of his horns after he bedded down in a patch of sage. My second arrow proved much more effective than my first despite being taken at a range I never would have considered under different circumstances. He never made it out of his final bed.

See? Nothing to it...

19.

Smaller Bulls, Greater Satisfaction

The Indian summer weather was typical for central Montana in September, with pleasantly warm days and crisp nights when temperatures dropped enough to leave a rim of ice around the previous evening's dishwater. Such conditions practically define archery elk season here, and the annual rut was progressing right on schedule, with herd bulls collecting their harems, spikes and raghorns working up their nerve on the perimeter of the action, and cows already growing tired of the whole process. I already wished I could see the season through to its conclusion in early October, but I couldn't.

For some reason, I'd scheduled a trip to Africa during my favorite time of year at home. I couldn't explain why even to myself, but I had just a few more days to put our annual elk in the freezer. I had already reached the conclusion that I didn't need any more antlers on the wall and had resolved to shoot the first mature elk that offered me an opportunity.

I was hunting alone on that trip, and I missed Lori's company. I also knew that if I did kill an elk, I'd miss her company even more, since my horses had already gone down the road with my ex-wife and I'd have to pack out anything I shot on my own back. When I rolled out of my sleeping bag, elk were already bugling wildly at the head of the basin where I'd camped. Packing an elk out solo might not be much fun, but if I killed one nearby it would at least be possible.

There's nothing I dislike more on an elk hunt than a wind that refuses to declare its intentions. One can engage in magical thinking, pretend that the wind isn't doing anything it all, and ignore it when planning an approach to the quarry. Trouble is, the wind is always doing something. Absent a prevailing trend it may betray you by switching repeatedly during the crucial phases of the final approach, especially in mountainous terrain. I decided to circle around the head of the basin and hope morning thermals developed enough strength to provide some consistency.

Two hours later, I was perched high on the ridge above the basin wondering where all the elk had gone. The concentrated bugling I'd heard at first light had dissipated, and the thick cover below me only offered fleeting glimpses of an occasional cow. Finally, I heard a high-pitched squeal several hundred yards downhill. When I trained my binoculars on the area, I spotted a lone spike trudging in my direction looking dazed and confused.

I knew there were bigger bulls in the area, but I also remembered my earlier decision. A tender young spike was just what the doctor (me, in this case) ordered, and since I'd be packing him out myself if I were successful, I wouldn't miss the extra weight of a big bull on my back

As cautiously as possible, I began to move laterally across the hillside toward a point of interception.

When I first started bowhunting elk, I spent way too much time trying to *find* them and not nearly enough time *hunting* them, although it took me several seasons to figure this out. Elk habitat is big country—one of the reasons it's so much fun to hunt there—but that makes a whole lot of haystack in which just a few needles can hide. Young and tough then, I climbed a lot of mountains and spooked a lot of elk.

I eventually realized that despite their dispersal across a lot of habitat, elk leave plenty of sign that can narrow the search considerably. Furthermore, during the Montana bow season (which includes virtually the entire rut) their bugling makes them one of the easiest animals in North America to locate. I started doing more elk hunting with my brain and less with my legs, and soon wondered why I hadn't done so sooner.

One September afternoon, I was glassing a broad expanse of open country where mountain foothills bled out onto prairie and cropland. As I watched a small herd of elk leave the timber and head toward the alfalfa fields to feed, they all disappeared into a little fold in the terrain and didn't reappear for nearly an hour. Curiosity aroused, I noted some landmarks and hiked in to look the following morning. The small stock pond, which did not appear on any maps, was interesting enough, but what really caught my eye was the evidence of extensive wallowing activity in the reed-choked upper end of the pond. There wasn't a tree around, but I cobbled together a crude—and remarkably uncomfortable—ground blind in the reeds before retreating to some distant shade to enjoy a book, lunch, and a nap.

I arrived back at my blind an hour before I thought the elk were due and spent the interval swatting bugs and touching up my blind, only to be disappointed when I heard elk bugling their way downhill one coulee away. With no cover between us higher than my ankle, I decided to sit tight rather than attempting an approach that would likely accomplish nothing but running the elk out of the country.

A Montana bull elk during the rut.

The next half-hour's worth of mosquitoes, mud, and wet feet didn't say much for that decision at first, but then I spotted a lone elk walking downhill toward me without making a sound. I could tell at once that the elk was a bull, but I didn't appreciate his size until I dialed him in with my binoculars, at which point I began to experience a serious case of elk fever.

The bull wound up studying the wallow from a position well out of range on the opposite sidehill. When it became apparent that he wasn't going to close the gap without some encouragement, I offered a series of soft cow calls. He then started walking slowly down the hill while studying the reed bed as if he were trying to convince himself that the cover really could hide a potential girlfriend. He finally came to a hesitant stop somewhere around the edge of my bow range.

I never did determine exactly how far that shot was, but it was one of those situations in which the little voice deep in my brain says, "You can do this!" So, with the elk perfectly broadside, I did.

In a matter of seconds, the bull was down in plain sight on the open hillside.

I played that game in other locations for several seasons without failing to punch my elk tag, having a lot of fun and killing some really nice bulls. However, I slowly began to realize that I missed my old, aggressive run-and-gun approach to elk hunting—the way it let me approach winter lion season in peak physical condition, the variety of wildlife I encountered, the grouse that I regularly packed home for dinner.

Above all, I missed the challenge.

When I reached the position where I thought the spike should be without seeing any sign of him, I backed up against a rock to break up my profile and settled down to wait. Perhaps 20 minutes passed before I heard a bugle from the timber below me. After confirming an upslope breeze, I cow-called down the hill. The results could not have been more dramatic.

Back when I first started hunting elk, bugling was all the rage. Diaphragm calls hadn't even been invented, and most hunters simply squealed into a length of hose. After spending several seasons listening to that racket and bugling in more hunters than elk, I decided to stop bugling and make myself sound like a cow elk instead.

That tactic had already proved productive for several seasons, and as soon as I saw the spike zeroed in on my position, I sensed that it was about to do so again. The ability of game animals to pinpoint the source of a call never ceases to amaze me, whether I'm banging antlers together in November or yelping at a gobbler in the spring. The spike came in as precisely as if he'd been given a vector by Air Traffic Control. When he turned broadside at 15 yards, my recurve sent a cedar arrow through his chest.

I felt confident about the hit as the little bull tore away down the hill, but I began to grow concerned when I set out on his trail half an hour later. There was virtually no blood, but I could follow his running track easily enough through the forest duff. (Panicked elk leave more obvious tracks than calm ones do.) Although I was aware that the air temperature was rising quickly, I considered backing off and giving the track a little more time. Then I crested a little rise and nearly tripped over the stone-dead spike. The autopsy revealed that my broadhead had done all I could have asked, for the chest cavity was full of blood, reminding me that a stricken animal running downhill can cover a lot more ground than one with a similar wound can on the level.

Then the *real* elk hunt began, as I broke the bull down into quarters. I might have boned it out on the spot, but I wanted to get the meat hanging in a cool place is quickly as possible. Besides, I was only a mile from my truck, although a direct route would require crossing one steep draw. I got the quarters out in good shape, but I'm not sure I could do it again at my current age.

I have some very nice elk antlers on my wall, but as I reflect on those events, I'm not sure those big bulls provided me more satisfaction than all the rest, including one that was "only a spike."

20.

The Crazy Season

Companionship

"It's a lot easier being the guide," Lori observed as we watched the billy pick his breakfast from the scarp 1500 vertical feet above us. "I've got the fun job this time around."

She knew whereof she spoke. Five seasons previously, she'd drawn a coveted Montana goat tag for these same Crazy Mountains, and we'd spent a week together there in the high country. There was no weapon restriction on the tag, but she'd stuck with her recurve bow throughout. She didn't kill a goat; the only reason we didn't devote more time to the effort was that she'd also drawn a sheep tag for the Missouri Breaks. (Lori should have headed to Las Vegas that year.) I was proud of her decision. A lot of folks around town didn't understand why she didn't pack in a rifle and kill a billy, but I did.

This year my turn had come round at last, after 30 years of futile application. Now Lori could sit at the bottom of the hill, glass, and critique my stalks while I made the tough final ascents. She was set to enjoy herself and I didn't blame her.

I too was hunting with bow and arrow, so the smart money was on the goats. At least we knew the terrain after our earlier adventure. The Crazies are a deceptive mountain range. Located in central Montana 80 miles southwest of our home, you can drive all the way around them in an afternoon, but there are no roads into the goat country (and I hope it stays that way). Despite their circumscribed perimeter, the Crazies contain some of the most rugged country in Montana, which is to say in the Lower-48. I had never suffered any illusions that this would be easy.

According to local rumor, the Crazies' name derives from a madwoman who retreated there in search of tortured peace during the pioneer days. She could scarcely have picked a better place to escape the busyness of civilization, such as it was back then. Sheer peaks rise precipitously from tangled valley floors strewn with talus that invites a broken ankle at every step. Bears abound, and the Crazies shelter the largest concentration of wolverines in the contiguous states. Psychically, this was Lear's blasted heath; now it was up to me to come to terms with it.

We'd made the long, uphill hike to our old campsite the day before, arriving to a welcome sense of neglected familiarity. Less than an hour out of camp that morning, I'd spotted the top of a goat's back disappearing behind a rock just above the creek bottom. Certain that the goat was feeding uphill to bed down for the day, I made a mad scramble to intercept it. Four hundred yards above the creek, I peeked over a boulder to find a goat standing 15 yards away broadside. One glance at its horns told me the animal was a nanny. My tag was valid for either sex, but did I want to shoot a nanny in the first hour of the hunt? I didn't. So, there we were, watching a billy feed in terrain that invited technical climbing gear and supplemental oxygen.

Shortly after Lori offered her sunny assessment of her role in the days ahead, we watched a billy vanish into a patch of scrubby juniper high above us. An hour later, it still hadn't emerged. "You *did* come here to hunt goats, didn't you?" Lori finally asked.

"I'll look down at you from time to time," I said as I girded up my loins for the assault. "If the goat reappears, you should be able to see him, but I probably won't. You know the hand signals."

Two hours later, I'd clawed and scrambled my way to goat level. Looking down the mountain toward Lori, I saw her staring back at me through her glasses with no new information to convey. Morning thermal updrafts had developed, and since goats are more alert to danger from below than above, I worked my way across the ledges so I could hunt my way downward through the scrub with the wind in my face.

An hour later I emerged at the bottom of the stunted evergreens having found no sign of the billy. Although Lori could see all the way around the stunted trees, when we rejoined at the base of the mountain, she told me she'd never seen the goat exit the cover. The mountain seemed to have swallowed the animal, granting me nothing to show for my effort but a few scrapes and bruises. Leave it to goat hunting to redefine one's concept of a good time.

Since the creek tumbling along the valley floor held trout, we'd packed a fly rod and a skeleton fishing kit into camp. By sunrise the following day we were already tired of freeze-dried backpack fare, and Lori carried the fly rod in its aluminum case when we left camp. She said that she just wanted some decent food on our plates that night, but I suspected her real aim was something more exciting to do than give hand signals while I crawled around the cliffs with the goats. Why was I starting to feel as if the lucky member of the party was the one who *hadn't* drawn the goat tag?

Different day, same story... and the same long, fruitless climb up the mountain and back. Lori hadn't abandoned me to fish though; she'd stayed glued to her glasses the whole morning while I scrambled around in the rocks with a billy that just wouldn't let me maneuver into bow range. "Time to go fishing!" she announced cheerily when I rejoined her at the bottom of the rockslide. No argument from me; I wasn't good for more than one honest goat stalk per day.

"Look at the size of that one!" she said once we'd worked our way down to the creek and peered into a beautiful crystalline pool. The sight below justified her enthusiasm. I knew the creek held some beautiful native cutthroats, but the specimen lying in the current against the far bank looked as if it weighed three or four pounds. Lori spooked that one with a cast the breeze drove awry, but she caught several smaller cutts from the same pool, each as gorgeous as any trout I've ever seen.

That didn't do our dinner aspirations any good though; cutthroats in Montana streams are appropriately protected. Another pool a mile back toward camp held a pleasant surprise, however: legions of eager, pan-sized rainbows. I hadn't killed a trout in years, but these were exceptional circumstances. Introduced rainbows are the biggest environmental threat native cutthroats face; besides, we were hungry. For once, the laws of man and nature stood in perfect accord. A half dozen alien rainbows sizzled in the frying pan that night. Trout have never tasted better.

Down to our final night in Round One without having taken a shot, we were trudging back to camp the following afternoon when Lori urgently tugged at my sleeve and whispered, "Goats!" I'd been looking where you're supposed to look—uphill—while Lori had alertly spotted the goats below us, right in the creek. A quick glance as we dropped behind a rock confirmed that at least one of them was big enough to shoot. Unfortunately, a steep ledge separated us from the creek below. "If they go up the other side, we'll never get to them," I said. "Our only chance is to hope they come uphill this way toward us. We need to get downwind right now!"

With the goats visually eclipsed by the steep ledge above the creek and the sound of the current masking my steps, I hustled back down the trail as quickly as possible. Soon the sound of hoof on rock below confirmed that the goats had done just what we needed them to do. But when I turned back into the breeze to prepare for the slam dunk shot they were about to offer, I saw Lori crouched behind a boulder 60 yards behind me. The goats tried to cross the trail between us, but when they winded Lori they clattered away down the ledge and out of our lives.

An experienced bowhunter herself, Lori immediately realized what had happened. "I was just trying to stay out of your way!" she wailed. "I should have known better!"

"It's okay, honey," I reassured her. And it was. A goat in the trail suddenly seemed too easy, too unlike mountain goat hunting.

A quarter mile down the trail I suddenly realized I was walking alone and stopped. When Lori caught up to me, she was in tears. "After all the effort you put in," she sobbed. "I just can't believe I made such a stupid mistake!"

I leaned my bow against a tree and put my hands on her shoulders. "I wouldn't have traded your company up here for the biggest mountain goat in the world," I told her. And I meant it.

Solitude

After three days of R&R, I was on my way back to the Crazies while Lori fulfilled the definition of a Cajun Trust Fund: a wife with a job. My days as a physician at our local hospital had ended three months before—I needed more time to hunt, fish, and write – but Lori was still gainfully employed part time as a nurse. A mile up the trail, I began to sense how badly I was going to miss her.

But there is a difference between being alone and being lonely, and I thought about the distinction as I downed a macaroni and cheese dinner in the dark that night. Paradoxically, I've always found loneliness a phenomenon of crowded places, while wilderness solitude evokes a different response entirely. I would certainly miss my wife in the days ahead, but the challenge of tackling the goats and the mountains that held them one-on-one felt seductively appealing.

While the bow may not be a particularly efficient means of putting meat on the table, that same inefficiency allows the bowhunter tremendous amounts of time and opportunity to observe and study the object of the chase. No quarry is more worthy of that attention than the mountain goat, I realized the following morning as I glassed another billy. *Oreamnos americanus* is a biologically unique species. The only animal I've ever pursued that resembles it is the Himalayan tahr, although the two species are not biologically related. Both animals inhabit similarly daunting terrain and display the same massive forequarters and rolling, ursine gait. Since our goat arose in the New World and the tahr in the Old, these similarities represent parallel evolution rather than common genetics. Both species adapted to fill a niche no other large animal wanted: high alpine cliffs, where they face no competition for food from other ungulates and minimal threat from predators. (Here in North America, eagles nab some kids, while falls account for the rest of the high first year mortality.) Seldom seen in the wild by most Americans, goats are fascinating animals that I can watch all day. Good thing: bowhunting goats involves a lot of watching.

Note to self: solitude allows plenty of silent time for such internal monologues. Are these interludes worth the price of absent human company? Get back to me on that later.

Those days rolled on, my spirits buoyed by the majesty of the setting and a run of gorgeous weather. But the equinox was approaching, and in Montana that celestial event often heralds the first real storm of the season. Clouds began to gather as I hiked back down the trail to camp on the last night of summer, and as I muddled my way through dinner (Spam and tortillas, absent Lori's fly rod), rain began to fall along with the temperature.

As I lay in the tent that night and listened to the patter of raindrops swell to a roar, it occurred to me that one function of wilderness is to redefine the notion of comfort. At home, the gathering storm would have been a minor inconvenience at most, with the security of our house's roof safely masking its implications. Here, the thin fabric of the tent overhead was all that separated me from serious discomfort if not hypothermic disaster. For once, I really knew how good I had it thanks to nothing more than the re-written rules of wild places.

The downpour had stopped by the time I awoke, but gale force winds were howling down the canyon in the wake of the storm front's passage. The new snow line began just a few hundred feet above camp, and the goat cliffs lay covered in termination dust—the traditional Alaskan term for the first snow fall at the end of the brief arctic summer, serving notice to seasonal workers to start packing their bags. Lori was expecting me back home that night and the logical course of action would have been to break camp down, hang the gear in a tree, and walk out. But each day I'd learned more about the goats and their habits, and I couldn't resist another morning of hunting.

Back at camp just before noon, I spotted a lone goat at the top of a cliff across the stream and down the valley as I was packing up. Already fatigued, I asked myself a simple question: Was I a man or a mouse? After studying the sheer cliff below the goat, I decided on the latter. However, I left my manhood an option. Because of the terrain, the closest approach to the goat might begin back down the trail I planned to walk out. I resolved that if I could still see the goat when I drew even with him, I'd shed my heavy pack and make the stalk.

For better or worse, the bedded goat was still visible when I reached the crucial point in the trail. Feeling invigorated, I cached my pack and started to climb. Two hours later, I peeked over a rock to study the lie from a better perspective. After further consideration, I decided that the best approach would be to climb around the back side of the mountain and stalk the goat from above.

That seemed like a good plan, and it was—up to a point. After two more hours, I had worked my way into a position 60 yards above the goat. With thermal currents still bathing my face and abundant cover in an old avalanche chute, I felt so confident of my ability to reach bow range that I was already making plans to spend the night on the mountain with the dead goat if I had to. Then the wind faltered. The goat's head shot up and he disappeared over the edge of the cliff into terrain no mortal man could enter.

My long afternoon of work had unraveled just like that, leaving me to start the long hike out toward Lori and home all over again. I admit that I was talking to myself by the time I started down the last mile of trail in the dark, but at least no one was talking back... yet.

Lori taking a break in goat country.

Epilogue

By the time mountain goat season ended in November, I'd spent 25 days in the Crazies, over half of them alone. I lost 25 pounds, one per day of mountain time, but I didn't miss them. My tally read as follows: three blue grouse, three ruffs, six rainbow trout, one deep bruise on my flank, numerous abrasions and lacerations on my hands, one near collapse, and one out-of-body experience. Credit for the last two goes to a combination of dehydration, extreme exertion, and high altitude—or so I thought. I imparted no deeper meaning to them at the time.

That list does not include a mountain goat. I had chances. I passed up several more nannies and failed to convert on two good opportunities, which is a euphemistic way of reporting that I missed. Unless I spend enough time back in Alaska to reestablish my residency there, I may well never have a chance to hunt mountain goats again, which makes me sad. But toward the end of the season, I realized that I was pursuing the goat in much the same way Ahab pursued Moby Dick, with a ruthless singularity of purpose that left me immune to all the reflections about life and love I'd experienced earlier. I did not enjoy that feeling, and when I recognized it for what it was, I stopped hunting goats.

It's hard to write a hunting story in which no one shoots anything without sounding sappy at some point. Going on about the meaning of the experience eventually begins to start sounding like an excuse. True enough; I wanted to kill a goat and I didn't. But I can honestly report that my month in the Crazies left me feeling wiser and—paradoxically, since wisdom is usually associated with age—younger. I felt wiser because I'd learned new appreciation for my wife and best friend at the same time I was expanding my ability to feel at home with myself. I felt younger because I confirmed the ability to do what I'd done outdoors at age 30, even though doing so hurt a lot more at 60. Those insights may not make up for the goat I didn't kill, but they sure came close.

Now for the rest of the story. As physicians are notoriously wont to do, I blew off those two strange episodes and rationalized them as previously described. When similar symptoms eventually began to recur at home, my excellent primary care physician said they sounded like complex partial seizures and recommended several tests including an MRI of my head. Since hunting season was still in progress, I ignored this advice until Nurse Lori put her foot down. The eventual MRI revealed a tumor on the right side of my brain, which was subsequently removed surgically, with a good prognosis.

The things one can learn while hunting mountain goats…

Section III

The Pacific

21.
Monsters from the Basalt Wall

As I eased through the lush grass, I tried to ignore the mosquitoes (*mozzies* in Australian parlance) and concentrate on the rich array of exotic bird life overhead. I was hunting the headwaters of the Fletcher River where it emerges from the world's longest lava flow, locally known as Great Basalt Wall. A flock of Pacific black ducks broke through the gum trees, making me long briefly for my shotgun. Sacred ibises wheeled in the sunlight and when a pair of huge brolga cranes glided past overhead their ratcheting cries reminded me of sandhills on the Alaska tide flats. But then a dark, hulking form appeared briefly twenty yards ahead and vanished into the foliage. A bird watcher no longer, I checked the wind and fumbled an arrow onto the string, mentally preparing myself for another encounter with the great wild boars my late friend Billie Baker respectfully called Basalt Warriors.

With a faint but adequate puff of breeze in my face, I eased forward slowly through the ankle-deep water, using my ears to guide me. Moments later, I heard the sound I sought: a faint slosh as the hog rooted through the mud for its breakfast. As I closed the gap, I finally detected a glistening black patch of hair and hide several bow lengths ahead of me in the grass. Unfortunately, it was impossible to tell what part of the pig I was studying.

Based on my earlier glimpse, I knew the hog was a mature boar, although I couldn't tell how large. With decades of experience under his belt, Billie had a remarkable ability to evaluate hogs based on nothing more than a brief look at a boar's head in thick cover, a skill I had yet to master. But with no season, no limit, and a hardworking rancher anxious for us to kill as many marauding swine as possible, I decided I'd take the shot as soon as I could safely identify ribs and worry about the size of the boar's tusks later.

But after a long, tense wait, a flock of sulfur-crested cockatoos flushed from the top of a nearby eucalyptus issuing their characteristic, raucous alarm cries. The alerted boar suddenly stopped foraging. While all pigs have relatively poor eyesight, old boars seem to have a sixth sense that alerts them to the presence of danger at close range. Combined with the racket from the cockatoos, that was enough to let him know something was wrong even if he didn't know where or what. When the tops of his ears appeared, I realized he was looking in my direction. Then a deep grunt broke the silence followed by an even more ominous sound: the click of ivory on ivory. Faced with the timeless choice between fight or flight, he seemed to be favoring the former.

A Basalt Warrior that fell after a long, careful, stalk.

On my first trip Down Under the year before, I heard all kinds of stories about charging hogs that I initially—and naively—dismissed as hot air. Then Lori and I attended a large bow shoot in northern Queensland at which everyone was dressed in shorts, and I noticed that most of the experienced bowhunters I met bore deep scars on their legs. In his fine chronicle of Australian bowhunting *Born to the Bow*, Billie documents several serious charges and one bad mauling. By the time I heard that boar chomping, I knew enough to take the sound seriously.

Since I still had the wind and the boar seemed uncertain of my location, I decided to wait matters out and hope for a shot. Finally, the pig exploded from the grass in a geyser of water and shot past without ever offering a target. No matter: when hunting the Basalt Wall, it's sometimes wise to settle for a draw.

Here in Montana, I live next door to the second longest true spring creek in the world. The longest is the Fletcher River, half a world away in northern Queensland. As all that clear water percolates slowly downstream, it creates a vast wilderness of swamps and marshes on Toomba Station, a huge working cattle ranch. Thanks to his longstanding friendship with ranchers Ernest and Robin Bassingthwaighte, Bill Baker outfitted the hunting on this vast property and managed it exclusively for the bow. Large herds of free ranging axis deer (chital) represent the ranch's glamour species, and on my first visit I was fortunate enough to stalk and kill a nice stag. But as much as I enjoy hunting these beautiful spotted deer, it was somehow the Basalt Warriors rather than the chital that defined the hunting experience there for me.

Feral swine are not native to Australia, whose indigenous mammals are all marsupials (save for the egg-laying duck-billed platypus). Some hogs probably arrived from mainland Asia with early seafarers, and those stocks were eventually supplemented by pigs from Europe during the era of British colonization. Once they reached northern Australia, swine found lush, moist habitat free of natural predators, and populations exploded. Notoriously hard on native habitat, pigs are regarded as an ecologic nuisance in Australia and hunters are generally encouraged to take them at will.

Because of the remoteness of the terrain and the limitations of hunting with bow and arrow, Toomba hogs grow large even by Australian standards, with mature boars commonly weighing over 250 pounds. Their tusks and temperament are even more impressive. For some reason, the Basalt Wall consistently produces some of the best trophy boars in the South Pacific. Due to high population densities, boars spend a lot of time fighting over sows and the scars they bear—and their aggressive behavior—reflect their need to battle constantly.

Pig hunters here at home are familiar with the fighting shield, the dense layer of cartilage boars develop beneath the skin on their shoulders and upper chest to protect their forequarters from rivals' tusks. While I was aware of this phenomenon from boars I'd killed in Hawaii and our own South, I'd never seen shields as well developed as those on big boars from the Basalt Wall, which probably reflects the amount of time they spend fighting. A broadside shot may not allow arrow penetration if it catches the back edge of that thick gristle, which is why shots taken slightly quartering away are preferable. Heavy arrows and sharp, non-replaceable blade broadheads are a must. My new Aussie friends routinely coat the business half of their shafts with Vaseline, which they believe improves penetration, a trick I've adopted for both hogs and bears here at home.

Soft morning light suffuses the eastern sky, leaving a towering stand of eucalyptus silhouetted against its glow. Game is on the move, and I've already passed up shots at a large sow and a young boar in separate encounters. Here on the Basalt Wall, it's only a matter of time.

No kidding. An imposing form suddenly appears against the grass, backlit by the rising sun. The swaybacked outline, massive shoulders and wickedly protruding snout identify the animal at once as a mature boar, interested perhaps in the sow that recently followed the same trail. Thanks to their solid profile and lack of anatomic landmarks, picking a spot on a hog can be difficult and I remind myself to bear down and concentrate. I've been closer to other pigs that morning, but as soon as my hand reaches its anchor point on my face the shot feels perfect. When the boar turns slightly away, I release. The mental camera that always clicks whenever I shoot at game registers this much: entrance just in front of the last rib at a perfect angle, penetration up to the brightly colored fletches. Done deal—or at least it ought to be.

Giving the boar the respect he deserves, I wander farther into the swamp and burn some film before returning to take up the trail. Blood proves sparse as expected, since the entrance wound is a bit high, the broadhead is buried in the opposite shoulder, and hogs don't bleed much from an arrow wound. Hogs are like bears in that nothing goes down quicker after a perfectly placed arrow, but few game animals are harder to recover after a hit that is anything less. In this case, a plain trail of newly compressed grass leads quickly to the dead boar, barely 50 yards from where he stood when I shot him.

A fine animal with genuinely imposing tusks, he's every inch a Basalt Warrior. But somehow, this hunt has been about so much more than dead game. From the curious wallabies that hop past during nearly every stalk to the new friends Lori and I have made, hunting the Basalt Wall represents an immersion into another world to which I'm always ready to return.

22.

My Heart of Darkness

We'd spent ten minutes studying the three bulls grazing in the open meadow 60 yards below the ridge, long enough to know that two were youngsters and the third a shooter... maybe. Since Australian bowhunter Dan Smith was the designated hitter that first night on northern Australia's remote Melville Island, he began to ease forward through the gum trees while Bill Baker, Brad Kane and I spread out to help keep an eye on the buffalo. All three of us were glancing around at the trees as we moved, not because we needed more cover but because we wanted to know the location of the nearest escape route in case the hunters became the hunted.

Although he was moving with admirable stealth, Dan had barely taken a dozen steps when something alerted the buffalo to our presence. The two young bulls immediately snorted and trotted off into the scrub, but their big brother proved more belligerent, an adjective that was to occur to me repeatedly during countless close encounters with buffalo over the following week. Instead of retreating, he studied our position as if he were trying to decide which one of us had just shot his dog, and then he began to advance up the hill.

Several minutes later, the bull stood facing us some 20 yards from Dan while I mentally gauged my leap into the lower branches of the nearest tree. The frontal shot angle was obviously unacceptable, but to his credit Dan held his ground. At that range, I had no trouble determining that the bull was a representative but by no means exceptional specimen, and I knew that Dan was willing to hold out in hopes of the latter. After a long face-off, the animal turned and I saw Dan's bow arm start to come up, but he hesitated just as the bull evidently decided that he'd seen enough of us. After one last, contemptuous snort, he wheeled and galloped back down the hill in a cloud of dust, leaving us to breathe a collective sigh of relief in the wake of his departure.

"Tell me, Dan," I asked once the tension started to ease. "Did you hold off because he looked too small or because the situation looked too scary?"

"A bit of both, mate!" Dan acknowledged with a laugh.

Welcome to the Tiwi Islands, where the land is wild, the game imposing, and time in the field seldom passes for long without an opportunity to test one's mettle.

A ton of trouble. A Melville Island bull engaged in the buffalo stare.

This book deserves a segment on "The Blackness of the Buffalo" analogous to Melville's chapter "The Whiteness of the Whale" in

Moby Dick. Perfect lightness or perfect darkness seems to represent all the human mind needs to understand each of these imposing creatures. The first time I saw a wild Asiatic buffalo lumbering toward me through the lush green cycads that blanket Melville Island, its mud-streaked ebony hide bespoke *trouble* as eloquently as the contempt in its eyes.

Australia has always been a source of biological anomalies. No placental mammals are native to the island continent. Descended from the Asian red wolf, the dingo arrived from the mainland courtesy of Malay traders before first European contact. Other than that, Australia was originally populated entirely by marsupials like the kangaroo, plus the world's sole egg-laying mammal, the duck-billed platypus.

New arrivals during the colonial era realized that they, like nature itself, abhorred a vacuum. They began to introduce a variety of large ungulates, ranging from pigs and goats (which now wreak ecological havoc throughout the country) to a half-dozen Eurasian deer species to camels. (No kidding. Australia is now home to the world's largest free ranging camel population.)

Asiatic buffalo went aboard Noah's ark to Australia in the early 1800s, where their first stop was Melville Island, a lonely strip of tropical wilderness in the Arafura Sea that could have served as landfall for Robinson Crusoe. From there, colonists engaged in another exercise in *it seemed like a good idea at the time* by introducing the animals to the Australian mainland. The plan was to domesticate them as a source of meat and hides, but the buffalo had other ideas. They proved impossible to contain and were soon marauding everywhere across the country's wild Top End.

Unlike our North American bison, these animals are related to the African Cape buffalo, to which they invite obvious comparison. Physically, the two are similar in size and body structure, although the horns on the Asiatic version are crescent shaped rather than down-curved. However, based on several seasons of extensive experience with them, I feel that they lack the malignant edge of the Cape buffalo's personality. However, we never lost track of the fact that they were large, dangerous animals that could and did kill people in the Outback every year.

That first exploratory trip was noteworthy for the absence of two pieces of equipment one might regard as essential. The first was my own bow. Prior to departure, I'd experienced a sudden, severe neck problem resulting in nerve injury and loss of function in my right arm. While urgent surgery made me cancel a scheduled trip to Africa, the opportunity to be part of the first group of bowhunters to visit Melville Island was too exciting to pass up. There's only one first exploratory trip to virgin country. Leaving it to my friends and waiting until the following year just wouldn't have been the same. By the time I left for Australia, my right arm was still far too weak to draw a bow capable of anchoring a buffalo, but I left anyway, determined to act as scout, tracker, photographer, and camp fisherman even if I couldn't hunt.

The second missing item was a backup rifle. As a longtime admirer of bowhunting legend Bill Negley, I'd always respected his eventual decision to leave all firearms behind during his last bowhunts for the African Big Five. While I've hunted all North American dangerous game without backup and spent plenty of time close to elephants and buffalo in Africa with no rifle around, I also recognized that Australian buffalo are huge, unpredictable animals with a deserved reputation for aggressive behavior. However, one inevitable effect of having a rifle along on a bowhunt is to make dangerous game less dangerous, and after a long discussion in Darwin the night before our departure for base camp in Snake Bay, the four of us made a unanimous decision: when we headed out to our camp in the bush, the .458 would stay behind. While we experienced several situations during the hunt that made us question that decision, in the end we all agreed that we'd learned a whole lot more about buffalo than we would have otherwise as a result.

Although my useless right arm kept me from carrying my own bow on that first trip, I found plenty to do—scouting new cover, spotting game, tracking, skinning, and, best of all, supplementing our meager larder. We had only been able to import a minimal amount of food to the island. By prior agreement, we salvaged the buffalo meat for distribution among the island's indigenous Tiwi population, and we anticipated being able to subsist on some of it ourselves. Unfortunately, we quickly learned that meat from any bull old enough to shoot was too tough to chew, even though it tasted fine. Had we been able to bring along a good Dutch oven we could have solved that problem, but weight restrictions on the flight from the mainland left us no means of cooking other than open fire and one anemic gas stove.

Although a fly rod may seem an inefficient survival tool, I always carry one on wilderness hunting trips. My 4-piece 7-weight has served that purpose well all around the world, from feeding sheep hunting camps with char and grayling in the Brooks Range to providing our party with sea-run char on exploratory hunting trips to Siberia. I couldn't imagine it failing to do the same in the fertile waters surrounding Melville Island.

We were camped on the island's remote east end, far from the little Tiwi community of Snake Bay. The area's only inhabitants were Laurence and Marjorie Priddy, members of Australia's "Lost Generation," whose parents had hidden them in the Bush when authorities rounded up Aboriginal children and packed them off to boarding schools to "civilize" them by erasing all traces of their traditional culture. Twice a year, Laurence walked to Snake Bay for a bag of rice. Other than that, the couple subsisted on vegetables raised in their garden and barramundi, Australia's signature estuarine gamefish.

The evening after we'd each invested an hour trying to chew our way through a bite of Bill's buffalo, I showed Laurence my fly rod and suggested a fishing trip the following morning. "That's fine, Don," replied Laurence, who had evidently watched some fly-fishing television shows somewhere. "But there'll be no kissing them and throwing them back in the water. When we catch barra, we kill them and eat them."

"Perfect," I replied.

Early the following morning, I met Laurence at his house and climbed into his ancient "tinny," as Australians call their small metal skiffs. The creek in front of his house was flowing briskly inland on a strong building tide, and we let the current carry us across a long, open flat toward the jungle. It soon became apparent that if one of us bailed constantly with the coffee can bobbing in the bilge, we could just keep pace with the water pouring in through the tinny's perforated bottom. The ever-present possibility of swamping or capsizing left me acutely aware of the area's ominous apex predator—the saltwater crocodile.

For as it happens, the ranges of both buffalo and barramundi overlap almost perfectly with that of the "salty," a prehistoric monster that even fearless Aussies regard with profound respect. I'd already seen evidence of their presence the day before, a huge, waddling drag mark that led into a buffalo wallow and didn't come out, motivating me to give the mudhole a wide, cautious berth. When I pointed to croc tracks covering the creek's muddy banks, Laurence confirmed that the water was full of them. This was not the place to swamp a skiff.

To my disappointment, the brisk tidal flow had muddied the current, never a good sign for a fly rod angler. Laurence encouraged me to have at it anyway, and I did. To my delight and surprise, on my third cast something whacked my streamer out in the turbid water and then gave me a glimpse of a yard-long length of silver flashing in the tropical sun before it threw the hook. Newly alerted, I didn't miss the next strike and eventually managed to haul the 15-pound fish (my generous estimate) over the tinny's gunwale. In accordance with prior agreement, I did not kiss it and toss it back in the water. That was my introduction to a fish that has haunted my imagination ever since.

I finally expressed my reservations about the cloudy water despite landing two more fish. Laurence paddled us toward the rapidly vanishing shoreline and directed me toward the nearby jungle. "The water will be clear up in those little pools, Don," he assured me. "But be careful in there. Don't want you stepping on one of our snapping handbags."

Croc tracks littered the mud as I slogged across the flat. Entering the shade of the gum trees felt like reaching Conrad's heart of darkness. The water was indeed clear, but the stumps and snags littering the little series of pools would make landing a fish the size of those I'd already caught challenging if not impossible. I shot a roll cast through the debris and received an immediate strike. The leaping barra soon had my fly line festooned across the snags like tinsel on a Christmas tree, and when the fish threw a half-hitch around one, I chose to break the leader deliberately rather than wade in and try to salvage the fly. No snapping hand bags for me.

By the time I had finished replacing my fly and leader, I began to experience the eerie sensation that I was not alone. I scanned the water for croc nostrils but saw nothing worrisome. My sixth sense proved accurate however, for when I glanced up into the trees, I saw a buffalo bull staring back at me from the shadows no more than four rod lengths away. When the animal showed no interest in yielding the right of way along the series of shrouded pools, I decided we had enough fish for dinner.

As indeed we did, but just barely. Barramundi enjoy a tremendous reputation as food fish, and our evening meal that night confirmed it. From then on, I was charged with providing fresh fish for dinner every night. That was a tough job but somebody had to do it, and I did. To the chagrin of my concerned Aussie companions, not even the crocodiles could keep me out of the water.

Those missions began my love affair with barramundi, which continues to this day.

By the third day of the hunt, Dan had enjoyed multiple close-range encounters with buffalo, including several bulls that I frankly would have taken in a heartbeat. But only the hunter himself can decide when an animal meets his personal standards, and as anxious as we all were to see what happened when an arrow struck one of those huge, black bulls, we respected Dan's decision to hold out for one that met his.

By that point, however, I could see Billie's own bow arm start to twitch. Although he was one of Australia's most accomplished and respected bowhunters, he'd never killed a buffalo and not because of lack of effort. Even the most experienced bowhunters often seem to have a "curse" species (my hunting partners felt free to laugh about my own mishaps with Sitka blacktail deer before I finally killed a few), and the buffalo was his. He'd logged countless days in the outback chasing buffalo only to be undone by the usual litany of factors that can be a bowhunter's undoing, from treacherous winds to country that didn't contain animals as anticipated. Now, surrounded by buffalo in a pristine wilderness setting, his own eagerness had grown palpable.

Our original plan had been for Dan to take the first bull and me the second, if my arm recovered sufficiently to let me draw an adequate bow. But with Dan being choosey and my arm still at half-strength, we reached an obvious conclusion over breakfast that morning. We would split our party in two, and Dan would hunt with Brad while I did my best to help Billie break his curse.

At first light, Billie and I bailed out of the Landcruiser to hunt our way down a long, winding creek to the sea. We'd found buffalo there the morning before as the animals worked their way uphill toward their bedding cover after feeding all night on a large grass flat just above the beach, and Dan had passed up a respectable bull after a careful stalk. With a steady sea breeze in our faces, we knew we'd enjoy a favorable wind until mid-morning, and the brush along the creek provided ideal stalking cover.

Half an hour later Billie hit the brakes a few steps ahead of me as the first wave of buffalo appeared right on schedule. With just enough time to take cover in the bushes, we soon had animals in bow range although all proved to be cows, calves, and young bulls. While cows are substantially smaller than bulls, their horns can be even longer, and they are notoriously unpredictable whenever they perceive danger to their calves. I kept this fact firmly in mind as the first cow-calf unit wandered past a dozen steps away, especially since the animals' sudden appearance had caught us a little farther from the nearest climbing trees than I would have liked.

It took the herd nearly an hour to work its way by. Although some of the animals eventually caught our wind, they managed to trot off uphill without spooking the whole group. "I guess that's it, mate," Billie finally sighed as the last of them disappeared behind us, allowing a welcome opportunity to break radio silence and stretch our knotted muscles.

"But the big bull was lagging behind the main mob yesterday," I reminded Billie. "Let's wait a bit before we head farther downhill." Just then, a flash of ebony appeared in the foliage ahead, and our binoculars quickly confirmed that this was the animal we were after.

In no apparent hurry, the bull was feeding noisily as he came into view, and Billie took full advantage of the cover and the racket to close the gap. At 20 yards, I watched him ease an arrow onto his string, but by pure chance the animal turned to face him. Although still unaware of us, he no longer offered an acceptable shot angle. Riveted to my field glasses, I watched the unsuspecting buffalo feed his way to a distance from Billie that we later measured at nine paces. At that point, the huge animal glanced up, realized that Billie's camouflaged figure hadn't been there earlier, and began one of the tensest stare-downs I've ever witnessed.

The bull's belligerent attitude had already eliminated the need for an elaborate stalk since he been tolerating our presence from the moment he first made eye contact. The problem was that he was facing us head on, and a frontal shot with a bow on any big game animal—let alone one that large—is a recipe for disaster. There was nothing for us to do but wait, and nothing to do while we waited except gauge the distance to the nearest gum trees and decide how we'd try to climb one should the situation go to hell in a hurry.

As the bull gave us the stink-eye I glanced at my watch, which is how I know that hunters and buffalo all stood motionless for exactly 29 minutes. The arrow on the riser of Bill's bow began to shake. I struggled to control the cramps developing in my legs. The buffalo began to drool and run his tongue inside his nostrils in order to pick up more of our scent, a doomed effort since we had been careful to put the wind in our faces as soon as we spotted him.

Finally, the bull appeared to decide that we just weren't worth his time and started to turn and walk away. The moment the axis of his body reached a full broadside angle, I watched Bill come to full draw and release the arrow. The impact made a sound like a baseball bat hitting a pumpkin as the stricken bull seemed to hesitate between flight or fight. Fortunately, he chose the former, and the long spell broke as we listened to him crash off into the brush. My legs were so shaky that had my outstretched arm not come up solidly against a gum tree, I might have fallen to the ground.

We easily located the dead bull 50 yards back in the brush. Bill's long quest for a buffalo with his bow was over, but three seasons' worth of adventure on Melville Island had just begun.

By the last day of the hunt, interesting events had taken place in and about my neck and right shoulder. Finally, the strength in my biceps and deltoid was beginning to return. Although nowhere near full strength, I found that I could draw Billie's #69 recurve to the level of my navel, and in camp I was consistently hitting empty cans at 20 yards with this unconventional style. I decided I was ready to give it a try, although I made it perfectly clear to my mates that I planned to be conservative and would decline any shot that didn't feel perfect at the moment of truth.

That afternoon, we struck out for new country: a remote inland lake that Laurence said held countless crocodiles within its waters and numerous buffalo about its banks. Since it was too early in the day to hunt, we took a detour past a saltwater creek to fish on the making tide. Barramundi were pouring up the creek. For an hour, we took turns casting and watching for crocodiles while I enjoyed some of the most exciting fly-fishing in memory. Finally, with a cooler full of fresh fish for dinner, we set off in search of a miracle.

After another hour of driving and a short hike through the scrub, we broke out upon a remarkable sight: a broad lake choked with lily pads, teeming with tropical water birds, and surrounded by buffalo. After checking the wind, we eased down the inlet creek—ever mindful of lurking crocs—and wound up 30 yards from the edge of a herd numbering dozens of animals just on the other side. Since the cover across the creek was sparse and no one relished the idea of wading the stream, we appeared to be at a stalemate. But then a cow spotted something and snorted, and our evening grew interesting indeed.

As a handful of cows scattered, the bull behind them began to advance. Several minutes later, he stood facing us in the middle of the stream a dozen yards away. While we'd had several similar encounters with belligerent bulls that week, something about this animal's attitude made me nervous—along with everyone else, I learned later. Nonetheless, I eased an arrow onto the string and resolved to shoot him if he opened up and offered a perfect shot.

While I'm usually crestfallen when such a close encounter comes to naught, I have to admit that I breathed a sigh of relief when the bull finally turned to gallop off. For just an instant, he presented a quartering angle that I would have taken if I'd been in perfect form, but I wasn't. As the bull tore off through the herd, he spooked the whole mob and for several minutes we stood and watched the spectacle of buffalo churning wildly across the shallow lake. Somehow, that seemed a perfect way to end a remarkable trip.

"You were going to shoot that bull if he stopped, weren't you mate?" Billie asked once the commotion died down.

"Yeah," I admitted. "I was."

"I was afraid of that," he noted with a laugh. "Don't worry, mate; you'll get him next year when your arm's back in shape."

I certainly hoped so. And I did.

It all seems so long ago now, as if these events had taken place in a galaxy far, far away. Bill Baker is dead, a victim of gastric cancer. Political turmoil in the local Tiwi community has left the island closed to visitors. We just happened to be in the right place at the right time.

However, this coda doesn't mean it was all for naught. The experience was always about more than hunting buffalo. It was about friends and fish and exotic wildlife, about the excitement of exploring a brave new world of tropical wilderness. Brad, Dan, and I remain good friends. I still return regularly to Far North Queensland and the Northern Territory, to visit friends and explore new salt water with my fly rod.

And whenever I head back home, I miss everything about it, even the crocodiles.

23.

Pick a Spot

The setting could not have provided a starker contrast to my last deer hunting experience, which took place four months earlier, during the Montana whitetail rut. The weather then had been relatively mild by local standards, but I still had to bundle up head to toe in wool and slog through snow the minute I set foot outside the house. Now I was dressed in shirtsleeves, and the air was alive with the sound of exotic birdsong. Rather than a background of solid snow, my eyes treated me to a view of the broad Pacific when I stopped to rest on my way up the hill.

Credit goes to my old friend Doug Borland for the scouting essential to this hunt. We'd both been hunting Hawaiian axis deer for years, enjoying some hard-won success along the way. The year before, he'd located an area with abundant sign that didn't require quite as much climbing to reach as our usual cover, and we'd enjoyed several close encounters there without managing to put a deer on the ground. Since Hawaii was right on the way from our Montana home to the PBS banquet in Portland (well, if you use your imagination), I was back again for another try.

We'd modified our usual axis deer hunting tactics the previous year. We both love pure spot and stalk hunting, and most of our experience with the species had come that way, including some notable successes. But axis deer are so sharp—more on this subject later—that stalking one in Hawaii's alpine represents an exceptionally difficult challenge even by traditional bowhunting standards. Despite those occasional successes, we'd blown a whole lot more stalks than we'd brought to fruition. Given the game density in the new area Doug had located, we'd decided to set up ambushes along trails instead. We'd both experienced close-range encounters with deer there earlier, but with this species, reaching bow range simply means that the hunt has begun in earnest.

That afternoon, when Doug and Ernie Holland peeled off toward simple ground blinds Doug had constructed prior to our arrival, I continued up the hill into new territory. The deer were bedding on top of a ridge during the heat of the day and moving to lower elevations to feed in the evening, much like elk. After studying the sign, I chose to set up downwind from the confluence of two trails where a patch of brush offered some natural cover.

Then I snipped out a few shooting lanes that would allow me to shoot toward both trails, dug up a spot in the dirt so I could sit and maneuver quietly, and sat down to wait.

The British Empire, upon which the sun once never set, was responsible for the dispersal of many traditions about the globe, ranging from bad cooking to the language that dominates world commerce today. Wildlife and outdoor sport were part of this diaspora, and species as diverse as brown trout, mallards, and red deer owe their current worldwide distribution to the British. So does the axis deer.

The species (*Axis axis*, or chital) is native to the Indian subcontinent. As a child reading James Corbett's memoirs of hunting man-eating cats (*Man-Eaters of Kumaon*), I noted with interest how Corbett would track the course of a tiger through the jungle at night by listening to chital and sambar bark as the cat moved through their territory. Sadly, free ranging wildlife is nearly gone in India now, so it is unlikely that any of us will ever have a chance to hunt these deer in their native range.

Fortunately, the British who colonized India were generous enough to share their bounty with countrymen far and wide. As a result, I have been able to hunt free ranging chital successfully in Hawaii, Australia, and Argentina. They do occur closer to home, in Texas. While most of us associate Texas axis deer with exotic game farms, in which I have no interest, free range chital were introduced to Texas in 1932 and have reproduced successfully in 32 counties, although I have no experience with them there.

The British brought their sporting traditions to Australia's "fatal shore" (the title of an excellent book about Australia by Robert Hughes) when they settled there in the early 19th century, but they soon realized that their new home contained no big game mammals. Through their Acclimatization Societies, the colonists addressed that natural deficiency for better or worse by introducing feral populations of animals ranging from Asiatic water buffalo to camels, feral pigs and goats, and six species of deer, including the chital.

Axis deer were introduced to Argentina in 1906. Although I am unable to document direct British influence on this introduction, British residents of Argentina and Chile did have Acclimatization Societies that were responsible for the introduction of the brown trout to these countries, so I infer their involvement in the introduction of Old World deer as well. Axis deer reached Hawaii in 1857 as a gift from the British government in Hong Kong to King Kamehameha V.

Australia, Argentina, and Hawaii all share certain characteristics that enabled these introduced deer to thrive: a mild climate like India's, abundant forage, and, most significantly, an all but complete absence of the natural predators they faced regularly in their home environment, especially the big cats. (There are cougars in Argentina, but no felids inhabit Australia or Hawaii except feral house cats.) The deer have fared so well in all three places that biologists now worry about their impact on native plant species and habitat.

I have developed a tremendous respect for chital no matter where I've hunted them, and not just because I share the widely held opinion that they are the most beautiful of all the world's deer. Whitetails set the standard for wariness among American bowhunters (although those experienced with African plains game may question that opinion.) A comparison between chital and whitetails proves interesting. I think the chital's senses are every bit as acute, and their vision may be better. Axis deer seem to lack some of the whitetail's spooky "sixth sense" intelligence, but their reaction times are even quicker. Chital lack predictable rut behavior, don't respond to calls or rattling (I've tried), and rarely inhabit terrain suitable for tree stands. And the winner is…?

Asked to name the animal that meant the most to me after a successful hunt, I seldom hesitate. That animal was my first axis deer. Although I've told the story before I think it bears repeating because of the insights it offers about hunting this challenging species.

That hunt also took place in Hawaii. Our day began with a steep uphill hike through rain drenched jungle brush. Just shy of the alpine, I set off in one direction while Doug and our Hawaiian friend Walter Naki continued in the other. An hour later, I'd met a strong blast of wind burbling over the top of the mountains. Soaking wet and chilled in cotton hunting clothes, I hunkered down beneath a bush contemplating the irony of surviving all those seasons in Alaska only to die of hypothermia in Hawaii.

An hour later, the sun broke through the clouds, and I set off around the side hill into the valley beyond. I was traversing a narrow draw on wet, slippery footing when a commotion erupted in the brush below me. The wind had carried my scent down into the bottom of the gulley, sending an axis hind bounding up the other side.

She offered no possibility of a shot, but the noise she made roused two stags from their beds farther up the draw. When the pair reached the top of the opposite side, the larger of the two paused quartering away, staring intently in the direction the hind had taken. The stag stood at least 40 yards from me and possibly farther, but I somehow felt confident that I could kill him even though the shot was beyond my usual range. And I did. I still had to get the deer down off the mountain, but that exercise turned into a labor of love before it was over.

Now to those insights I promised. First, hunting axis deer in Hawaii is a whole lot tougher physically than most people imagine. Second, because of its inherent difficulty, the bowhunter may need to test the limits of his range. I'm certainly not advocating irresponsible shots. I'm simply suggesting that if you are faced with a difficult but reasonable shot, you better take it because, in contrast to many other bowhunting situations, it's unlikely to get any better. Third, success on an axis deer hunt requires the simultaneous occurrence of two unusual events: perfect execution by the hunter and a mistake on the part of the deer. Fourth, when one chital spooks, others will often mill around in confusion rather than racing away from the area. A careful hunter may be able to take advantage of the disorder.

Pick a spot? This Hawaiian axis stag offers plenty to choose from.

Australian axis deer inhabit a geographically restricted range along the Queensland coast, and I consider myself fortunate to have experienced several opportunities to hunt them. During those hunts I enjoyed numerous stalking opportunities, but I only released one arrow. Fortunately, it proved to be a good one.

That hunt marked the start of my transition from spot and stalk tactics to ambush hunting for chital. It began one morning when Bill Baker and I watched a line of axis deer with a tremendous stag at the rear work its way through an isthmus between a lake and a steep wall of boulders as they returned to their bedding area in the Great Basalt Wall. Rather than risk spooking them by an ill-advised approach, we carefully noted some landmarks and returned in the dark the following day.

Since Bill was eager to obtain some video footage of a successful axis deer hunt with traditional tackle, he lagged behind with his camera while I carefully worked into position behind a downed tree the deer had passed the day before. After a long, motionless wait, I saw deer filtering toward me down the lakeshore, but something told me that they were going to pass wide of my log. After I oozed 15 yards laterally, the lead hind veered again onto a vector that would take her right into my lap. I had apparently out-thought myself, but at that point there was nothing to be done but await developments.

When the hind stopped mere feet away, I had to endure one of the longest stare-downs of my bowhunting career. Fully expecting an explosion of alarm barks at any moment, I closed my eyes and slowed my breathing down until it resembled a hibernating bear's. When I finally heard the hind walking off on my upwind side, I knew that the hardest part of the hunt was over.

But I still had to kill the stag. By the time I felt comfortable enough to open my eyes and look around, I felt disappointed to see that the stag at the end of the line wasn't the exceptional specimen we'd seen the day before. But not too disappointed—when he paused in front of me, I sent an arrow through his ribs and watched him pile up 30 yards away.

I learned some lessons from that encounter as well, prime among them being that if you can survive initial scrutiny by an axis deer or a member of its herd, you have a reasonable chance of getting away with some delicate close-range maneuvering. That realization proved valuable during that later Hawaiian hunt.

Sitting in a ground blind cobbled together from natural materials bears little resemblance to similar vigils conducted from pop-up blinds or other more elaborate structures. My "blind" did little more than break up my outline, so I had to hold motionless. Absent a chair to sit on, I had to be ready to move quickly from the ground into shooting position without being detected. Rocks and thorns beneath me eliminated any possibility of comfort.

Since sustained discipline is practically impossible in such conditions, the trick is to pick up approaching deer as far away as possible. All that requires is vigilance, and mine was rewarded when I saw a flicker of movement in the brush shortly after I'd settled in. By the time the flickers became deer, I was up on one knee in position to shoot in the direction they seemed most likely to take.

The first deer in line were hinds, as usual. By the time I could identify a dozen spotted forms moving toward me I hadn't seen a single antler, and no more deer were visible behind them. Did I want to sacrifice the possibility of a stag that probably wasn't even there for a shot at a deer with no horns?

Damn right I did. We rarely eat store bought meat when we're in Hawaii, preferring the finer, cheaper, and more gratifying fare we can obtain from the hills and the sea. I'd eaten enough chital to recognize it as some of the finest venison in the world. (I use the term venison in the European sense, to refer to all wild game meat and not just that from deer.) The cupboard was bare back at our condo, and a plump axis hind was just what we needed to get us through the rest of our stay.

But I learned years ago not to count on venison before it's on the ground, and even as the lead hind reached bow range, I knew I still had a long way to go. And sure enough—the old rip veered off at the last moment on a course that would take her on my downwind side. She had enough of a quartering tailwind for me to hope she wouldn't spook immediately, but I knew it was only a matter of time.

More deer had walked into bow range by then, but they were all quartering toward me. Since there is a difference between testing the limits of your bow range and taking a shot at an irresponsible angle, all I could do was wait. Then the inevitable alarm bark erupted behind me, and the brush was full of deer bouncing around like popcorn in a hot pan.

That first chital on the mountainside years earlier had taught me that it was too early to stop hunting. I remained in position, and when a mature hind appeared broadside at 30 yards and hesitated, I took the shot. The *splat* that followed reminded me that while spine hits may not be pretty, they sure are effective, especially when they eliminate the necessity of a difficult nighttime tracking job miles from the nearest road in weather warm enough to make meat spoil quickly.

Even with the deer lying at my feet, the day's challenges weren't over. Because of airline weight considerations, I'd taken my trusty Randall knife out of my duffle before we left home. With the tropical night fast descending, I learned that the folding knife I'd substituted at the last minute wouldn't cut butter much less field dress a deer. Fortunately, Doug and Ernie were better equipped, and after we regrouped we soon had the venison dressed, bagged, and on our backs for the walk out by headlamp.

When the steaks came off the grill the next night, I remembered why axis deer don't need to carry horns to make them worth whatever effort it takes to shoot one.

24.

Getting Your Goat

> The local nymphs, the daughters of Zeus himself
> flushed mountain goats so the crews could make their meal.
> Quickly we fetched our curved bows and hunting spears
> from the ships and, splitting up into three bands,
> we started shooting, and soon enough some god
> had sent us bags of game to warm our hearts.
> —Homer: *The Odyssey*, translated by Robert Fagles

Beautiful and apparently endless, the foothills of New Zealand's spectacular southern Alps stretched away forever beneath a cloudless sky as Lori and I perched atop a boulder and scanned the vista through our glasses. We were a week or two early for the red stags' annual roaring season, and the ridges remained silent except for the gentle sigh of the breeze. Fresh sign told us the stags were out there somewhere, but despite the open terrain they were doing a remarkably capable job of staying hidden. Suddenly a gleaming patch of black caught my attention in the rocks below. It was early in the afternoon for the tahr to be moving, but I turned my glasses in that direction hoping to catch a glimpse of one of those magnificent transplants from the Himalayas. Before I could focus my binoculars, the up-slope breeze carried the true nature of the animal's identity to my ears and nose simultaneously. The shiny dark hide belonged to a foraging flock of feral goats' lead billy.

As the rich chorus of bleating rose up the hillside, we watched a half-dozen more goats scamper nimbly up the rocks in our direction. With a favorable breeze and broken terrain favorable to stalking, the band of goats seemed to be issuing a deliberate challenge that Lori wasn't about to turn down. Shedding her pack, she set off down through the boulders while I settled back to enjoy one of my favorite spectator sports: watching a hunting partner stalk game with a bow.

Despite my vantage on top of the boulder, I quickly lost track of Lori's progress through the scree. Suddenly I heard loose rock sliding farther up the hill and turned to see an entirely different band of goats picking their way across the cliff above me. While I enjoyed a less advantageous wind, I still thought I could hustle up through the rocks in time to intercept the animals before they reached my scent line. Confident that my wife could handle herself and her own goats, I placed my pack next to hers and set off uphill through the rocks.

The cover couldn't have been better—open enough to let me keep the animals in sight but sufficiently broken to hide me—and when I reached the goats' level without being winded, I felt confident of a shot. Studying the flock, I identified three mature billies scattered among an assortment of nannies and kids. When one of them stepped out in the open 15 yards away and lowered his head to browse, I picked a spot on his chest, came to draw, and sent the arrow through his chest. As the goats scattered across the hillside in an explosion of clattering rocks, my billy faltered and collapsed and that was that.

Back where we'd left our packs, I met Lori trudging up the hill with a chagrined look on her face and a quiver full of clean arrows. "There were just too many goats!" she explained. "I set up perfectly on one of the billies, but nannies and kids kept getting in the way until one of them finally smelled me."

"Don't worry," I said with a grin as I pointed up the cliff where my fallen billie lay. "We've got plenty to do until the tahr start to move."

Once again, I'd salvaged a slow day in the field courtesy of an unlikely resource: the noisy, odiferous, largely unappreciated feral goat.

For most American bowhunters, the word *goat* evokes images of a stately, white-maned creature roaming the alpine peaks of Alaska or British Columbia. In fact, our familiar mountain goat isn't really a goat at all, but a distant relative of the antelope family. (And to confuse matters further, our pronghorn isn't really an antelope, but—you guessed it—a goat. Sort of.) The true goats are an Old World family of hoofed animals that includes the ibex, markhor, and tahr, of which none currently enjoys a greater worldwide distribution than *Capra hircus*, the feral version of the familiar domestic goat.

Hardy travelers adaptable to a wide variety of habitat, goats enjoyed great popularity among settlers and colonists who introduced them throughout the world during the era of European exploration. Because of their susceptibility to predators, wild goats fared best in isolated island ecosystems free of large members of the cat and dog family. Today, feral goat populations thrive throughout the Pacific, where I've hunted them from Hawaii to New Zealand. Closer to home, they inhabit several of the Channel Islands off the coast of California and numerous locations about the Caribbean. Goats breed prolifically and many areas support high population densities. Because they represent a non-indigenous species that's particularly hard on local habitat, seasons and limits are often generous to nonexistent, creating potential opportunities for bowhunters.

Saving the planet isn't the only reason to pursue wild goats with a bow. While largely disdained as table fare by our own society, goats remain an agricultural staple in many cultures, valued as a source of meat as well as milk and cheese. I've enjoyed barbecued *cabrito* in Texas and Mexico, and when I did my internship in Montreal my rare weekends off usually began with the Friday night goat roast at the Jamaican grocery store up the street. So, if you share my aversion to shooting anything you don't plan to eat, take heart. If food value is the prime concern, it's best to concentrate on taking a tender young kid, but if you've successfully collected a nice set of spiral horns for the wall, never underestimate the power of a crock-pot to work magic on a tough old billy.

In areas free of predators—and that usually means us—feral goats can be easy to approach. But while their noses and ears are fair at best, their vision is superb, and once they've been hunted they quickly become quite challenging to stalk. On a recent trip to Hawaii, I spent a day on a steep mountain that receives a fair amount of hunting pressure. Although I saw hundreds of goats and passed up shots at a few nannies and kids, I never even got within bow range of one of the mature billies I was after.

A feral billy from the South Island of New Zealand.

While they occasionally lack wariness, feral goats more than compensate for this shortcoming by their habitat preferences.

Remarkably sure-footed and fearless, goats regard steep terrain as their natural security cover and inevitably retreat to the scariest cliffs around at the first indication of trouble. In Hawaii, I've watched feral goats run helter-skelter down sheer cliffs more rugged than any wild sheep habitat I've ever hunted. And there's a moral to this observation. Never hunt that kind of country alone and wait until the animals have moved out of the cliffs to feed before planning a stalk. A wounded goat will almost always head back to the closest cliffs at a dead run, so try to do your shooting some distance from the escape cover. Otherwise, recovering the animal may well make you wish you'd missed cleanly.

Two thousand feet below me, the calm surface of the Maui Channel looked like a postcard image of Hawaii, and when I scanned the surface with my glasses, I could see humpbacked whales cavorting in the sun. But I hadn't spent four hours climbing straight up through layers of volcanic rock and dense jungle vegetation to spend the day as a whale-watching tourist. As the goats fed slowly in my direction, I considered edging closer, but I'd promised myself I wouldn't take a shot unless I was at least a hundred yards from the edge of the cliff. I knew what kind of terrain lay below the grassy plateau, and I didn't want any part of it.

Patience proved its own reward that day, and when the little band finally reached my ambush site, I waited until a billy lowered his head to feed before I came to draw and released. If I'd ever seen a situation that absolutely demanded perfect arrow placement, this was it. While the animal apparently never knew what hit him, the goats all stampeded for the cliff at the muffled twang of my bowstring, and I watched anxiously until the billy slowed, faltered, and finally collapsed in plain sight.

Sharing the results of a successful hunt has always been a favorite part of my Hawaiian bowhunting experiences, but I wasn't sure what kind of reception my prize would earn back at sea level. While wild pigs enjoy centuries' worth of tradition in Hawaiian cuisine, goats are regarded as newcomers to the islands, and I'd never heard any of my Hawaiian friends express much enthusiasm for them on the table. Too tired to worry about it when I finally staggered down off the mountain that night, I simply threw the boned backstraps into a soy sauce marinade and placed it in the refrigerator to worry about the following day.

It's amazing what curry powder, hot peppers, and fresh Maui onions can do for just about any edible meat. When everyone showed up for dinner the next night, the goat curry proved as popular as the pork teriyaki and grilled fish. "*Ono!*" my friend Walter Naki beamed as he slurped down a mouthful, and since that's the highest compliment a cook can hear in Hawaiian, I went to bed that night knowing that the long hours of climbing beneath the relentless tropical sun had been worth the effort they demanded.

Section IV

Around the Country

25.

Swamp Things

Even Lori has trouble looking great dressed head to toe in a camouflage bug suit, but neither of us felt any concern for our appearance as we eased our way down the trail deep in the swamp adjoining central Georgia's Flint River. Stately gum trees towered overhead as mosquitoes hummed about our heads, erasing any doubts about our choice of clothing. The mid-August temperature hovered near 90 with a humidity to match, but we were moving slowly and concentrating too hard on the possibility of game to notice the sweat pouring down our backs. Despite the heat and the bugs, the swamp cast an enchanting spell and I felt delighted to be there.

Lori and I were enjoying some genuine southern hospitality courtesy of our friends Cory Mattson and Greg Campbell. Wild hogs were our quarry, and as we still-hunted carefully into the breeze I kept thinking about the life-sized giant boar we had seen that afternoon at Greg's folks' place. His father Eddie was a true old time bowhunter with an impressive collection of mounts from animals taken all over North America, but none stirred me more than the boar taken a few years back right there on the Campbell property. Sporting tusks the size of chisels, the pig looked as if it would push five hundred pounds on the hoof. Lori wasn't sure she wanted to run into a boar like that at close quarters, and I wasn't sure I did either.

Suddenly I caught a glimpse of movement in the grass thirty yards ahead of us and motioned Lori to a stop. The afternoon light was already fading beneath the dense canopy of leaves overhead, but after a moment of patient study I felt certain I could identify black bristles moving through the foliage. Lori agreed, and with no further ado she nocked an arrow and began to work her way toward the feeding hog.

I always find watching a bowhunting partner stalk an animal as exciting as making the stalk myself, especially when the hunting partner is my wife and the quarry is a potentially belligerent species whose exact size is yet to be determined. As I watched Lori narrow the gap toward shooting range, I remembered some advice from Greg, who probably knows as much about stalking wild hogs with a bow as anyone. When hogs are rooting actively in high grass, he recommended moving on them quickly, taking advantage of their poor eyesight to reach bow range before the capricious river bottom wind had an opportunity to ruin the stalk. Patience is a valued instinct in the bowhunting game and old habits die hard, and as I watched Lori ooze forward at a snail's pace there was nothing, I could do but hope the breeze held long enough to give her the shot she deserved.

When she finally came to a stop barely five yards from the waving grass, I wasn't sure my nerves would survive the tension. After a long point-blank face-off, the hog finally picked up her scent and exploded from the cover like a cork from a champagne bottle. This was my first decent look at the pig, a black two hundred pounder that would have provided a lot of great eating and great memories. "What happened?" I wondered aloud as she turned toward me with a smile.

"He was facing me the whole time," she explained. "There never was an acceptable shot, so I just tried to wait him out."

After congratulating her for her discipline, we turned and hunted our way back toward the truck, where we found Cory with a depleted quiver and a fresh round of stories. He had one hog waiting for us to load and had sent an arrow through the middle of another, leaving the blood trail until morning because of some uncertainty about his shot placement.

Southern hog hunting can be many things, but boring is rarely one of them.

The wild hog is one of the world's most successful and widely distributed game animals. Despite their remarkable variation in appearance and habits, all wild hogs belong to the same species—*Sus scrofa*—which originated in Eurasia. Because of their food value hogs were among the first large animals to be domesticated, but hunters in Europe and Asia accorded their wild progenitors near legendary status as game animals based on their intelligence and occasional ferocity. Because they travel well, domestic pigs accompanied human settlers away from the Old World in all directions. Some of these animals inevitably escaped into the wild where their superb adaptability allowed them to thrive in a variety of new habitats from the Pacific to our own South.

Four centuries ago, the Spanish explorer Hernando DeSoto first introduced hogs to the American mainland, where they rapidly established wild breeding populations throughout what is now Florida and Georgia. Successive waves of colonists brought barnyard swine with them, and as those animals escaped from captivity, they interbred with wild stock. Then sportsmen introduced relatively pure strains of wild European boars to the area, and these animals made their own contribution to the gene pool. The result is the hodge-podge of porcine genetics responsible for today's mixture of wild southern hogs, which range in appearance from feral "piney rooters," to animals like the monstrous "Russian" boar in Eddie Campbell's den.

All these varieties of pigs share certain common characteristics with similar but unrelated species around the world, from javelina in the American southwest to African wart hogs. All have poor vision but keen noses. They are highly intelligent and reproduce with remarkable efficiency. As enthusiastic omnivores, they eat everything from crops to crawdads, and will alter their feeding habits freely depending on the availability of various food sources.

Wild hogs can also be belligerent. Back when I was hunting the Soviet Far East, I noted that the Russian woodsmen considered wild boars every bit as dangerous as the region's notorious bears. How dangerous are the wild hogs closer to home? I asked Greg Campbell, who has had as much experience with them as anyone. He's never been charged seriously, but he still treats them with respect. After several forays into hog country, I've wound up regarding them much as I do black bears: I don't worry when I'm stalking them, but I acknowledge that wounded or cornered pigs can be dangerous.

Because of their weak vision, pigs are quite stalkable, with shots in close cover often coming at very close range. But first you must find the pigs. Local knowledge of their habits and food sources certainly makes the job easier, which is one reason I enjoy hunting with southern friends like Greg and Cory. As a rule, pigs leave abundant sign wherever they feed, and if you aren't seeing lots of it, you should probably look elsewhere. Also, don't hesitate to listen carefully when still-hunting at prime time early and late in the day. Pigs are noisy animals, and in thick swamp habitat it's often easier to locate them with your ears than your eyes.

Pigs are tough animals. Their heart and lungs are well protected by their forequarters, and their vitals are located relatively low and forward. I learned this lesson the hard way hunting in Florida with my friend Don Davis a few years back, when I made what I thought was a good shot on a boar and spent the rest of a long, hot afternoon proving that I had hit the animal above the lungs. Some recommend the quartering away shot because of the forward location of pigs' vital area and the tough cartilaginous shield protecting the anterior thorax. As with bears, I still prefer the classic broadside, but I've learned to remind myself before I shoot that there is a lot of arrow-resistant bone and gristle on the forward half of a broadside pig.

From a legal standpoint, most southern states regard wild hogs as unwelcome intruders, a biologically correct position. Since they can be hard on crops, pigs are seldom popular with local farmers. In the states where I have hunted them there are no seasons or limits on wild hogs, so take plenty of arrows.

As a final bonus, wild hog meat turns out to be delicious even though it is much leaner than domestic pork, which it resembles hardly at all. Wild hogs can carry both brucellosis and trichinosis. If you remember to wear rubber gloves when field dressing pigs and cook all meat thoroughly, these concerns shouldn't prevent successful hog hunters from enjoying the result of their efforts on the table.

Lori with a feral hog meant for the barbeque.

Back in the swamp early the next morning, Lori and I made an unproductive still hunt along the river while Greg and Cory took up the trail they had allowed to rest the night before. In typical wild hog fashion, Cory's stricken boar had headed for the nastiest cover it could find, and by the time we rejoined them, both hunters were covered with scratches from the all too abundant green briar. But they had a happy story to tell, as Cory had literally fallen on his stone-dead hog barely fifty yards from where he had shot it. The hit was indeed a trifle back of perfect, but no one was complaining, including the hog.

As we loaded the boar into the back of Greg's rig and headed for home to dress it, I stopped to appreciate all that Lori and I had enjoyed during our too brief stay in wild hog country: exciting hunting, great companionship, and a unique wild ecosystem, all at a time of year when most bowhunters are usually waiting for opening day.

Reflecting their adaptability and wide distribution, Lori and I have successfully hunted feral hogs in more places than any other bowhunting quarry, including Australia, Hawaii, California, Texas, and Florida as well as Georgia (on another trip). Although they were biologically the same animal in all those far-flung locations, variations in habitat and terrain made each of those hunts feel different from all the rest. None proved more interesting and enjoyable than the time we spent along the Flint River, even though I never loosed an arrow.

Lori may look busted, but she killed this javelina.

26.

Pigs Along the Border

I'm not sure there's a polite way to say this, but my lovely wife Lori is a pig person. At least she's a pig *hunter,* which sounds a little bit better. Ever since she killed her first javelina in Texas, she'd been after me take her back to the land of prickly pear and road runners so she could have another go at those fascinating little desert pigs. When Ricardo Longoria invited us down to hunt his family's property on both sides of the Rio Grande, we jumped at the chance. I think Lori was even more eager to make the trip than I was.

Before going further with this chapter, a biological note. Javelina (*Tayassu tajcu*) are members of the New World family *Tayassuidae*, which also includes the white-lipped peccary, found farther south in Latin America. Despite their many pig-like features, they are not members of the Old World family of pigs, which includes animals such as the wart hog, bush pig, and the familiar domestic (and frequently feral) swine, *Sus scrofa* (see Chapter 25.) Despite this distinction, javelina (properly known collared peccaries) are often referred to as "pigs" in our Southwest. Although technically incorrect, I will sometimes refer to them as such out of habit.

Three nights after we closed down the whitetail season back home in Montana, I drove a back road on Ricardo's ranch at last light and found Lori bubbling with excitement and tales of stumbling into javelina by the dozen. Her enthusiasm hadn't kept her from making a good stalk and putting an arrow through one—after a miss, as she freely confessed. After listening to her description of the hit, I decided it wouldn't hurt to give the track a little time, for two reasons. Javelina come with a small, oddly positioned vital area, and despite her confidence in the shot I thought from her description that the arrow placement might have been a bit back. Furthermore, picking your way through the dense thorn brush that infests the border country can be difficult enough by daylight. With a crisp December night falling around us, we decided to leave the track until first light the following morning.

As it turned out, our precautions proved unnecessary. As unfamiliar birdlife greeted the sunrise the following morning, we walked to the spot where Lori had seen her pig vanish into the brush and located it immediately. Her arrow had struck an inch or two farther back than perfect, but her sharp broadhead had taken out the liver and one lung and that had been plenty.

"What do you want to do now?" I asked when we had the pig hanging safely in the skinning shed back at the *hacienda,* for we had a variety of choices ranging from quail to whitetails.

"Look for some more javelina," Lori replied without a moment's hesitation. As I said—a pig person, through and through.

I first met the javelina in the deserts of Arizona decades ago. The terrain they inhabit there is beautiful, and hunting javelina provided me with welcome opportunities to escape the cold winter weather back home. A lot of time passed before I had an opportunity to chase them again, and when I did, it was in the brush country on both sides of the border between Texas and Mexico. The hunting conditions there differ substantially from what I found in Arizona, with thicker brush and less elevation to the terrain, which makes glassing more difficult. Even when you've located pigs, approaching them to close range through thick brush can be a challenge.

The south Texas terrain we hunted contains sandy ridges covered with live oak, which makes comfortable stalking conditions.

Unfortunately, that habitat doesn't contain high densities of javelina, although a few pigs there can produce more shot opportunities than a lot of pigs in nastier cover. I soon learned that stalking along the shallow arroyos that laced the countryside was a better tactic than roaming blindly through the cactus. Pigs—feral hogs inhabit the area as well as javelina—like to feed in the relatively moist soil along the dry creek bottoms, and the open, sandy washes provide quiet stalking conditions. They're a good place to look for arrowheads too, as Lori proved one morning when she returned with a pocketful of them.

Javelina there run a bit larger than their Arizona relatives. I didn't have an opportunity to weigh any of those we shot, but I'd guess they averaged five or ten pounds heavier than those we killed in Arizona. They're still small animals by big game standards, which makes them a tricky target for the bow. Part of the problem is mental. Because of their small size, you tend to shoot for the middle of the animal as you would if you were hunting rabbits. But javelina act like big game when they're hit, and anatomically correct arrow placement is as important as it is on deer. Furthermore, javelina seem to be made mostly of head, paunch, and gristle. The vital area is small and located low and forward. Some experienced javelina hunters advocate shooting them directly through the shoulder. That's certainly the shortest route to the important part of the pig, but a direct hit on the point of the shoulder can produce penetration problems even on animals this size, as I once found out the hard way. My advice is to wait for a shot angle that has the animal quartering slightly away and try to slip the arrow as close behind the shoulder as possible. Above all, don't underestimate your quarry's tenacity just because of its small size.

Most experienced bowhunters regard javelina as easy to stalk, and they are. They don't have good eyesight and they make a lot of noise when they're up and about, factors that make it easy to approach to close range and draw a bow undetected. However, they have very good noses and anyone who isn't watching the wind carefully isn't javelina hunting. They also have good ears, although the noise they make when feeding helps disguise careless footsteps by the hunter.

Javelina don't enjoy a great reputation as table fare. That's unfortunate, for they can be quite tasty when properly handled. Furthermore, I think we all enjoy hunting more when we can look forward to eating the result of a careful stalk and a good shot. The trick is to avoid letting the pungent musk on their hides contact the meat. The best way to do that is to work in concert with a hunting partner, with one member of the team handling the hide while the other butchers the meat.

When you're camped out in the desert, grilling fresh pig over a bed of mesquite coals certainly sounds tempting. Unfortunately, that's one of the least appetizing ways to prepare javelina, which tends to be dry and on the tough side, unless you've deliberately shot a youngster for the table. I like to cook javelina slowly with moist heat, and a crock pot serves that purpose well. Just don't believe everything you've heard about their inedibility. Treat the meat with the respect it deserves, and you'll earn your reward at the table.

Javelina are biological anomalies unrelated to the swine elsewhere around the world.

Lori and I found the ambience in southern Arizona so appealing that we eventually bought a house just north of the border. For several years we spent our winters there, enjoying lovely weather that provided an enjoyable contrast from the snow and cold back home in Montana. Another of the area's welcome features was the abundance of public land at a time when access to private land in Montana was rapidly becoming restricted. We found the ability to go hunting virtually anywhere we wanted especially enjoyable.

As non-residents we had to draw tags to hunt javelina, although they were easy to obtain in the remote districts around our rural home. Since we had both shot plenty of javelina by that time we didn't always bother, especially since we were preoccupied with the excellent hunting for Coues deer and quail nearby. We frequently hosted visiting bowhunters, however, and since many of them had never seen (much less hunted) javelina before I aways enjoyed the opportunity to go out with them and relive the excitement of initial encounters with what was once an exotic animal for me and still was for them.

Old friends from Alaska, Doug and Olga Borland showed up one year to attend the famous Tucson Gem and Mineral show, where they did a lot of buying for their retail art outlets in Southeast Alaska. One of the best bowhunters I know, Doug has enjoyed a remarkable record of success on challenging species such as Dall sheep and mountain goats, but he had no prior experience hunting javelina and had never seen one. After several hard days of quail hunting in the mountains nearby, Lori and I decided to give the bird dogs a rest (a convenient excuse for giving ourselves a rest) and try to introduce Doug to a javelina.

Doug had spotted some at long range the day before, so we decided to go back to that valley from another direction and hope we could relocate them withing stalking distance. Hunting desert quail (Gambles and scaled quail) isn't physically demanding, but the Mearns quail we prefer to hunt inhabit rugged mountainous terrain that can challenge anyone's physical conditioning. After three straight days of up and down behind our hard-charging German wirehairs, my legs were reminding me of my age, and I welcomed the opportunity to sit in some shade and glass the vast desert terrain below us.

Searching with binoculars is a classical means of hunting javelina, but it's a strange business. Even in areas with abundant sign, the desert can easily become a vast and lonely place. When (more properly *if*) a squadron (the correct term for a group of javelina) crosses my field of view, the effect is startling no matter how often I've been through it before. What are those bizarre looking animals doing here and not on some far-away continent? How could I have missed game as obvious as these busy black dots for hours? (The answer is that javelina often bed down midday in the best shade they can find, in which position they blend into the background so well they can be extremely hard to spot.) Doug saw them first that morning, half a mile away, and after studying the terrain and making appropriate guesses about the wind, we set off on a route to intercept them.

Thirty minutes later, we were sitting on top of a little ridge watching two dozen javelina scurry around through the brush and dry grass beneath us like beetles. When Doug set off on final approach, Lori put the telephoto lens on her camera while I settled back to watch the show. One of the pigs had bedded in a favorable position by that time. I'm quite aggressive with javelina, since I know how much I can get away with undetected and I want to seal the deal before the treacherous desert breeze betrays me—a tactic like that described by Greg Campbell for southern hogs in the last chapter. Unfamiliar with these concepts, Doug was moving as if he were stalking a full-curl ram on an Alaska mountainside. "Move on him, Doug!" I pleaded aloud to Lori.

Then the inevitable happened. In response to the sound of crunching gravel behind me, I turned around in time to see a half-dozen javelina walking casually along the ridge right at us. Absent tags and bows, all we could hope to do was take advantage of the photo opportunity, but Lori had too much lens and her images turned out to be nothing but unrecognizable black blobs. We had the wind, and the pigs eventually paraded past us at a distance better measured in feet than yards. Why do the best shot opportunities always fall to the observers rather than the shooters? I have yet to figure that one out.

By the time we turned our attention back to the amphitheater below us, Doug was on point with an arrow on his bowstring. Since the bedded pigs he'd originally started for were still out of bow range, he was obviously alert to something we couldn't see. Just then, the largest javelina I have ever seen emerged from the grass in front of Doug and he came to full draw. A polite friend would probably fail to report the sight of his arrow sailing over the top of a javelina that looked like a black bear, but etiquette has never been my strong suit. Besides, Lori captured the entire sequence on film.

Doug's January javelina hunt wasn't over yet though. The following morning, he called to report a good hit on a pig and request our assistance with the recovery. Despite some uncertainty on his part, his arrow placement had been perfect. After locating the pig easily, we field dressed it using the two-man technique outlined earlier and left the field with a game bag full of prime javelina meat. Back at home, Olga brined the hams and cut it into pastrami. That weekend, we watched the Super Bowl while enjoying the best Reuben sandwiches I've ever eaten. So much for "inedible" javelina!

Back on Ricardo's ranch, I was ready to follow up Lori's success by shooting a javelina of my own after waiting years since my last one. Sunrise found me working my way along the bottom of an arroyo lined with grassy banks, hunting with my ears just as I had learned to hunt bush pigs in Zimbabwe. From high on the bank, I heard the unmistakable rustle of low-slung bodies moving through the grass below me. As I eased laterally toward a strip of sandy soil that offered a potential shooting lane, a bristly boar emerged from the cover in front of me less than ten yards away.

It's not often that you get to shoot straight down at an animal when you're hunting from the ground. That unusual perspective brought me to a halt for a moment, but I finally managed to visualize a spot I liked, and my recurve sent the arrow through the pig's thorax and out its opposite shoulder. There were no recovery problems that day, for after a few frenzied grunts and kicks, the javelina collapsed in plain sight.

That's when I realized I'd been away from javelina country too long. As I slung the dead pig over my shoulder and headed back to the *hacienda* for breakfast, I felt the kind of satisfaction that always comes from a well-placed shot no matter what the size of the quarry. On that beautiful desert morning, that was enough.

Section V

Field Notes

27.

Hunting with the Bushmen

As a culture, we have lost the honorable art of sitting still. Bowhunting and wildlife photography have given me lots of practice and I do it better than most, but I still have my limitations. As I watched Ghao settle into the dirt at the base of the shepherd's tree, I realized I was watching a master in action. He didn't fidget. His eyes didn't drift shut. He simply sat, elegant and motionless, and waited for the next phase of the stalk to begin as if he had all the time in the world, which I suppose he did.

We had kept pace with the wildebeest for over two hours while the sun burned the last of the overnight winter chill from the sands beneath our feet. The herd was grazing slowly into the wind, and the big bull we were after refused to detach himself from his company long enough to let us try to slip in for a shot. Left to his own devices, I'm sure Ghao would have headed off into the bush to look for a more promising track, but I wanted a wildebeest. So, there we sat.

As the dark, strange-looking animals frisked about the dry pan, the sounds of the veldt filled my ears: the buzz of insects, the three-note dirge of the doves roosted in the acacias, a springbok ram's distant snort. Yielding to the spell of the place, I soon found myself watching and listening patiently. As we waited for the animals to make their next move, I found myself reflecting idly upon our remarkable circumstances: a visiting American bowhunter and a representative of the world's oldest surviving hunting culture, improbably joined together against the long odds of capricious winds and wary eyes.

During all my bowhunting adventures around the world, I'd never run into people quite as intriguing as Ghao and his fellow Bushmen.

The San

An ethnically and linguistically unique people, the Bushmen— or San, as they refer to themselves collectively— were among southern Africa's original inhabitants, ranging in nomadic fashion from modern Zimbabwe and Zambia all the way to the Cape. No one knows just how long the San have been around, but their rock paintings date back at least 5000 years. Early in the last millennium, the area experienced an influx of pastoral, Bantu-speaking tribes from the north. Agriculturalists and cattle-tenders, the new arrivals' social structure conflicted sharply with the Bushmen's hunter-gatherer lifestyle. Furthermore, the northern tribesmen introduced a new concept to the region, one that the San had managed to avoid: organized warfare.

The results were inevitable. Relentlessly displaced from their original homelands, the San slowly retreated to the inhospitable Kalahari, where their finely honed survival skills and an incredibly harsh environment provided them with a natural means of insulation from their enemies. While the arrival of European colonialists four centuries ago certainly increased their isolation, the San had given up most of their original territory long before our own ancestors arrived on the scene. And they endured only by the most demanding means imaginable: learning to thrive in terrain that others could barely survive.

Short, finely featured, and almond colored in complexion, the San appear physically distinct from other indigenous African peoples. Punctuated by baffling clicks, their unique speech has intrigued linguists for years. Their democratic social customs also distinguish them from other inhabitants of the region. As a bowhunter, I must admit that all these unique traits paled before my appreciation of their hunting and tracking abilities. Simply stated, they are the best, and every time I've hunted with them, I've come away from the experience in awe.

Reserved without being diffident, the Bushmen are quick to laugh and provide unfailingly good company in the field. The only flash of animosity I ever saw from them came one morning when we stumbled across a horned adder while trailing a gemsbok. The Bushmen quickly armed themselves with sticks and beat the nasty looking little snake to a pulp. As they explained via the usual linguistic ramble between their local dialect, Afrikaans, and finally English, "We might walk this way again tomorrow."

Today, most Bushmen live in Botswana and Namibia. Many have lost contact with their traditions through inevitable cultural assimilation. Those who have not often live in geographic isolation compounded by formidable language barriers. My own opportunities to hunt with the San have come through Allan Cilliers, a widely renowned Namibian PH who enjoys a unique relationship with the Bushmen based on years of experience with their culture. Despite his own accomplishments and abilities, Allan clearly holds the Bushmen in esteem, and it's equally obvious that the sense of respect extends both ways. In Allan's camp, the Bushmen are more hunting partners than employees. Even the simplest walk through the bush with Allan quickly turns into a fascinating lecture on the local flora and fauna and how the Bushmen utilize them in their daily life. Furthermore, Allan's huge, game-rich hunting concession borders immediately on Bushmanland, a huge trackless area where the San still enjoy their traditional way of life in as unspoiled a manner as possible.

Bushman Archery Equipment

While architects and engineers have debated the relationship between form and function for years, the design of Bushman archery tackle begins on an even more basic level: they had to make do with the raw materials at hand.

Bushman bows are simple affairs. Whittled down from a variety of woods, especially the brandybush (*Grewia flava*), they are usually only 30 – 35 inches long and draw no more than 20 pounds. Oil derived from the sour plum (*Ximenia caffra*) keeps the wood from cracking in the dry desert heat. Strings come from a variety of materials including hide and sinew, but most are made from plant fiber harvested from a tough succulent known as mother-in-law's tongue (*Sanseviera aethiopia*) which the Bushmen roll into cord on their thighs. The Kalahari San fashion lovely cylindrical quivers from the root bark of the umbrella thorn (*Acacia luerdertzii*). Farther to the south, bark from the aptly named *kokerboom* (quiver tree) serves the same purpose.

As often seems to be the case in indigenous hunting societies, bow design ultimately reflects the availability of suitable arrow materials, and the traditional Bushman hunting arrow clearly represents the most sophisticated and imaginative element of their hunting tackle. Shafts are made from sections of a variety of stiff grasses similar to our own river cane. These grasses are not widely distributed, and on our last trip into hunting camp Allan thoughtfully stopped by the side of the road as we passed a thicket of the stuff and harvested a supply for his hunters.

Between joints, the cane is quite straight and true, but single segments are too short to make an effective arrow. The Bushmen solve this problem by whittling a male-male ferrule from giraffe bone with which they can link two segments together, resulting in an arrow approximately 20 inches long. Shafts are unfletched and completed with a simple self-nock. Tips traditionally came from carved bone, but nowadays most are made from scavenged steel filed into delicate triangular heads. Steel points seem to represent one of only three concessions to modern society, the other two being the surplus Namibian military jackets the Bushmen wear during cool Namibian winters and tobacco.

By itself, this simple, lightweight equipment lacks the punch needed to bring down gemsbok and other large antelope. Bushmen hunters overcome these limitations by poisoning the tips of their arrows. Under certain conditions, they use a variety of plant-derived toxins for this purpose, but most arrows are treated with potent poison derived from several species of flea beetle grubs. Bushmen harvest the larvae from known locations at certain times of year and store them to treat arrows as needed. Based on descriptions of the poison's effects, I surmise that it effects the autonomic nervous system, leading to incoordination, stupor, and eventual collapse. The poison takes hours to days to work depending on the nature of the hit and the size of the animal and does not affect the edibility of the meat.

The toxin is applied only to the distal segment of the shaft, not the tip itself, so the arrows remain relatively safe to handle. Arrows tend to break off at the ferrule, leaving the toxic segment embedded in the quarry. Arrow making remains a highly esteemed art in Bushman culture. Hunters frequently pass arrows back and forth as tokens of gratitude and respect, and in the elaborate formula Bushmen used to divide meat among the band after a kill, the maker of the lethal arrow receives first share no matter who actually fired the killing shot.

Hunting Techniques

Bushman hunting practices ultimately depend upon their legendary tracking skills, which we'll discuss below. But first, a few observations made about the methods they employ in the field, especially as they contrast to our own.

Hunting with Ghao, I was surprised to note that when we came to open areas, I often spotted game at a distance before he did even without my binoculars. At first, I thought there might be something wrong with his eyes, but I quickly realized that when he needed to, he could spot game in the brush better than I could. I finally realized that he just didn't care about spotting animals hundreds of yards away. Seeing game told him nothing that he didn't already know based on the sign underfoot.

The Bushmen seemed indifferent to terrain features when planning stalks and were often quite willing to advance upon sharp-eyed animals in plain sight. They get away with this because of their spooky ability to anticipate the quarry's head movements. Ghao always seemed to know just when to freeze. Bushmen only stalk game early in the morning and late in the afternoon when there are long shadows on the ground, and they regard stalking at midday and during low light as a complete waste of time.

In traditional Bushman culture, hunting is very much a group effort, largely because of the need to have lots of help at hand upon the successful conclusion of a hunt to avoid meat loss to spoilage or scavengers. When I hunted with two or more of Allan's trackers, I noticed that they conversed in animated fashion on the trail, especially when the track demonstrated some confusing feature. In this regard, their unique language seemed especially adaptive as their flurry of clicks usually disappeared into the chatter of mopane leaves rustling in the breeze. Allan reports that he has often observed the Bushmen holding one of these discussions within earshot of wary game without spooking the animal.

The Bushmen use two gaits to close within bow range. The first is a stooped-over duck walk they can sustain at brisk speed indefinitely. The second they call the "leopard crawl": down on all fours, with long feline strides that result in almost no change in profile. The short, light Bushman bows prove ideally suited to this kind of stealthy maneuvering.

Once within bow range, the Bushmen shoot with a quick, plucking style: a short draw, free floating anchor, and thumb release. Shot placement as we know it matters very little. The idea is simply to get the tip of an arrow into the animal somewhere and let the poison go to work. Several times when we stalked together, Ghao obviously expected me to take a shot at what I considered an unacceptable angle and rolled his eyes in frustration when I declined. I tried my best to explain my reservations in pantomime, but I'm not sure I ever made much of an impression.

Tracking

The Bushmen truly distinguish themselves from the competition when it comes time to track game. Over the course of multiple trips to Africa, I've hunted with many African trackers whose skill level ranged from not much better than my own to very good indeed. But none could begin to approach the remarkable level of skill I observed when hunting with Ghao, Tsisiba, and the rest of Allan's incredible crew.

The soil in Allan's hunting area consists mostly of soft, sugary sand. Granted, that kind of footing can hold lots of tracks, but individual hoof prints rapidly lose their distinction. Furthermore, game densities are so high that most ground contains tracks left by multiple animals. Nonetheless, the Bushmen could easily follow the trail of an individual animal through this riot of sign at a dead run. They could also tell exactly how far away the animal was, its condition, the precise nature of any wounds, and what it was likely to do next, even when tracking at night by moonlight.

One day during our last visit with Allan, Lori shot a kudu bull. As she described it, the shot placement sounded perfect, but she was shooting from a pit blind and Lori doesn't stand that far off the ground. The steep upward track of the arrow resulted in a one lung hit and an opportunity for the Bushmen to do what they do best.

As we listened to Lori's description of the shot, one of the younger trackers started immediately for the edge of the brush where Lori had last marked the bull. Ghao called him back sharply and delivered what sounded like a stern lecture. As Allan explained, Ghao was chiding him for ignoring the first part of the track even though we all knew where it led. Ghao explained that it was always important to take the track from the very beginning, to learn as much about the animal as possible. In fact, by the time we reached the acacias Ghao knew the age and size of the kudu, exactly what Lori's arrow had done, and what the likely outcome of our pursuit would be—opinions that all proved remarkably accurate.

I'll spare readers most of the long, hot miles through the thorns. The only tracking hitch came in a flurry of sand. As the trackers sat down to smoke and consider the situation, Allan explained Ghao's interpretation of events. Lori's bull had run into the middle of a large herd of kudu. She had hit in the left side of the chest. The arrow was still embedded, and the sight of the bright fletching protruding from its chest had scattered the herd to the right as it ran. Half an hour later, Ghao had sorted out the mess and we were back on track again.

After five hours and several miles, Ghao stopped trotting and began to creep forward like a cat, aware that we were about to contact the wounded bull. Several hundred yards farther ahead, he suddenly pointed to a dense patch of thorns from which two spiral kudu horns protruded, and it was time for a strategy discussion. Allan's rifle offered an effective if unattractive option. Ghao explained that based on the spoor he felt the kudu was distracted and that Lori should be able to slip in for a killing shot. After some last-minute discussion between the two of us, I watched her do her best version of a leopard crawl into the brush.

After one of the longest hours in my life, Ghao suddenly leapt to his feet in excitement. Moments later, the bull charged past trailing another one of Lori's brightly fletched arrows from its previously healthy side. When the kudu piled up a hundred yards away, Lori enjoyed the distinction of becoming the first modern woman archer to kill a big game animal in Namibia—with a little help from her friends.

*Two of my Bushman friends prepare to sort out
the tracks at a Namibian waterhole.*

Back in the dry riverbed, the wildebeest have finally started to stir. Rising slowly from the base of the shade tree, Ghao tests the wind. Using hand signals and crude diagrams scrawled in the dirt, we offer one another thoughts on our next approach, each shaking off a suggestion or two from the other like pitchers who want to throw curves when their catchers are calling for fast balls. Finally, we reach a tentative agreement of sorts and begin to ooze forward through the brush.

And suddenly I realize just what a remarkable life experience bowhunting can be. Here we are, two men separated by apparently impossible gulfs in culture, language, and background, setting off together on one of the most difficult tasks our species can face. A simple realization tempers my high spirits: as a 52-year-old American, I will never be able to emulate Ghao's remarkable talents. While he was learning how to stalk and track, I was studying calculus, English literature, and biochemistry, noble efforts that suddenly feel strangely meaningless.

A century ago, our culture tried to destroy Ghao's with rifles, roads, and fences. Today, we threaten the same end through the process of assimilation: radios, money, and all the empty promises of easy living. I have no idea how the story of the San will conclude. But in the meanwhile, I'll do my best to keep to the shadows and start every track at the beginning, just as I'll remain grateful for the opportunity to appreciate the potential skills that lurk inside us all.

28.

The Art of the Ground Blind

Baked medium rare by the hot prairie sun, I had let my attention falter as I curled up in the dirt like a mule deer instinctively seeking a precious measure of shade. After a morning spent chasing elk through a five-mile circle that seemed to run uphill all the way from camp and back, my legs appreciated the rest. I even told myself that this was strictly midday down time and that I didn't even care whether any antelope showed up at the little waterhole while I let my legs recover from all that up-and-down hiking. Of course, that fiction wasn't likely to survive an appearance by the antelope.

The sun and the soft sounds of the prairie had nearly lulled me to sleep when an odd gurgling noise roused my attention. Easing to my knees, I peeked through the sagebrush I had piled into a makeshift ground blind to see a fine antelope buck watering barely ten yards away. Accustomed to the remarkable distance vision of this wary species, I experienced a moment of doubt as I began to ease my longbow into position. The animal almost looked *too* close, and my blind consisted of nothing but a single length of camo netting and a few raw materials gathered hastily on the spot. But I had been through all this before, and I knew that if I could keep moving as slowly and deliberately as possible my makeshift setup should allow me to make the shot.

Coming to full draw seemed to take forever, and despite the point-blank range I made myself concentrate on picking a spot before I released. The buck stood quartering slightly away, and the impact of the arrow against the inside of his opposite shoulder nearly knocked him down. It was what I call a monster hit, the kind that leaves no room for doubt the moment the arrow leaves the string. And sure enough; the big buck barely made it 30 yards across the sage before he collapsed.

Brilliant shooting? Hardly. Meticulous hunting technique? Not after I've admitted being halfway to dream land the moment the buck showed up. If there was any credit to be derived from this memorable kill, it came from the simple ability to piece together an effective ground blind from scratch.

Hunting archers have been ambushing game from the shelter of logs and rocks since time immemorial. Contemporary bowmen stalking game in big country still need to develop and practice the skills necessary to master those simple methods. However, there is a lot to be said for sitting and waiting for game to come to you, a strategy that often goes best with the aid of a stand or a blind. The explosion of interest in tree stand techniques over the last few decades has left many of today's bowhunters convinced that there is no other effective way to ambush wary game. Fortunately, that's not true, since suitable trees don't always grow where we'd like them, especially when hunting species that favor open habitat. Here, we'll examine ways bowhunters can use ground blinds—ranging from simple to complex—to supplement naturally existing cover and insure close, certain shots even under challenging circumstances.

Ground blinds come in many different forms, ranging from simple patchworks of natural materials to commercially manufactured portable blinds to semi-permanent structures that could pass for low-income housing. Choosing among these options involves inevitable tradeoffs. Simple blinds offer the advantages of being cheap, light weight, and readily portable. More elaborate blinds offer superior concealment and comfort at the expense of reduced mobility and starker contrast to natural surroundings. Choosing among these options depends on individual preference, terrain, and the nature of the quarry being hunted.

A bowhunter accustomed to life in a tree stand may initially be put off by some of ground blinds' disadvantages. Tree stands offer superior visibility, and despite the outcome of the hunt described earlier, ground blind hunters generally need to be alert to the possibility of shot opportunities that appear and disappear rapidly. Minimalist blinds require the hunter to exercise more caution than tree stands during the process of drawing the bow, while full-concealment cloth blinds pose some special shooting problems of their own.

However, ground blinds also offer advantages above and beyond their practicality in areas that lack trees. Well-made cloth blinds provide excellent scent control. In Africa, I've been amazed how often wary game has approached one from dead downwind. Ground level shots offer more vital area than those taken from above. Tree stands rarely fool turkeys since birds are programmed to look up, and ground blinds of various sorts provide the best opportunities for these wary critters. Ground blinds can be extremely comfortable when you are settling in for an extended wait. In contrast to tree stands, you can doze off in them safely, which is why I love them on hot September days between early and late elk hunts.

The simplest version of the ground blind that I use is nothing more than a strip of camouflage netting, a system that costs next to nothing and is light enough to carry easily in a day pack. In brushy terrain, I simply drape the netting from any conveniently located branch and hunker down behind it. While this approach doesn't offer definitive concealment, it can make the difference when it comes time to draw on wary species such as turkeys. Fine mesh nylon mosquito-type netting works poorly for this purpose because it is difficult to attach quickly to foliage and tends to shine in oblique light. I prefer heavy, punched out military style netting woven onto a fishnet of thin, tough cord. This stuff is durable, hides me better, and best of all sticks to brush like Velcro. With a little practice, you'll be able to use it to set up an effective blind in less than a minute, at least in suitable cover.

In a slightly more complicated version of the theme, my favorite turkey blind consists of a 15-foot strip of mesh netting, one tree step, two light tent stakes, and a strap-on tree seat. When I'm setting up the blind, I look for a mature conifer with a trunk thick enough to conceal my outline and dead branches at approximately eye level (which fortunately describes 90% of the ponderosa pines that carpet prime Montana turkey cover). Begin construction by placing the tree step head-high on the side of the tree from which you expect the bird to approach. Hang the edge of the middle of the netting from the step and hook each upper corner to a dead branch. Fasten the lower corners to the ground with the tent stakes to keep the netting from flapping in the wind. The result should be an open V of netting with the point facing the bird's likely route of approach. Set out decoys ten yards from the open end of the V and attach the seat to the tree facing the decoys. The seat's purpose is to allow you to hold still *in shooting position* during the bird's final approach.

Ideally, you should set up to take the shot over the top of the netting as the bird closes on the decoys. It helps to set up with clear shooting lanes on both sides and in front, with a few other pine trees nearby to allow you to draw while the bird's vision is eclipsed. While this simple blind obviously doesn't offer total concealment like commercial cloth blinds, it is cheap, light weight, and can be set up quickly after a little practice. I strongly recommend experimenting with this system in the yard before trying it in the field, both to familiarize yourself with the set-up and to learn what heights and dimensions fit your shooting needs best.

Among North American hoofed game, no species justifies familiarity with ground blind technique like the pronghorn antelope. Notoriously difficult to approach in open terrain, pronghorns do offer the patient bowhunter ambush opportunities at waterholes and fence crossings. The problem, of course, is that these strategic locations rarely come equipped with trees. Windmills offer an alternative in some locations, but consistently successful pronghorn hunters almost all learn to master the art of the ground blind.

Cloth blinds and even collapsible plywood structures certainly have their place in this game, but there are simpler ways to accomplish the same goal while preserving mobility. Despite their legendary eyesight, antelope are only good at seeing just two things: motion and change in horizon contour. They are poor pattern recognizers, and to borrow a photographic concept, I'm convinced they see the world through an open aperture, which means a narrow depth of field. The bottom line is that once an antelope has approached, anything sufficient to break up your outline will often allow the careful hunter a close, controlled shot.

If you enjoy digging deep pits beneath the hot prairie sun, be my guest. In suitable terrain, I generally find this unnecessary. When constructing quick ground blinds for antelope, the most important principle is to reduce your exposure to the horizon. In country like eastern Montana, where waterholes are usually found behind small earthen dams, dirt banks usually suit that purpose well. It may take a little bit of digging to get yourself seated below the level of the bank, but that is generally all that is required.

Don set up this ground blind along a whitetail scrape line.

Even in open terrain, I can usually construct an adequate ground blind from on-site materials, the same kind of camo netting described earlier, and a couple of loops of baling twine. The Greeks learned 3000 years ago that the tripod is world's most stable structure, and it still is. If you scavenge three sticks from the area, tie a loop of twine about their top, and spread the legs like a tipi you will have a serviceable tripod. Do that again and you will have the two front corners of your blind. Run an additional stick from each tripod to the top of the bank behind you, lay a third stick between the tripods, and you will have a sturdy blind framework. Wrap the netting about the whole thing, stake out the corners, add a little brush around the edges, and *voila*. For a total investment of fifteen minutes and a few dollars, you're hunting antelope. You can take the whole thing down when you leave, stash the frame in the sagebrush until you return, and no one will even know you were there.

As much as I enjoy the satisfaction of this do-it-yourself, quick and easy approach to ground blinds, nothing can match the comfort, convenience, and total concealment offered by commercially made, internal frame cloth blinds that I'll refer to generically as pop-ups. I learned to appreciate good ones hunting in Africa, where the game is almost supernaturally wary, and circumstances often require the hunter to remain perfectly concealed for hours on end. Their principal disadvantages compared to the simple systems just described are bulk and cost, which makes it especially unsettling to return to a waterhole and discover that an ornery elephant has stomped your blind into the ground overnight. (Oh well; at least you weren't in it!)

Newcomers to pop-up blinds need to be aware of several peculiarities in their use. The first requirement is to be sure the blind allows adequate limb clearance. Some models have low tops, which can pose a real problem for longbow shooters. Furthermore, shooting through narrow windows takes a bit of adjustment, since depth perception can easily be compromised. Peeking cautiously over the edge of the shooting window can lead to loss of binocular vision, which can cause instinctive shooters fits. If you do shoot instinctively, train yourself to reach full draw with both eyes on the target when shooting from a cloth blind. Avoiding these potential pitfalls requires what should be a familiar word: practice! If I were planning a first-time trip to Africa or a western antelope hunt, I would make every effort to practice shooting from a ground blind prior to departure. And once you are in the field, don't forget to take practice arrows with you to the blind to keep yourself sharp under actual hunting conditions.

Remember what I said earlier about antelope and horizons – the most important part of the blind is often what lies *behind* you. At waterholes, I often place brush behind me to eliminate my silhouette and supplement the set up with stick tripods and netting in front. Don't forget that the most effective blind is always the one you have with you or make on the spot.

Experienced bowhunters learn to look for ground blinds that involve no construction at all simply because nature has provided them free of charge. I am especially likely to take advantage of these opportunities when I'm turkey hunting. While Montana turkeys often roost in cottonwood bottoms, most of the habitat I hunt consists of ponderosa pine forest. Wind knocks down a lot of pines, and nothing make a better ground blind than a fallen ponderosa that still has needles on the branches. I always look for them when I'm walking, and don't do any exploratory calling without one nearby. Sometimes I augment the natural blind with a strip of "sticky" netting to cover an opening, but more times than not even that is unnecessary.

As usual, there is more than one way to skin a cat. From the simple satisfaction of piecing together an effective blind from materials at hand to the convenience and reliability of well-made commercial models, ground blinds can be as varied as the needs of the bowhunters who use them. Becoming familiar with their intricacies allows the hunter an opportunity to explore the excitement of new hunting situations, and when used properly they can increase the chances for the close, controlled shots that should be every bowhunter's goal in the field.

So, tinker, practice, and above all use your imagination. And remember that the absence of trees does not mean the absence of bowhunting opportunities, even for the wariest species we face.

29.
The Story Underfoot

Years ago, when I was just a kid, my father wanted to talk me into picking the rocks out of the garden next to our house outside of Boston. In an inspired bit of chicanery worthy of Tom Sawyer, he suggested that I could look for arrowheads as I worked, a ruse that promptly aroused my youthful interest. Incredibly, the third piece of stone that I kicked out of the dirt turned out to be—you guessed it. As soon as I rushed back inside to show the perfect flint point to my father, the tables turned. I spent the rest of the afternoon watching my parents grub eagerly through the garden, where they completed my original task without finding anything more interesting than rocks and dirt. Even so, I ended the afternoon with something even more valuable than a splendid beginning to an arrowhead collection: an appreciation for the value of looking down.

Here in Montana, I have friends who campaign arrowheads as methodically as I campaign elk, reasoning out the location of buffalo jumps and slaving away for hours beneath the hot prairie sun. While I remain a casual arrowhead hunter at best, I still stumble on a point or two every year, usually while I'm on my way back to the truck after doing something more conventionally exciting. But the occasional artifacts I come across still move me in ways that are difficult to articulate and that certainly exceed the conventional value of my finds. Holding a freshly recovered arrowhead immediately establishes a visceral link to the past and effectively defies the cultural hubris that suggests western history began with Lewis and Clark. It is one thing to read about indigenous culture in a book and quite another to bend down and come up with a tangible piece of it in your hand.

Higher mammals—our own species included—come programmed to view their world at eye level. We rarely look up – an oversight I gladly exploit when I hunt deer from tree stands. Our reluctance to look down is just as oddly fixed. Artists attempting to capture the feeling of Western life seem to enjoy an unremitting fascination with mountain peaks and distant horizons whether they choose to work in paint, film, or the written word. Given the extent of our spectacular skylines here, that's probably natural. However, this fixation is also something of a shame. As it turns out, the best stories often lie right underfoot.

There is always a story underfoot. No one reads it better than the Bushmen.

As an outdoorsman who learned the art of tracking on a schoolboy trap line years ago, I'm amazed by the number of hunters who seem all but oblivious to the wealth of sign on the ground beneath them. Several seasons back, I turned the dogs loose on a fresh lion track in a nearby mountain range. After four hours and more tough miles than I care to remember, I followed the pursuit back down out of the hills and across a snow-covered county road on the canyon floor. There was a late season elk hunt in progress, and as I stumbled down onto the road a pickup carrying two older, orange clad hunters slowed to a stop in front of me. When the driver asked what I was doing, I thought of making up some story to explain myself, but it wasn't that kind of day, so I told him.

"Lions?" he replied with an amused snort. "Son, there haven't been any cats in these hills for years!"

This conversation took place while his pickup sat straddling the fresh track of the entire chase—cougar, dogs, and all. The sign would have been obvious to a lion hunter a hundred yards away, but the story remained invisible to him. No wonder he knew there weren't any lions in those hills. He had never looked for them.

For the hunter, tracking skills often begin as a practical means to a well-defined end. The ability to decipher sign quickly and accurately can make an important difference when it comes time to put meat in the freezer. However, the thoughtful outdoors enthusiast soon learns to appreciate tracks and signs on their own abstract terms. Stumbling across an unusual track—one left by a wolverine, say, or a lynx, or a bear in a place there aren't supposed to be any bears—evokes the intimate delight of a shared secret. Tracks always have a story to tell. Reconstructing a dramatic woodland event like a cougar kill from the sign alone feels like exploring the mysteries of a carefully textured novel. As one hunting partner likes to point out, fresh snow never lies, and he's right. The trick, of course, is to get your face down on the ground and listen to what the tracks are trying to tell you.

Here in Montana, where I live now, we enjoy an abundance of outdoor glamour species ranging from pheasants to elk to trout. In this milieu, it's easy to forget that we may be walking right across the choicest bounty of all. Nothing illustrates this principle quite like the pursuit of wild mushrooms, an endeavor that combines potential gourmet rewards with long miles, fresh air, and even the hint of danger. Despite my natural aggression when it comes to most hunter-gatherer activities, I remain a bit of a wimp when it comes to mushroom picking, perhaps because in my professional life I have seen firsthand what a few bites of the wrong amanita can do to the human liver. The woods contain plenty of easy targets for light-hitting mushroom pickers, and even those who never choose to push the envelope beyond such sure bets as morels and shaggy manes can find plenty of rewards in the field on a wet year.

In our household, no species of mushroom arouses excitement quite like the morel. While part of that enthusiasm derives from the morel's unique table quality, its appearance in the spring adds to its appeal. Early May represents peak morel season, a time of year when I particularly appreciate any excuse to be outside, confirming my sense of renewal and congratulating myself on surviving another long winter. Something about morels' appearance and habitat seems to invite their discovery. After a mile or so of fruitless searching, the sight of that first morel evokes the feel of spotting a rare bid or big game. I can remember morel discoveries that left me as excited as if I'd stumbled onto a bugling elk in September. That kind of enthusiasm probably derives as much from spring fever as from the legendary gourmet quality of the find, but it's still a grand endorsement for a mushroom the size of my thumb.

Despite the apparently brainless nature of mushroom hunting, it's interesting to note that not all gatherers are created equal. Some of my friends never seem to get the hang of walking through the woods with their eyes focused downward. Perhaps they're instinctively afraid they will miss something, and they have a point. While hunting morels, I've blundered into everything from turkeys to bears, to the occasional surprise of all parties concerned. But if I'm missing things by looking at my feet, others are missing them in equal measure by refusing to do so, as my collection bag usually demonstrates at the end of these outings. I remain content to study the distance at other times, and nothing vindicates that concession like a skillet full of morels fresh from the spring woods.

A fresh morel mushroom, a welcome bonus on many spring turkey hunts.

It is May, the season of hope, when a few inches of moisture can make the difference between prosperity and disaster in the agriculture community. Turkey season has ended, and spring rains have turned the creek chocolate brown to the delight of local farmers and the temporary frustration of fly fishermen. Walking along the edge of the newly turned field, I keep my eyes focused downward, searching for the glimmer of polished flint in case the plow has unearthed a gift from some ancient hunter. But by the time I reach the edge of the coulee, the only artifact I've found is the remains of an old beer can, evoking a moment of despair over the legacy our own culture seems determined to leave future observers.

"Look!" I can imagine some delighted hiker exclaiming to a companion in the year 3000. "A Bud Light can! Late-Clintonian, probably just prior to the millennial cataclysm!"

"Indeed. Remarkably accomplished for such a primitive people, weren't they?"

With this brief outburst of cynicism behind me, the yawning coulee beckons like an invitation. Somewhere in its depths a ruffed grouse drums, and the slow, two-cycle putt of the bird's self-advertisement seems to shake the ground. Picking my way downhill, I finally arrive at the floor of the timbered draw, where a carpet of new spring grass lies spread out in a mosaic of dappled light. It is time to suck in my breath and focus my concentration on a layer of the natural world most casual hikers will never see.

Weaving my way through the cottonwoods, I gradually find myself oblivious to anything more than four inches above the ground or ten feet away. The process becomes hypnotic after a while as civilization's usual yap recedes, leaving me little more than a blank receptacle for certain visual cues. A fresh set of turkey tracks appears in the mud along the stream, but they hardly register, like an advertisement in a foreign language. Even a series of whitetail scrapes leftover from the previous autumn—ordinarily a valuable piece of intelligence—fails to arouse anything more than passing interest. Then after nearly a mile of back and forth through the creek bottom, the first morel appears.

The sight of certain species in the wild always arouses a visceral response beyond the sum of its parts. Large predators exemplify this principle, and no matter how many times I see bears and cougars I doubt that I will ever grow casual about the experience. But a *mushroom?* Well, yes, as it turns out. And this mystique only derives in part from my enthusiasm for morels' table qualities. There's just something about the appearance of that first dark, brooding form peeking its head above the new grass that reminds me of the obelisk at the beginning of *2001*. Down on my knees, I approach my find with all the anticipation of a prospector who has caught a flicker of yellow at the bottom of a clear mountain stream.

Discovering one morel almost always implies the presence of more. In any given area, the fruiting bodies that we perceive as individuals are just multiple expressions of a vast organic whole linked together by a subterranean network of mycelia. Even so, morels seldom appear in high densities, and this morning it takes me another hour of concerted searching to collect enough for dinner.

When I finally stretch, secure my specimen bag outside my daypack so spores can disperse as I walk, and start back up out of the coulee, I'm tempted to raise my eyes and enjoy the scenery more conventionally. But my efforts have left me programmed to keep looking downward, a frame of mind that earns one last reward. As I set my quads against the contour lines for the last pull up out of the draw, a flash of ivory catches my eye from the carpet of organic debris the recently departed snow has left behind. Suddenly, I realize that I am staring at a shed antler from a large whitetail buck.

And not just any whitetail, I realize as I reach down and retrieve my latest find. The split eye-guard, the main beam curved around as if to touch its mate's tip and form a perfect circle— I *know* this deer! In fact, I rattled him in to bow range at the head of the coulee last November only to muff the opportunity for reasons beyond the scope of this discussion. But now I know he made it through the season, and at least the hardest part of the winter. The evidence lies in my hand, too hard and tangible to deny. The found antler feels as personal as a calling card delivered by a gentleman prior to a duel. *All right, buddy,* I think to myself as I add the antler to the contents of my pack. *You made it. Congratulations. See you again this fall.*

And that's enough for one spring morning. I have outwitted no quarry wilier than a fungus and returned with no trophy grander than what one deer has left behind of his own free will. But as I return to the world of busyness and clutter, I do so knowing that I can see a bit more clearly, all because of the appreciation of an old childhood lesson. The ground beneath our feet offers more than a surface to walk upon. Viewed properly, it can become a source of wonder.

30.

The Blue-Collar Super Slam

Bowhunters seem fatally addicted to controversy at times, so let me make one point clear at the start. I'm not out to rain on anyone's parade. Taking all 29 officially recognized North American big game animals (the Super Slam) with a bow is an accomplishment. I am delighted that someone finally did it with traditional tackle.

However, long before that desert bighorn fell, I had reservations about the underlying concept. I've never been shy about sharing those reservations in print. Anyone capable of adding big numbers can prove that completing the Super Slam requires tremendous time and financial resources, especially the latter. Lots of luck in long-odds tag drawings can help, but even that can't eliminate the need for expensive guided hunts for many species. The Super Slam as currently defined is beyond the reach of the 95% of us who are bound to jobs, lack large sums of disposable money or corporate sponsors, and don't have the kind of luck in the tag drawings that belongs in Las Vegas. No offense intended toward anyone, but shouldn't hunting goals depend on skill and determination as well as resources? I like to think that even successful Super Slam hunters would agree.

The idea of the Super Slam grew out of a concept popular in sheep hunting circles for years. The original Grand Slam consisted of taking all four recognized North American wild sheep species (a quartet that biologists narrow down to just two species, but that's another story). The idea was often incorrectly attributed to pioneering big game hunter Jack O'Connor who, when asked about it, dismissed the Grand Slam as a "caper." Guides, outfitters, and other commercial hunting interests endorsed the idea enthusiastically, since it allowed them opportunities to earn big money from wealthy clients who "had" to have a desert bighorn or Stone sheep to complete their Slam. As hunters became more mobile and better heeled, the idea of the Super Slam perhaps became inevitable.

Since my brain is always busy—too busy, according to some—a thought occurred to me. What if we defined a new Super Slam, potentially within reach of hunters of ordinary means? Here are the rules. You would have to be able to hunt each animal without hiring a guide. No drawings for tags would be required; if you can't buy a tag for the animal over the counter, it's off the list. Only free-range species would be available, with no game farm animals allowed. Finally, opportunities would have to be equally available to residents of all states. What would this egalitarian set of rules do to the current list of Super Slam species? Of equal interest, what animals could we add to take up the slack?

Bye, Bye, Baby

Let's begin by studying the current list of 29 to identify those that don't meet the criteria outlined above.

Deer (5): There's some good news here for deer enthusiasts, as all five species (actually two species, with five subspecies), make the grade.

Sheep (4): Sorry, high country hunters. All four North American sheep require a guide or a lot of luck in the drawings. Alaskans may protest that they can hunt Dall sheep without a guide or a drawing tag, but we agreed that opportunities must be available to residents of every state.

Caribou (5): Because of non-resident guide laws in Canada, only Alaska's barren ground subspecies qualifies. Non-resident hunters can hunt them without a guide and do not need to draw tags.

Bears (4): Only the familiar black bear makes the list. Hunting brown, grizzly and polar bears require a guide (except for Alaska residents in the first two cases and we've been over that before).

Elk (3): The tule subspecies requires a drawing tag or guide, but both the Yellowstone and Roosevelt elk remain fair game.

Moose (3) Only the Alaska-Yukon moose qualifies. Canadian moose require a guide in Canada or a drawing tag in our own Northeast, and Shiras moose require a drawing tag.

Cougar and pronghorn (2): Fair game! Eastern hunters will need to travel a bit, but both are widely available with over-the-counter tags (in some areas) and no guide required.

Musk ox, buffalo, and mountain goat (3): Again, Alaska residents can do all three but the rest of us can't without hiring a guide or hitting the jackpot in a drawing.

Amazingly enough, the list of 29 we began with has shrunk all the way to 12!

Blue Collar Trophies

Now it's time to think outside the box. I'm amazed by how much fun I've had over the years hunting North American game that doesn't even make the officially sanctioned list. The distinction between big game and small can be arbitrary. Don't worry; I'm not suggesting that we take up the slack with multiple species of bunnies, grouse, and squirrels (not to say that I haven't spent a lot of time in the field hunting them). But there are a number of North American animals that I hunt like big game even if they aren't on the officially approved list, and most meet all the criteria for inclusion in the hypothetical Blue-Collar Super Slam outlined earlier.

Collared peccary: AKA javelina, this one is a slam dunk. The species is unique to North America and a bowhunter's off-season dream. While drawing tags are required in Arizona the odds are such that almost anyone can get one, and no drawing tags are necessary in Texas.

Feral hog: Granted, they're an introduced species. But American bowhunters probably spend more time hunting them than any other wild mammal except the whitetail. The general no-season, no-limit regulations fit right into our blue-collar program.

Bobcat: A widely distributed, underrated quarry. Western houndsmen know that a mature bob is almost always harder to tree than a cougar.

Coyote: Why is the wariest, wiliest mammal on the continent considered a varmint and not a game animal? Beats me.

Wild turkey: As bowhunting turkeys has grown in popularity, most of us now recognize the challenge they pose. And if the official Super Slam can turn one species of caribou, one species of moose and two species of deer into five, three and five entries on the list respectively, I'm calling for the Full Monty: eastern, Osceola, Merriam, and Rio Grande! (Hunting the Gould's subspecies in the United States requires drawing a tag.)

Sika deer: Since we've allowed introduced species onto the list with the obvious inclusion of the feral hog, it only seems fair to include a few others that have established self-sustaining populations. Traditional high fence prohibitions apply, so I'm not going to name every Texas exotic. Maryland hunters assure me that their free ranging sikas are a tough quarry in every respect. Based on my own limited experiences with them in the Pacific I can believe it.

Axis deer: Again, no game farm animals allowed, but Hawaii's free ranging axis deer are available to anyone with enough legs and heart to hunt them. Free range axis deer also inhabit some parts of Texas.

Nilgai: Free ranging populations of this Eurasian import are available in Texas.

Feral goats: Skeptics should read the early historical accounts of bowhunting goats on California's Channel Islands. They've largely been eliminated there, but they're still readily available in Hawaii.

Wolf: While wolf hunting has been controversial in the Lower-48 states since they were de-listed from Endangered Species Act restrictions, they are now legal game in several western states with no disqualifying restrictions in most. Seasons and limits have long been generous to non-existent in much of Alaska. Although I had several memorable encounters with wolves up north, I've never shot at one and very few bowhunters have ever killed a wolf. This may be the toughest of the lot.

Red fox: Far more widely distributed than the wolf and nearly as smart.

Voila... we've added 14 back, making a total of 26: Sitka blacktail, Columbian blacktail, whitetail, Coues deer, mule deer, barren ground caribou, black bear, Roosevelt elk, Yellowstone elk, pronghorn, cougar, Alaska-Yukon moose (all from the original list), plus javelina, feral hog, bobcat, coyote, Osceola turkey, eastern turkey, Rio Grande turkey, Merriam turkey, sika deer, axis deer, feral goat, wolf, nilgai, and red fox.

All these animals can be hunted without guides or special tags, by residents of any state. Some readers may protest that the amount of travel a few of them require still puts them out of reach. The goal was to make the hunting reasonable, not free; besides, hunters east of the Mississippi now have multiple new species to pursue close to home.

Of course, making lists like this invites discussion. One could make a case for the alligator, for example. Obtaining alligator tags is still complicated and confusing. If that situation changes, I'm all for including them in the Blue -Collar Slam. If the grizzly is successfully de-listed in the Mountain West it may belong there too, but I'm not holding my breath.

So, kick the idea around and have fun with it. I haven't memorized the hunting regulations in all 50 states, and regulations change constantly, so some of this information may be inaccurate by the time you read it. I'm sure some readers will point out possible candidates I haven't considered. One way or another, the idea provides a comprehensive bowhunting goal that can be undertaken without the kind of expense entailed in buying a house. I'm not much of a scorekeeper myself, but the notion is interesting enough to make me think about tackling some of the tougher ones I haven't taken. And the mental exercise emphasizes one of bowhunting's most appealing characteristics: you've never really done it all.

31.

The Once and Future Predator

"There still remains, even in the United States, some areas of considerable size in which we feel that both the red and the gray (wolves) may be allowed to continue their existence... Yes, so also thinks every right-minded ecologist, but has the United States Fish and Wildlife Service no responsibility for implementing this thought before it completes its job of extirpation?" Aldo Leopold, 1944.

By all accounts, Bear # 346 – a.k.a. the Falls Creek male -- enjoyed a long, successful career along the Rocky Mountains' eastern front. But when he finally met his end in 2001, the response among the many Montanans who knew of him could not have been more divided. Preservationists saw his destruction by officials of the federal Wildlife Services and the state Department of Fish, Wildlife and Parks as another sad chapter in Montana's long, uneasy relationship with the top of its natural food chain, while local ranchers and the veteran wildlife agents who had pursued Bear #346 for over a decade breathed a collective sigh of relief. How could so many people interpret the same event so differently?

All would agree (or almost all... unanimity remains practically unheard of in discussions of this topic) that the Falls Creek male was both exceptionally large and good at what he did. Unfortunately, what he did was kill cattle, an economic mainstay and cornerstone of life along the Front Range. Authorities now believe the 650-pound grizzly killed his first calf in 1984, and during the next 17 years rang up a dinner tab estimated at $200,000 worth of Montana beef.

It's not that those responsible for local cattle and their welfare didn't try to stop the feeding frenzy. Between the time FWP biologist Keith Aune collared the bear in 1985 as part of a research study and the day a crew from the state Department of Livestock darted him from the air, the big grizzly matched wits with experienced hunters and trappers from both state and federal wildlife agencies and eluded them all. "Among the most notorious livestock killing grizzlies in Montana," Wildlife Services supervisor David Nelson noted, "the Falls Creek grizzly was famous for his uncanny wariness." In the end, Bear #346's cunning contributed as much to his reputation as his size and his appetite.

At the ripe old age of 22, Bear #346 finally died by lethal injection at the FWP laboratory in Bozeman on April 18, 2001. Were his pursuit and destruction overdue or overdone? Differences of opinion—often passionate—will likely divide local residents for years to come, echoing a recurrent theme in the argument over large predators and their proper place in the West.

There are no easy answers.

Gray wolves, grizzly bears, mountain lions... each species could serve as a poster child for the growing movement to restore large predator populations across the American West. Large, powerful animals command a unique degree of attention among human observers whether that response eventually translates into admiration, fear, or loathing. Let's face facts: it's a lot harder to ignore a grizzly bear than a snail darter, whether your objective is to save the world or build a dam.

In various capacities, I've spent more time up close and personal with all three of these species than most participants in the debate over their future. And yes, each has made a profound personal effect upon the way I view the world. But this time around, the story really isn't about the wildlife. For just as I consider myself a hunter, hiker, writer, photographer, and unabashed enthusiast of wild places, I'm also a citizen of Montana, with a remarkably complex network of ties to parties on all sides of the dispute over the future of large predators. A week's worth of discussion about wolf reintroduction with ranchers, hunters, biologists, environmental activists, and the neighbors down the road can make anyone feel like a UN observer in a war zone. Believe me.

After a decade in the national spotlight as reluctant host to Yellowstone's surplus bison, Montana has served as a focal point for conflict over animal management policies for years. Much of the impetus for the preservationist viewpoint arose elsewhere, an immediate source of resentment for many Montanans. When I sought out a source for preservationist opinion for this article, I deliberately chose the Bozeman-based Predator Conservation Alliance simply because I wanted to hear from a source close to home.

I never asked PCA staffers Sara Folger and Dave Gaillard their ages, but within minutes of meeting them in their pleasantly cluttered Bozeman office I found myself thinking of them as kids. This impression derived not from any suggestion of immaturity on their part, but from their obvious dedication to their work. I found it a pleasure to interview people who chose their jobs because of what they believed in as opposed to what that job might pay them, and during our discussion I found myself admiring my hosts' integrity even when I disagreed with some of their views.

Folger described the PCA as a membership-driven private organization dedicated to "saving a place for America's predators." While the PCA does some work with legislative proposals and Environmental Impact Statements, the staff views its primary mission as advocacy and education, convincing the public of the intrinsic value of large predators and teaching people better ways to live near them. The PCA deliberately eschews the headline-grabbing confrontational tactics employed by some activist groups.

I asked Folger if she thought ranchers should be compensated for livestock losses due to predators. "My personal position," she replied, "is that I think it (loss to predators) is the cost of doing business." Gaillard offered a gentle dissent, acknowledging that "if our goal is getting wolves re-established in the northern Rockies, compensation… has been important to make that happen." On the subject of predator management, modest disagreement is not unusual even among those on the same side of the fence. Folger also explained that the PCA supports dealing with predators actively engaged in livestock predation by "non-lethal" means.

Hunting has always been an emotional issue for advocacy groups, and I found myself especially interested in the PCA's views on the subject. "We've been officially opposed to hunting imperiled predators," Gaillard stated, a bit of redundancy given that state and federal law already prohibits hunting endangered species. He reported that his group did not wish to see wolves hunted again in Montana, although this position does not coincide with the mandate of the federal wolf recovery effort.

"We have some ethical concerns about a lot of hunting practices," Folger added. Asked for specific examples, she named bear baiting (illegal in Montana for decades) and hound hunting. "We're all personally opposed to the notion of taking a pack of dogs out on the ground and chasing down an individual animal," she stated. "It doesn't seem like fair chase to me." When asked if she had ever actually observed such a hunt, she acknowledged that she had not.

But despite obvious philosophical differences on certain issues, we did find common ground. "Europe has its cathedrals," Gaillard pointed out in an eloquent summary of his group's position, "while America has its wilderness." And in a final candid moment he noted: "We're the first to acknowledge that we don't have all the answers."

Welcome to the club.

By coincidence, Ed Bangs and I knew each other two decades ago when we both lived on Alaska's Kenai Peninsula. We enjoyed many common friends and at least two common passions: bowhunting and wildlife. At the time, I was an overworked physician, and he was a biologist at the Kenai National Moose Range. Now I'm a bum who writes and he's the Wolf Recovery Coordinator for the Fish and Wildlife Service (or was at the original time of this writing). At least one of us can still claim to have a high-stress job. We hadn't seen each other for years, and when I walked into his Helena office, my first impression was that I hoped I'd aged as gracefully as my host.

Bangs offered a quick synopsis of the wolf recovery effort's historical background. The last wolves were eradicated from Montana in the early 1930's, ironically by the federal agency that eventually evolved into the Fish and Wildlife Service. Except for occasional loners that drifted south across the Canadian border, no wolves inhabited Montana for the next several decades. In the 1960's, the Canadian government began its own wolf recovery program, leading to increased numbers of wolves migrating southward. In 1973, Montana wolves fell under the protection of the Endangered Species Act. Under the auspices of the Fish and Wildlife Service, the Wolf Recovery Program introduced the first transplanted wolves to Montana in 1995.

At least from the perspective of those who endorse the recovery effort, the results were spectacular. The Recovery Program has completed the biological goals of its initial mission. When I suggested that this accomplishment had no doubt earned a mixed reception, Bangs replied with a knowing laugh.

Since the most vehement opposition to wolf introduction in Montana has come from the ranching community, I asked Bangs to quantify livestock losses inflicted by wolves. "In northwestern Montana," he replied, "it averages about six cattle and five sheep per year." According to his data, predators account for a little over 2% of all livestock losses on the range. However, he acknowledged that those losses are not randomly distributed, and that individual stockmen can occasionally be hard hit.

What about the issue of compensation for those losses? Bangs pointed out that his agency is not involved in compensation, and that payments to ranchers for losses due to wolves are made by a private organization, Defenders of Wildlife. He also echoed the view I'd heard earlier from the PCA that at least on public land occasional losses to predators amount to a cost of doing business. Such losses, he pointed out, are factored into the discounted price of public grazing leases. How effective has the private compensation program been? "I think it helps," he replied. "I think it builds some tolerance… A person who supports wolf recovery is saying: I understand why you could be opposed to this. That may be as beneficial as the economic part."

I asked about the view that livestock-killing wolves should be dealt with by "non-lethal means." "It doesn't work," he replied simply.

We agreed that Montana hunters have expressed mixed opinions on wolf recovery. We'd both heard hunters voice concerns about the impact of wolves on ungulate populations, which he estimated as a potential 5-10% reduction in herd numbers in the limited areas wolves inhabit. But he'd also spoken with many hunters willing to accept such nominal losses in return for the intangible benefit of sharing the field with another large predator. What about the eventual possibility of hunting wolves in Montana? If appropriate safeguards are maintained, Bangs strongly supported return of their management to the state, which would likely include regulated hunting. (Since this article was originally written, this has come to pass.) In direct contrast to the PCA view I'd heard in Bozeman, he did not oppose a properly managed wolf hunting season in Montana as long as population numbers justified one.

Given the intensity of opinion wolf recovery has aroused in Montana, I wasn't surprised to learn that Bangs has regularly endured personal harassment including death threats while doing his job. But I was surprised to learn this abuse has come from opponents and advocates of wolf recovery in nearly equal measure.

"A wolf kills a cow," Bangs related with a philosophical smile, "and the ranchers start calling. I do my job and kill the wolf, and I get it from the other side."

As always: no easy answers.

We've heard from those who want more predators, those who want fewer, and those charged with negotiating the tricky politics in between. It only seems fair that I offer an opinion of my own.

Doing so arouses a measure of trepidation, since I felt considerable sympathy for all the parties I spoke with in the preparation of this piece, and my own synopsis includes views likely to offend almost everyone. First, a simple statement of principles. I hold large predators in high regard and hope sustainable populations will inhabit Montana in perpetuity. I support Montana ranchers, not just because I count many of them as friends, but because I believe that stability in the traditional farm and ranch community is ultimately in the best interest of wildlife. I believe hunting plays a vital role in the viability of wildlife populations and deplore the antagonism that has developed between the hunting and non-hunting segments of the conservation community. With that much on the record, I would offer a simple suggestion: manage Montana's large predators as game animals whenever biologic considerations allow.

Distasteful as the idea may be to some, the historical record supports this model. Driven by scientific principles rather than emotion, game management has allowed target species to rebound to historic carrying capacities throughout North America. Organizations led and funded by hunters have restored both habitat and wildlife populations for species as diverse as waterfowl, wild turkeys, and elk. Game animal status affords large mammals protection and respect underwritten by potential economic value. Game animals create their own constituency, and to the degree that protection boils down to politics, predators need all the friends they can find.

While the notion of hunting endangered species sounds repugnant, it's also moot. As noted, state and federal law already prohibit the practice. Of the three predators mentioned in this article, only the mountain lion currently qualified as a game animal at the time this was written. (The state now has a regulated but controversial wolf season.). And the cougar has thrived —not coincidentally, in my opinion—during its evolution from varmint to game species.

From the rancher's viewpoint, treating predators as game animals would prevent the ability to shoot them at will—but that option isn't viable already. Dealing with individual problem predators would be no more difficult than it is now, while predator populations could be controlled (although not eliminated) through regulated hunting. And as many Montana ranchers have already learned regarding other species, game animals may be more economically valuable over time than livestock.

The predator-as-game concept will no doubt prove particularly difficult for many preservationists to accept emotionally, and emotional responses are difficult to argue. But as I reviewed the PCA newsletters I brought back from my trip to Bozeman, I noted the number of issues they raised—unregulated prairie dog shooting, state agencies killing black bears and cougars to increase elk numbers, tax funded predator destruction by the federal Wildlife Services—that would largely go away if the involved species enjoyed the protections afforded game animals. At some point, preservationists may have to face hard choices between doing what makes them feel good about themselves and what makes sense for the long-term benefit of the species they're committed to protect.

A flawless solution to a difficult issue? Hardly. But when addressing a problem to which there are no easy answers, it always helps to keep an open mind.

Author's note: The original version of this material was written for *Big Sky Journal* in 2001. The regulatory and political management of large predators is evolving constantly, and many changes have taken place since then. While I have tried to explain those changes briefly, these notes will inevitably be dated by the time the material appears in book form. Readers should look to current information about the regulatory and biological aspects of the issue. I include the discussion here because the fundamental conflicts surrounding large predator management are relatively constant and should be of concern to all who care about wildlife, including hunters. DT

32.

Heavy Bows Revisited

Fueled by camaraderie and good cheer, I purchased the lightest bow I owned at the time during the PBS Banquet auction in Seattle. My old friend Dick Robertson had handcrafted this lovely little work of art, which included laminations from some favorite woods and delicate Pierce points in the riser. Dick happened to be at our table that night, and despite his continued assurances that he would build me an identical recurve at a fraction of the price, my hand kept rising in response to the auctioneer as if it had a life of its own. I felt no regrets the following morning even though, at a mere #58 draw weight, I had no idea what I would do with my acquisition.

By my standards at the time, that was ridiculously light. Over the next several seasons, I killed a few turkeys and antelope with "Auction Fever," but when I set out in search of heavier game, I always carried tackle in my usual #70-74 range. After all, those were the bows I'd hunted with for years, and since I could still handle the weight, I felt I should be hunting with all the bow I could draw.

Then my hubris regarding draw weight changed suddenly. As Lori and I were packing for an eagerly awaited ramble through southern Africa, I experienced a flare in an old cervical disc injury that rendered my right arm all but useless, as described in an earlier chapter. My trip to the Dark Continent became a trip to the operating room instead. When we returned home, persistent weakness in my right deltoid and biceps muscles prevented me from drawing anything, even the kids' bows left over from the days when son Nick and daughter Gen were receiving their introductions to archery.

I continued on a planned trip to Australia anyway, as a noncombatant, but if I meant to salvage my fall season, I was obviously going to have to rethink my entire archery program.

The definition of a "heavy" bow remains arbitrary. One bowhunter's heavyweight may be little more than a toy to another. While I think most would accept my definition of bows pulling #70 or more as heavy, I have friends who routinely carry #80 tackle even when they're hunting nothing larger than whitetails. When I ask them why, they tell me that their bows offer a better chance of penetration on marginal hits and that they see no reason not to hunt with the heaviest bow they can shoot without sacrificing accuracy. Since that's the same argument I use to justify my own choices, their reasoning leaves me little room for reply.

I once worked my way laboriously up to #85 in preparation for an African buffalo hunt that never happened. It wasn't easy, but I did it, although I never developed confidence in my accuracy beyond 20 yards. At least that situation justified the attempt to move up dramatically in weight—or so I thought. Subsequent experience with physically similar Australian buffalo taught me that #70 was perfectly adequate.

Two cultural factors seem to influence the definition of a heavy bow. The first is time. A generation ago, our predecessors rarely hunted anything with bows over #60, and I'm old enough to remember when even lighter bows were standard for virtually all big game. The second is geography. During my travels, I've noticed that bowhunters who live east of the Great Plains generally shoot tackle that averages around ten pounds lighter than what I'm used to, no doubt reflecting the fact that whitetails are the heaviest game most of them encounter regularly. In contrast, I've spent decades living and hunting in Alaska and Montana where elk, moose, and bear are everyday quarry. Heavy game seems to invite heavy bows, if for no reason other than that's what everyone else is shooting. Logical? We'll see.

Whatever one's personal views on the subject, it's important to emphasize that draw weight is only one of several elements that define an effective hunting tool. Draw weight and arrow speed don't mean much at the point of impact unless they're driving a sufficiently heavy shaft. That arrow, in turn, must be flying true to avoid wasting energy when it strikes, and it must be tipped with a proper broadhead. Those are considerations for another day, and I mention them only so readers won't accuse me of being naïve to their importance.

But there I was in late August, with bow season rapidly approaching. The good news: the injured nerve in my neck had finally started to recover and I was shooting again. The bad news: I still couldn't draw any of my usual hunting bows back to my familiar anchor at the corner of my jaw. But I could pull Auction Fever, and when opening day finally rolled around, I took to the field carrying the lightest tackle I'd handled in years.

Before heading to the elk cover, I decided to tune up on something a little less intimidating. After a week at our house in Alaska during which I spent a lot more time with my fly rod than my bow, I left work early one afternoon for a tree stand below the house with my antlerless whitetail tag burning a hole in my pocket. An hour later, a dry doe ambled up the hill toward the alfalfa field behind me. She eventually wandered off the main trail and offered a tricky shot through a window of brush, but the shaft passed completely through her chest, and I watched her collapse on the opposite side hill. Never mind the lack of horns. I consider any big game animal taken with a traditional bow an accomplishment, and since I'd been incapacitated so recently, that one certainly felt gratifying.

With that confidence builder behind me, I headed for the elk cover. My failure to kill a bull the following week had nothing to do with my bow. After passing up some small bulls and having the wind betray me to some big ones, I set out to fill my antlerless mule deer tag. That night, a doe made the last mistake of her life and my "little" recurve (I'd added quotation marks by this time) sent a cedar shaft clear through the length of her chest quartering away.

By October, I'd stopped being fussy about elk, and when a 5-point bull wandered by during an evening deer hunt, I killed him. But Auction Fever wasn't through with wapiti yet. Thanks to a new twist in the regulations, I held an additional cow tag. During the last week of the season, a small group of cows and calves surprised me on another deer hunt. Auction Fever drove another shaft home, making me the first bowhunter I knew to kill two elk in Montana during the same season. I couldn't help but observe that my lightest bow was killing elk just as dead as my usual tackle.

While I know others who feel differently, I've always considered bears the toughest test of archery tackle on our continent. But when I stalked in on a foraging boar mid-October, another shaft from Auction Fever broke ribs on both sides of the chest and I watched the stricken bruin collapse within 30 yards. So much for that challenge to my limited draw weight.

By the time the whitetail rut rolled around, I had started to draw my usual hunting weight bows again, but since the #58 had proven itself so handily on elk and bear I saw no reason to change. After looking over a lot of whitetails around the house, the 5-point I'd been concentrating on finally offered a shot. The result: another complete pass-through.

My rehabilitation program finally ended in the hills of west Texas that December. I'd seen some exceptional mule deer while hunting a friend's ranch, all of which managed to stay out of bow range. But on the last morning of the hunt, I engineered a stalk on a large fork-horn. Auction Fever sent my arrow through his chest and so far into the cactus beyond that I eventually had to search for half an hour to find it. Mission accomplished; over and out.

I would offer several conclusions from my experiences that fall. The news that a #58 bow will cleanly kill a wide variety of big game is hardly revolutionary. My surprise arises not from the bow's performance but from the unfounded strength of my previous convictions. Old habits die hard, and I now recognize that for years I had made equipment decisions based on assumptions unsupported by data.

The principle referenced earlier—shoot the heaviest bow possible without sacrificing accuracy—still makes sense. But after a season's experience with a lighter bow, an admission: I *do* shoot that bow better than I shoot my heavier tackle, even though I wasn't aware of this earlier. Practice at the range doesn't tell the whole story. Under hunting conditions, archers often must draw slowly to avoid detection and shoot at odd, contorted angles, circumstances that highlight the advantage of lighter bows. In retrospect, I can appreciate several circumstances when carrying a light bow worked to my advantage.

Have I totally recovered from my addiction to heavy tackle? Yes, but not necessarily by choice. Several seasons later, I sustained a badly torn rotator cuff in my right shoulder during a fall while carrying a heavy pack. Arthroscopic surgery revealed so much damage that the tendons couldn't be repaired completely. While trauma due to the fall was likely enough to explain the damage on its own, I'm sure that all those years drawing heavy bows left my shoulder prone to injury. The surgeon's opinion that a lot of the damage seemed old reinforced that view.

Even after a year of physical therapy, I couldn't lift anything above my right shoulder or pull any of my kids' old bows. My only option at that point was a reverse total shoulder replacement, which was a new procedure at the time. Since orthopedic surgeons at the University of Washington had more experience with it than anyone in Montana, I headed back to my medical school alma mater. After an initial evaluation, I wound up on the operating schedule.

When I arrived for my final medical clearance the day before I was due in the OR, the head of the team asked me bluntly: "What are your goals for this surgery?"

"I want to be able to shoot a bow, shoot a shotgun, and cast a fly rod," I replied without hesitation.

After a brief conference among themselves, the downfaced team leader made an honest admission. "This operation hasn't been around long enough for us to know if the prostheses will tolerate that kind of use. It will allow old ladies to reach the top shelf of a cabinet, but you're asking for a lot more. If the prosthesis dislocates... I don't know how to say this other than that you'll be screwed." That was the end of my shoulder replacement plans.

The good news is that after a year of minimal progress with rehabilitation, I suddenly and inexplicably began to improve. The bad news is that I still couldn't shoot any of my old hunting bows, not even Auction Fever. However, after making some modifications to my style, I could shoot a shotgun (after ditching my old, reliable 12-gauge for a 20) and cast a fly rod (proper form requires using your wrist and not your shoulder anyway, so I got rid of one old bad habit). Best of all, I could shoot my kids' bows again. I kept working at it, and by that fall I was killing deer cleanly with a sweet little #48 recurve from Dick Robertson's shop.

I still can't pull Auction Fever, but that bow is so pretty and so full of pleasant memories that I'm happy just looking at it. Hunting with it again remains an aspirational goal that I'll likely never attain. What about the rest of those great heavyweights? Plenty of memories reside in them as well, but at some point, realism had to rear its ugly head. One by one, I'm donating them to various worthy organizations like the Professional Bowhunters Society as auction items to raise money to better the future of hunting.

That seems like an honorable way for those bows and me to ride off into the sunset together. I just hope that no one blows out a shoulder shooting them.

33.

Snow Never Lies

Calm air, clear azure skies, and a uniform blanket of white covering the entire landscape save for the lower branches of the pines... I didn't need a thermometer to tell me it was a sub-zero day, and there wasn't another human being within miles. A perfect storm of weather events had created ideal tracking conditions: an ankle-high base of old snow with a thin, icy crust topped by an inch of virgin powder. The record of the previous night's wildlife activity I crossed included the elk and mule deer tracks I'd expected, but nothing more unusual than a porcupine's lazy drag mark and the delicate etching of a grouse's flight primaries where it had taken to the air. I walked in circles for ten minutes trying unsuccessfully to determine what had flushed the bird.

Then I cut the cat track. Learning the distinction between feline and canine tracks is one of the first challenges a winter tracker faces in the Mountain West, but with experience the difference becomes obvious, at least in good snow conditions. My first impression of this one was that it had been left by a sub-adult cougar, but something didn't look right. I followed the track carefully, my eyes alert for clues.

The process of identifying a strange track reminds me of a common tactic I often used when faced with an uncertain situation during my medical career: constructing a differential diagnosis.

This consists of making a list of everything the problem *could* be, followed by discarding possibilities one at a time based on the evidence. "When you have eliminated the impossible," as Sherlock Homes once pointed out, "whatever remains, however unlikely, must be the truth." That principle applies equally well to mysterious illnesses and unusual animal tracks.

When I followed the track under the canopy where the powder had been sheltered from the previous night's wind, the prints looked crisp and concise and definitely belonged to a cat, which left a limited number of possibilities. The stride seemed short and narrow for a lion, but the prints were too large for a bobcat. Then I realized that whatever had left the track hadn't been breaking through the thin crust beneath the powder. Dropping to my knees, I tested the strength of the crust with my fingertips and confirmed that a cougar should have been breaking through. Hmm… A cat with a print the size of a cougar's left by an animal a fraction of a lion's weight. *Voila!* I was on the trail of a Canadian lynx.

I had occasionally seen lynx when I lived in Alaska, but even there such close encounters of the first kind were rare. I'd never seen a lynx in Montana, but there was a clear record of one's passage. Think of tracking in terms of simple geometry. An animal is a point, but its track is a line that can extend for miles. It's obviously more likely to encounter the latter, especially when the animal is taking evasive action at the first indication of human presence. Such are the joys of tracking, and there is no better time to do it than during winter, when snow is eager to tell the observer so much about local wildlife.

Back in the day… Lori and Drive investigate a fresh cougar track.

I admit that I am addicted to winter tracking. To the concern of family and friends, I've been known to slam on the brakes at 50 mph while driving down a snowy road just because I thought I spotted an unusual track through the window. Granted, a lot of this enthusiasm developed from hunting experiences, but non-hunters need not worry. No animals are harmed in the course of this essay. That's a large part of tracking's appeal. You can enjoy the process and learn a tremendous amount about wildlife no matter what your intentions toward whatever you're following.

Unless you're an avid skier, it's easy to avoid the outdoors during a high-country winter. Since I would prefer to do something during the cold months besides read, write, tie flies, and gain weight, I'm always looking for excuses to get into the mountains. The backcountry is beautiful then despite the cold, and there is never a better time to enjoy it in solitude. Tracking provides a great excuse and opportunities are never farther away than the nearest National Forest.

Over the years, I have tracked all kinds of wildlife across all kinds of surfaces ranging from sand to pine needle duff to tundra, sometimes down on hands and knees looking for nothing more obvious than bent blades of grass or disturbances in the dew. I've even enjoyed the process in the company of the world's best, Africa's Kalahari Bushmen, for whom tracking is literally a way of life. (See Chapter 27.) Those experiences have left me with a deep appreciation for fresh snow, which we enjoy in such abundance in Montana that it would be a shame to overlook all that it has to tell us.

Sometimes tracking can serve a practical purpose. When dog food started disappearing from an overturned container beside the kennel that houses my bird dogs, a late October snowfall allowed me to identify the culprit as a black bear and chase it out of the coulee behind the house before it became habituated to free lunches. Tracking has allowed me to stay in shape over the course of many long winters, gain unique insights into wildlife behavior, and "see" unusual birds and animals, including a wolverine in addition to the lynx described earlier.

There is no more dramatic story in nature than a predator killing its prey, even if the event is nothing more involved than a raptor pouncing on a rabbit. Seeing one large mammal kill another in real time is a rare event, as reported earlier when I watched a grizzly kill a moose when I was guiding in Alaska, as described in Chapter 1. However, tracking has led me to many kill sites, where snow has told stories as easy to read as an open book. Want to know how a 100-pound cougar kills a full-grown elk? Follow enough tracks, and the snow will tell you. Shakespearean tragedy or just another day in the woods? Such events contain elements of both.

Tracking has also allowed me insights into unusual wildlife behavior that I never would have imagined otherwise. One such day began with a cougar track in the snow, followed by an enigma. Interpreting the sign demonstrated how tracking can illustrate unexpected aspects of wildlife behavior.

The conditions weren't optimal, for warm winds had turned the snow to slush on the south facing slopes. Confusing "snow tracks" left by clots of melting snow dropping from the trees dotted what powder remained. My two friends and I had to cast about frequently whenever the track disappeared on a stretch of rock where all the snow had melted, and we once lost it temporarily where the lion had climbed upward through a rocky cliff. The track belonged to a small cat, likely a young male.

We had covered a mile or two after regaining the track when I noticed something interesting in the snow ahead: a long drag mark running downward along the fall line. My first thought was that the cat had killed a deer and skidded the carcass down into the trees to hide it from scavengers, but there was no blood or hair along the disturbance in the snow, which also held intermittent jumping cat tracks. We followed the sign down the hill and found what I can only describe as a giant snowball. After climbing back to the beginning of the "drag" mark, we saw where the lion had used its paws to dig up snow and pack it together.

Farther along the sidehill we found two areas similar to the first, with a sphere of snow at the end of each. The cat had evidently spent the morning building snowballs and chasing them down the hill. Was it practicing its attack technique, working out, or just having fun? The sign didn't allow us to determine its motivation. We never saw the lion either. The snow had left a clear record of a cougar engaging in behavior that would have been virtually impossible to observe in person. That's why I love to spend my winters on foot in the hills, reading the white pages.

Opportunities to track winter wildlife abound on public land, with no license or special equipment required except a daypack with winter survival gear and perhaps a pair of snowshoes or cross-country skis. Tracking skills are best developed through experience. As a useful exercise, one can simply start out on the track of a common animal like a deer and follow it until you lose the trail or find what made it.

Exercise, solitude, mountain scenery, and an opportunity to learn more about wildlife… What a way to spend a winter day.

34.

Shooting Down

Some of us hunt almost exclusively from tree stands, while others agree with the late Glenn St. Charles that they compromise bowhunting skills and refuse to use them at all. Many, like me, fall somewhere in between, utilizing elevated stands in some situations but not in others. I certainly don't consider tree stands unethical, but I find game taken from the ground more satisfying, for the same reason I find a trout taken on a dry fly more satisfying than one taken on a nymph. A review of my field notes confirms that I've taken substantially more game from the ground than from trees, and nowadays I confine my use of tree stands exclusively to the pursuit of whitetails. But no matter where you fall along this spectrum, if you hunt from trees, you're going to have to learn to shoot accurately from them, which can be a bit more involved than it seems.

I've never considered myself a great target archer (and I doubt anyone else has either), but in the field I generally kill what I shoot at. However, a disproportionate number of my really bad misses—the chip shots that make you wonder "How in the #!&*! Did I do *that?*" as the deer bounds away unharmed—have come from tree stands. It shouldn't be that way. Tree stand shots are often close. An elevated position allows the hunter plenty of time to prepare for the shot. Game is usually relaxed and totally unaware of the hunter's presence. But I've certainly done it, and I still do even after years of experience. And so have a lot of other veteran bowhunters I know.

Several factors contribute to the difficulties involved in shooting from above, but let's start by examining the most basic: the archer's form. For the sake of our discussion, we'll assume you have form well worked out on the target range and are comfortable and competent out to 20 to 25 yards with your feet on the ground. (If not, you probably need to work on it before adding elevation to the equation.) What happens to your good, solid form when you climb up a tree and start shooting at targets on the ground?

Two basic form faults often arise to threaten accuracy, and both involve the geometric relationship between bow arm, anchor, and the dominant eye. Any three points define a triangle as do these, in this case a right triangle (at least theoretically) with its base composed of the short leg between your anchor point and the eye. When arrow and target are vertically aligned as they are at ground level, tiny changes in the position of the bow hand are all the archer needs to correct for range. But from a tree, you need to direct the arrow down—*way* down—and one common way to do that is to lower your bow hand.

But look what happens when you do that. The whole shape of that critical triangle—the one that you've worked all summer developing and burning into your "instinctive" muscle memory—changes. And you're going to miss.

The bow arm is just part of the problem. Absent deliberate correction, your dominant eye will now be higher than usual regarding the alignment of the arrow. Wing-shooters know what happens when they lift their cheek up off the shotgun stock to get a good look at that pheasant: they shoot high, because they've changed the geometry of their "aiming" triangle. (Good wing-shots don't truly "aim" any more than "instinctive" traditional archers do, but the principles of form are the same whether or not you consciously estimate range and look at the tip of your arrow—or the end of your shotgun barrel.)

You need to get your form back in shape when shooting from an elevated position, and fortunately that's easy to do once you've identified and understood the problem. Obviously, that bow arm still must go down when the target is below you, but there's a right way and a wrong way to get it there. We've seen what happens when you lower the arm and disrupt that crucial triangle, but look at what happens when you simply bend at the waist. With a bit of practice, you can do this in a way that keeps that crucial aiming triangle intact. Practice from an elevated position during the off-season by picking a spot on a tree at eye level and aiming at it just as you would from the ground on the practice range. Then, maintaining the position of both arms, bend at the waist until you're lined up on the ground level target. That's what your arms should feel when you're shooting at a deer.

It's still easy to wind up with your dominant eye higher than usual in relationship to the other components of the aiming triangle, but there's a simple solution to this problem. As you come to draw, *tuck your chin down*. This will restore the proper relationship between your eye and your anchor. Now you understand my mantra when I prepare to shoot a deer from a tree: *pick a spot, bend your waist, tuck your chin.*

With these basic elements of shooting form addressed, we can move on to some of the other reasons archers have difficulty shooting from tree stands. The next one is simple: lack of practice. It's easy to shoot regularly from the ground at a 3-D target in the backyard, or to head for the nearest range for a walk-around several times a week over the summer. But practicing from a tree stand is a hassle: hang the stand, climb up, buckle your safety belt, shoot a few arrows, climb back down… Even if your local range has elevated shooting stations, they're usually wide platforms that bear little resemblance to the small, portable stands you're likely to use during hunting season.

Furthermore, if you're new to tree stand hunting it may take you some time to get used to being in the stand even if you aren't trying to shoot at a target (let alone a deer). I still remember the first time I climbed into a portable stand a friend had set up for me. I was so rattled that an hour passed before I could let go of the tree and turn around. (This was so long ago that we hadn't even heard of safety belts, so I *should* have been rattled.)

The solution to these problems is obvious and doesn't really take much extra work. Pick a stand similar or identical to the one you plan to hunt from and hang it, perhaps even in an area you plan to hunt if it's close by. If you're a novice in tree stands, take a book and a pair of binoculars and sit there watching the wildlife for several evenings until you feel comfortable. Once you've reached that point, or right off the bat if you're a veteran, pack a quiver full of arrows up the tree and start shooting. (Target tips will work fine unless the ground below is solid rock.) Natural unmarked targets like leaves or blades of grass work best for me, but you can always toss a few paper plates on the ground at varying distances if you prefer. (Don't forget to pick them up.)

Practice during hunting season is just as important as practice over the summer, although many of us are so busy hunting we neglect it. When I'm hunting whitetails in November, I keep a 3-D target beneath my deck, which is about the same height above ground as a tree stand, and shoot some arrows at it every few days, or more often if I'm not happy with my shooting. There's another good way to stay sharp. I always carry a target arrow in my quiver and shoot it at a pinecone or a spot on the snow right before I leave my stand. In addition to keeping my shooting sharp, this habit serves to remind me of any obstructions to arrow flight or potential sources of limb interference, giving me an opportunity to adapt my shooting or fix the problem before it costs me a buck. Don't worry about spooking game. You're about to climb down the tree, which will make more noise than your bow.

This advice highlights another issue inherent to shooting from tree stands: the difficulties of maneuvering a bow at odd angles from tight quarters. The longer the bow, the bigger the problem (longbow shooters, beware!). Also, note that the closer the target is to the tree and the steeper the downward shot angle, the more contortions you'll have to go through to get a shot away without limb interference (and the greater the form problems outlined earlier). Closer is not always better when shooting from a tree. Even if a bow limb (usually the lower, but not always) doesn't hit something, the more you're worried about the possibility when you shoot, the greater the chance you'll miss.

The way to address this problem, of course, is to shoot from the stand once it's hung in its actual hunting location. I try to get up into each of my stands with a quiver full of arrows early in the season, or right after I've put the stand in place. This time around, I'm not worried about my shooting form as much as I am about identifying any peculiarities associated with shooting from that specific stand. Don't spend too much time on the slam dunk shots at the trails the stand was set up to shoot. Instead, reach around and try the odd angles, paying particular attention to limb interference. It may well be that you just can't shoot at a deer on the secondary trail running behind the stand. No shame in that, but it's better to find out about the problem now than to risk missing or wounding a deer there later. This is also the time to trim sone of those annoying little branches that can deflect an arrow in flight.

This kind of practice may convince you (as it did me) that the hardest shot of all from a tree stand is at a deer directly underneath you. (As noted, closer is not always better.) If you've mastered that shot, I salute you. I haven't, so I pass it up and hope the deer proceeds to a more favorable location. This conclusion has cost me some shots, but it's also saved me from some wounded deer, and I'll take that trade any day.

This shot illustrates another problem associated with shooting at a downward angle. The steeper the angle between archer and deer, the smaller the dimensions of the effective vital area become. This is simply a matter of anatomy. The top of a deer's chest is narrower than the sides are deep, and an arrow from above faces a more bone than it does on a broadside shot from ground level. Given that there's no way to change the way game animals are put together, there are a limited number of solutions to this problem. You can limit the height of your stands (the current trend toward stands at stratospheric heights is ridiculous), maintain a solid grasp of deer anatomy, and—most important of all—be willing to pass up some shots that you'd take from ground level.

Although I've referred repeatedly to tree stands, a lot of these ideas also apply anywhere steep terrain might require a shot from the top of a ledge, cliff, or rock. I've encountered such situations while stalking game ranging from bears to mule deer and goats. In fact, the first arrow I ever shot at a black bear many years ago resulted in a non-lethal shoulder blade hit because of just these factors. I'd made a long stalk in steep, mountainous terrain that put me less than 15 yards above the bear as it circled through the tundra eating berries. Unfortunately, I failed to consider the effect of the steep downward angle upon the size and position of the vital zone. Lesson learned.

The effect of gravity upon the ballistics of overhead shots is real but often over-emphasized. Imagine another right triangle with one leg the vertical height from the ground to the stand, the second leg the horizontal distance from the base of the tree to the target, and the hypotenuse the distance from the stand to the target. Gravitational effect on arrow flight is a function of the distance from the base of the tree to the target. Think of the arrow cutting through imaginary vertical lines of gravity. This distance will always be shorter than the hypotenuses of the triangle (the path of the arrow flight). Gravity's effect on the arrow is a function of the shorter horizontal difference between the base of the tree and the target. So, if you aim as if you are taking the shot at the 20-yard distance between you and the target, the arrow will act as if it's following the shorter 15-yard distance on the ground, and you'll shoot high.

This principle is accurate in theory but rarely has a significant effect in bowhunting situations. These ideas were worked out by rifle hunters, and the effect is much greater at the longer distances from which they shoot. They don't matter much at 20 yards. Furthermore, there is another factor at work that affects arrows more than bullets: drag, which will make the path of the projectile tend lower as a function of the distance the projectile covers in flight. Since arrows are bulkier than bullets, drag has more effect on them. In practice, the effect of drag tends to cancel the effect of gravity described earlier, making the arrow hit lower. Shooting at deer instead of 10-rings, I ignore both factors and shoot instinctively the way I always do. I discuss this subject here simply because readers are likely to hear about it in discussions among other archers, during which misinformation commonly arises.

It's not that shooting down is difficult; it's just *different*. The most diligent practice in the world from ground level won't prepare the bowhunter for all the variables when shooting from above. If you're going to hunt from tree stands or in steep, mountainous terrain, you owe it to yourself and your quarry to familiarize yourself with these quirks before taking a shot that really matters.

35.

Sterling's Arrow

This story begins a long way from my usual haunts in Montana and Alaska. For various reasons, I'd missed the PBS Banquet in 2006 and 2008, and the minute I walked through the door in Nashville in March 2010 I realized what a mistake that had been. Lori and I ran into so many old friends on our way through the lobby that it took us two hours to get to our room. Hunting stories buzzed back and forth like bees, and I rejoiced in the knowledge that some of them were probably even true. It's difficult to describe the atmosphere to those who haven't been there—a family reunion is the best metaphor I can produce. Those who have been to a PBS Banquet will understand without elaboration. The rest of you might consider joining what I consider our best national bowhunting organization, hands down.

Since I was the Saturday night banquet speaker—an honor I took very seriously—I felt preoccupied that evening and didn't give the exciting after-dinner auction the attention it deserved. That event is no place to look for bargains, not with hundreds of enthusiastic bowhunters looking for excuses to direct some money to their favorite cause. As the bidding wound down, I realized that Lori and I had failed to purchase anything. With only a few auction items remaining, I had a limited amount of time to make up for our inadvertent neglect.

That's when I saw Sterling's arrow. I attend a lot of bowhunting functions, and although I do my best to give everyone who wants it as much of my time as they can stand, there are usually a few old faces that I'm especially eager to see. Sterling and Krista Holbrook are two such people. Accomplished primitive archers both, we'd tromped a lot of the same ground in Alaska, where Sterling flew helicopters for years, even though we'd never hunted together.

Featuring a river cane shaft, a perfect self nock, barred turkey fletches, and an exquisitely knapped chert head, the arrow that Sterling donated to the auction was truly a work of art, and I simply kept my hand in the air until the bidding stopped. The following day it went into my rod tube as we departed from Nashville straight to a fly-fishing assignment in Venezuela. I inadvertently neglected to declare any "wildlife parts" on our return trip, and the feather fletches drew a few disapproving clucks from the customs inspector in Miami. But the arrow eventually reached our Montana home safe and sound, at which point I had to decide what to do with it.

At first it simply rested on the mantle over our fireplace along with a collection of bear and cougar skulls and mementos from decades of travel in the outdoors: a KGB hip flask from Russia, a knapped obsidian knife blade, boar tusks from around the world, porcupine quills from Africa, sting ray barbs from the South Pacific, primitive arrows from Brazil, and a long list of similar treasures too lengthy to catalog here. But the longer I looked at that arrow, the more I realized that art of this sort becomes doubly meaningful when it serves a function. This arrow was meant to kill a deer.

STERLING'S ARROW

Sterling's lovely- and lethal- stone point.

As regular readers know, although I'm a devoted traditional bowhunter, I'm not a primitive bowhunter. While I have great respect for those who have chosen to take bowhunting to this highest level of challenge, I've always found killing big game with my standard traditional tackle challenging enough. I'd never killed anything with a primitive arrow, at least not since I whittled sticks to shoot at rabbits and frogs back when I was a kid. Now Sterling's arrow sat there, practically daring me to turn craftsmanship into venison.

By November I'd put enough meat in the freezer to satisfy most of our family's voracious annual needs, and I began to pack the cane arrow around in my quiver waiting for an ideal opportunity to drive it through a deer. I was afraid to shoot the arrow at anything in practice for fear of damaging it, and as always, my principal concern was for the animal and the cleanliness of the kill, if there was one. Another reason for waiting until the end of the season to put my plan into effect was that I wanted good tracking snow on the ground in case of a marginal hit. Experienced primitive bowhunters may well laugh at the timidity of my approach, but please remember that I had no experience at all with stone points.

During the last week of the season, I passed up several shot opportunities I would have taken with my usual tackle. I wanted everything to be perfect: a totally relaxed deer at 15 yards or under, perfectly broadside to minimally quartering away. It's not that I didn't trust the arrow. This was an experiment of sorts for me, and as a scientist I understood the importance of eliminating as many unnecessary variables as possible.

Finally, I faced the opportunity I needed when a doe browsed past me on the last weekend of the season. (I could describe her as a "large, fat doe", but such descriptions have become a cliché. How often do you hear a writer describe killing a "scrawny, old doe"?) As she paused at 12 yards and turned ever so slightly away, I carefully picked a spot, drew back, and released. As the arrow flew out of my longbow like a laser and centered the clump of burrs on her side that I'd focused upon, I concentrated on absorbing every detail of the few crucial seconds that follow a hit.

I never cease to be amazed by the speed with which a motivated whitetail can move and the amount of ground one can cover even when it's dead on its feet, especially when it's traveling downhill. Once the woods grew silent again, I closed my eyes and replayed what I'd seen and heard: fletchings and half the shaft protruding from the exact spot I'd asked them to go, one tumble by the deer just before it reached a little patch of dog hair pine that cost me visual contact, and finally the sound of the animal impacting against our north-south border fence with the force of a runaway car—all favorable signs. Although I felt perfectly confident of the hit, I walked back up to the house to give the trail an hour and enlist some help from Lori.

The wait, if not Lori's assistance, proved unnecessary. The deer had left a blood trail that Ray Charles could have followed, not that I needed it in the newly fallen snow. Any concerns I might have had about penetration evaporated as the trail revealed blood blown out several feet on either side of the deer's bounding track. And there she lay, just beyond the fence as dead as a proverbial mackerel. The autopsy conducted as I field dressed the deer confirmed complete penetration of the chest cavity, by way of both lungs. I may not have needed my wife's tracking skills on this trail, but I certainly appreciated her presence as we set our legs against the hill to drag the deer up to the barn.

What to make of all this now? First, although this will hardly come as a surprise to readers familiar with the subject, events confirmed for me that a primitive arrow and stone head can absolutely kill an animal as surely as standard traditional tackle, and likely even more surely than some of the pathetic lightweight darts tipped with mechanical heads that fly from a lot of compounds nowadays.

Am I ready to convert to primitive tackle for all my hunting needs next season? No, I'm not, for a variety of reasons. Making your own tackle is the essence of the primitive experience, and I lack the necessary skills to do that now, although I've certainly had my interest in developing them aroused. The gratifying result I enjoyed was the result of a perfect hit on a thin-boned species at close range, circumstances that may not apply to many of the situations I encounter during a typical season.

Does that mean I've killed my last big game animal with a primitive arrow and head? Absolutely not. I found the entire experience enthralling, and Sterling's arrow turned an ordinary encounter with an antlerless deer into something memorable, perhaps the most important lesson of all. Each of us sets the bar at different levels in the degree of challenge we're willing to face in the field, and the number of such levels is nearly infinite. That's what keeps bowhunting such an intriguing activity, and why so many of us regard it not as a sport but a way of life.

Sterling's Arrow: The Recipe
Main shaft: Giant cane (*Arundiaria gigantea*)
Fore-shaft insert: Yaupon holly (*Ilex vomitaria*)

Glue: Pine resin mixed with charcoal
Wrapping: Chewed deer sinew
Fletches: Turkey and goose quills
Point: Knapped chert

Nobel Prize Ceremony, 1990.
The country boy from rural Texas meets the King of Sweden.

36.
Did I Ever Tell You About the Time...?

In the August 2008 issue of *Gray's Sporting Journal*, editor Jim Babb, writing about the death of Editor-in-Chief David Foster, identified two American traditions that Yankees have never mastered: gravy and funerals. No argument there, but I would like to add a third: storytelling.

Certainly not all great American writers have been southerners, but there is a difference between writing and storytelling. The latter should feel as if it is being spoken in a familiar and informal setting, even when it is unfolding from the printed page. Of course, the best can combine these forms seamlessly. William Faulkner's *The Bear* is one of the English language's great novellas, but, in substance at least, it could have been told around a wood stove in a Mississippi hunting cabin (after trimming a few two-page sentences).

I learned about storytelling at an early age, from my father. Like my mother, he had deep roots in rural Texas, where he grew up dirt poor during the Depression. My grandfather's status as a physician—one of the last from the horse-and-buggy era—had little impact on the poverty. While those were hard times, to hear him tell it later his childhood came right out of *Tom Sawyer* but with a much broader grounding in the outdoors. Hard times always look softer in retrospect.

Those stories unfolded at a time when I was even younger than my father was when many of the events he described took place. I heard most of them while sitting in a darkened living room in rural upstate New York. A fire, fueled by wood we'd cut ourselves, was usually crackling in the fireplace, and the flames added to the ambience of each story. Almost all those adventures involved the company of my father's best childhood friend, John Sanderson. Thus, I became familiar with one of the most personally compelling opening lines I know this side of *A Tale of Two Cities* or *Moby Dick*: "Did I ever tell you about the time John Sanderson and I...?" And so began the familiar process of enchantment one bitter December evening after I had returned from running my trap line, cold and tired but not quite tired enough to go to bed.

"Did I ever tell you about the time John Sanderson and I got scared?"

He had not. The possibility that something could scare either John Sanderson or my father, let alone both of them at once, seemed terrifying.

"Well, we were camped out one night down on the bank of the Brazos River. It was summertime, and we didn't have to worry about school. We were after catfish, and we'd set out several trotlines. You know what a trotline is?"

By then I did in theory thanks to his stories, although the local brook trout had given me no opportunity to exercise this knowledge in practice.

"It was clear and still that night, so quiet you could hear a pin drop. I had Drive with me that night, leashed up to a tree. You remember Drive?"

I certainly did. Drive was a redbone that had apparently treed most of the possums and coons in that part of Texas. Not only did I know Drive then; I never forgot him. That's what I named the first hound I ever raised and trained, even though he was a blue tick. He was still one of the two best hounds I've ever had, although I doubt I could make that case as convincingly as my father did for the original.

My father knew full well that I remembered Drive, just as he knew about my knowledge of trotlines. Only later did I recognize the wisdom of his technique. He never missed an opportunity to involve the listener directly in the storytelling process, even if the primary purpose of those questions was to confirm that the listener had not fallen asleep.

"Well, there we were, Drive and John Sanderson and I, just waiting another hour or two until it was time to light the lantern and check those trotlines." He paused. I sat forward and studied the fireplace, where the flames had grown ominous. The pause continued.

"Suddenly," he began in a voice loud enough to make me jump, "the loudest *bang* either of us ever heard shook the ground. It sounded like a huge bum had just exploded!"

That's not a typo. Thanks to some colloquialism I've never heard from another source, my father always pronounced the word "bomb" as "bum", even when we were discussing "H-bums" during the Cuban missile crisis.

"What did you do?" I asked after another period of silence. Sometimes the pauses in those stories were more effective than the words.

"Why, I untied Drive and the three of us ran back home through the dark as fast as we could. We didn't find out what really happened until the next morning."

"What *did* really happen?" I finally asked after I realized I wasn't going to find out until I did.

"Turns out a gas line had blown up over 20 miles away. A couple of houses burned down, and windows were knocked out over half the county."

"Were there any catfish on the lines when you went back to check them?"

"Yes, there were," he replied with a smile I could barely see by the firelight. And that was enough to let me go to sleep.

"Did I ever tell you about the time John Sanderson and I cheated each other?" my father asked. There was no fire burning then, for it was the night before the July opening of bass season, and I was too excited to go to bed. My father, as usual, knew the cure for my insomnia.

"Why would you do that?"

"Listen and I'll tell you," he replied as he packed his pipe and lit it, another deliberate means of letting anticipation build although I didn't recognize it at the time. "I'd worked hard all summer, chopping cotton for a dollar a day." I heard a lot about chopping cotton for a dollar a day when I was growing up. "That was because I had my eye on a brand new .22 down at the local hardware store."

"What kind was it?"

"I can't even tell you the make and model now. But it had a five-shot magazine, and that was a big step up from John Sanderson's little single-shot that we always took when we went hunting with Drive and John's dog."

"Did you buy it?"

"I sure did, and boy was I proud of that rifle. But after I'd had it for a couple of months, I noticed something odd. I just couldn't shoot it as accurately as I could shoot John's single-shot. And by the way, you know all about that gun of John's."

"I do?"

"You bet you do. It's that Winchester down in the gun cabinet, the one you used to shoot your first squirrel. Here's what happened. John really thought my new rifle was the ticket. Meanwhile, I'd figured out that his single shot was an unusually accurate .22. One day John told me that he'd love to buy my rifle from me, but he didn't have any money. So, I made him a proposition."

"What's a proposition?"

"Be quiet and I'll tell you." Suddenly the pipe needed attention. I waited patiently. "Well, I told John that if he'd give me his .22, I'd give him mine. Straight up."

"What does that mean?"

"It means neither of us gave the other any money. We just swapped guns. Now, John was sure he'd cheated me, since my new rifle was probably worth a lot more than his single shot. And I thought I'd cheated him, because I knew his single shot was a more accurate rifle. As it turns out we were both right, which means no one really cheated anyone although we both thought we did. That way, we got to stay friends."

I can attest to half of his assessment of the firearms involved in the trade. While I have no knowledge of the rifle he bought new, the Winchester Model 67 remains in the family. All my kids learned to shoot with it. And iron sights and all, it is still the most accurate .22 I've ever handled.

I do not remember if we caught any bass the following morning, but I never forgot the story of how that .22 began its journey to my own gun cabinet. That tale also taught me an important lesson in economics: a successful transaction is one that leaves each party confident he has snookered the other.

"Did I ever tell you about the time John Sanderson and I went hunting and I made the best shot I've ever made?" Winter had come again, and both the fireplace and I were begging for a story. I sometimes lied—fooling no one—in response to that formulaic opening question, but this time my denial was genuine. By then I had started to tag along after my father through the grouse cover and appreciate the respect other seasoned hunters granted his shooting ability. His best shot ever? This had to be good.

The best wing-shot Don has ever seen.

"What did you shoot?" I asked eagerly "A big deer?"

My father shook his head wistfully and reached for his pipe. "It's hard to believe now, but there weren't any deer in that country back then. All the ground was planted in cotton, and cotton fields aren't good places for deer to live."

"What did you shoot then?"

"If someone wouldn't interrupt so much, I might be able to tell the story." The censure failed to sting. It was always easy to tell when my father was joking and when he meant business. "We were walking home from the river one day, without the dogs. John was carrying his new .22 and I had my single shot, the one you've been using to hunt squirrels." According to the State of New York I was too young to be hunting anything then, but after an uncompromised grounding in the principles of firearm safety I had received a green light on the bushy-tails inhabiting our rural property. The ruffed grouse and the 12-gauge followed shortly thereafter.

"Did I ever tell you how I got that .22 from John?"

"You did." Under different circumstances I might have denied it just for the pleasure of listening to the story again, but I really wanted to hear about that great shot.

"Well, we came up across a rise overlooking a little tank and saw that a flock of doves had flown down the bank to drink."

"How can a tank have a bank?"

"This wasn't a tank like the one we use to water the horses. Where I grew up, little ponds and reservoirs were called tanks."

"So, the muskrat pond at the bottom of the hill would be a tank?"

"Not really. Sometime I'll explain the difference." The pipe began to receive a lot of attention, a gesture that I recognized as a signal to be quiet and let the story unfold.

"Now John and I considered ourselves pretty good shots," my father went on after an appropriate disciplinary delay. "So, we figured we'd sneak down this little ditch, come up over the top, and pick off a couple of doves with our .22s before they flew."

"Are doves good to eat?" New York didn't have a dove season, so doves were an unfamiliar and exotic species to me.

"There's not much to them, but they're delicious." My father was glad to tolerate another interruption to establish this important point. "When we got to the end of the ditch," he continued, "we spread out a few yards apart and eased through the last of the brush. We were trying to time it so that we both got to shoot at sitting birds. But John squeezed off a shot just as I was getting ready, and the next thing I knew there was one dove dead on the bank and the rest of them were flying off over the water."

"What did you do?"

"I must have been pretty proud of my shooting, because I picked out a bird on the edge of the flock and shot at it while it was flying. And you know what? It fell stone dead out in the middle of the tank." I didn't fully appreciate the magnitude of this accomplishment at the time, but I sure did after I spent a season carrying a shotgun through the grouse cover. I could still feel the lingering disbelief in my father's voice, and that was enough to leave me impressed.

"How did you get it if you didn't have a dog?"

"Drive wouldn't have been much use anyway. He was a hound, not a retriever like Bits. So, I had to strip down to nothing and swim out to get it."

"That must have been cold!"

"Not really, not in Texas at that time of year. But there were a lot of snapping turtles in that tank, so I was worried about my toes."

"Would a snapping turtle bite off your toes?"

"You bet he would." The muskrat pond at the bottom of our hill held plenty of little painted turtles, which I caught by hand with impunity. But I never saw a real snapping turtle until the following summer, when a friend and I were fishing for bass in the Susquehanna River and a big one swam by under our canoe. The turtle, which must have weighed 30 pounds, looked like a prehistoric monster. I gave a warning shout and we picked up our paddles. We didn't stop going for nearly a mile, and I never swam in the river again.

"Did I ever tell you about my first horse?" my father asked one night when he had come home from the hospital in an unusually subdued mood. The absence of John Sanderson's name in the introduction should have alerted me to the possibility of something out of the ordinary ahead. We had horses then and my father was an accomplished rider, in a small-town Texas weekend rodeo style far removed from the English saddles that were standard with the local horsey set where I grew up. Oddly, he had never spoken much about the horses in his childhood before.

"Well," he went on after my denial, "everyone in the county was poor then, and my father—your grandfather—delivered a baby for the wife of a farmer who didn't have any money. It was a hard delivery, and he had to use forceps to get the baby out."

"What are those?" I asked. In the second grade, my knowledge of anatomy, especially female anatomy, was severely limited.

"I'll draw you a picture sometime. I remember it because I made the house call with him, and dripped ether onto a piece of gauze across the lady's face while your grandfather delivered that baby." He paused and studied his pipe. "My God," he mused. "Ether anesthesia administered by a kid in a farmhouse lit by kerosene lanterns." Years passed before I fully appreciated the hazards of the situation he described.

"Then one day that farmer came riding over with a young roan gelding ponied up behind him and told your grandfather thanks for saving his wife and their baby. Your grandfather told me that horse was mine. I named him after my favorite singer." He paused, inviting a guess.

"Elvis?" I finally asked.

"This all happened long before Elvis was born. I named him Bing."

The name meant nothing to me. My father's explanation took some time and included some whistling. The rest of the story went on longer than usual as he described breaking Bing to saddle and riding him behind Drive. He took his time reloading his pipe, once and then again. I'd never heard a three-pipe story before. I finally realized that he was telling this story to himself as much as to me.

"Then one day I came home from school and noticed that Bing was unsteady on his feet. He always came running up to me when I went out to the corral, but this time he acted as if he couldn't see me. When your grandfather came home, I asked him to look at Bing. When he came back to the house, he asked me to sit down at the kitchen table. Then he told me that my horse had the blind staggers."

"What's that?"

"No one really knew back then and I'm not sure they do now."

"Is it bad?"

"It's fatal."

"Always?"

"Always."

"What did you do?"

"My father—your grandfather—went upstairs and came back carrying his pistol, the same old Colt .32-20 that's locked up in the gun cabinet. Then he handed it to me."

The end. Well. When I read J. D. Salinger's great short story *The Laughing Man* years later, I began to experience an eerie sense of déjà vu midway through the piece. By the end I recognized its origin. Salinger explained the motivation behind his character's morbid tale to his young charges clearly enough, but years passed before I understood my father's. The day he told me that story, the country's first bone marrow transplant recipient had died on his service at the hospital.

I'm not sure when I heard the last of those classic stories about my father's Texas childhood. He and I always remained exceptionally close, shared many experiences in the outdoors, and told lots of stories to each other as well as to family and friends. Sadly, it was never quite the same once I grew too big—or too old—to curl up next to him on the couch and watch the flames dance in the fireplace while he talked. But long before we reached that point, I knew with certainty that I wanted to be three things when I grew up: a doctor, an outdoorsman, and a storyteller.

Just like my father.

End note. Don's father left Texas during the Second World War and began a medical career that eventually led to his pioneering work in the field of bone marrow transplantation, for which he received the Nobel Prize in Medicine in 1990. After his death in 2012, the many tributes and accolades that followed all left out one important detail. He was the best wing-shot Don has ever seen, and he's seen a lot of them.

About the Author

After growing up in the Pacific Northwest, Don Thomas completed his higher education in California, Montreal, and Washington, winding up as a board-certified internist. He spent his 40-year medical career in rural parts of Montana and Alaska, where he was also a pilot, commercial fisherman, and bear hunting guide.

Despite his background in medicine, he always wanted to write and began doing so professionally in the early 1980s. Following old advice to write about topics he both knew and cared about, he turned naturally to the outdoors for subject matter. Since then, he has written over 1600 features and columns for a wide variety of magazines including *Traditional Bowhunter, Bowhunter, Gray's Sporting Journal, Big Sky Journal, Alaska, Retriever Journal, Pointing Dog Journal, Just Labs, American Flyfishing, Strung, Tail, Sports Afield, Outdoor Life, Field and Stream, Fish Alaska, Ducks Unlimited, Pheasants Forever, Quail Forever, Western Hunting Journal, Fly Rod and Reel, Outside Bozeman, Saltwater Flyfishing* and others. His writing has won numerous awards including the Traver Award for Flyfishing Fiction (twice) and the Tom Shupenis and Glenn St. Charles awards from the Professional Bowhunters society. He was also the Co-Editor of *Traditional Bowhunter* for nearly 20 years.

Don has also written over 20 books on subjects including, in addition to bowhunting, flyfishing, wing-shooting, gun dogs, conservation, and natural history. His work has appeared in numerous anthologies. Working together, he and his wife Lori have also contributed numerous photo essays to the same magazines.

Don belongs to many organizations working for the benefit of hunting traditions, wildlife, and conservation. Never one to avoid speaking truth to power, he wrote the prestigious back page column for *Ducks Unlimited* for 15 years until he was fired for criticizing a wealthy donor who was attacking public access rights in Montana. He regards that episode as the highlight of his career.

Don and Lori now live in rural Montana, where they hope to avoid the rapid development taking place elsewhere in the state. Their four kids are grown and gone, but they still have their Labrador retrievers, German wirehair pointers, and one Jack Russell terrier.

Don has always written under the byline "E. Donnall Thomas Jr." in honor of his father, who won the 1990 Noble Prize in Medicine and was one of the most capable and ethical outdoorsmen Don ever met. He omits the "M.D." to which he is entitled because he has never met a game animal that cared.

About the Photographer

A fifth-generation Montanan who grew up in a hunting ranch family, Lori Thomas had no experience with bows, shotguns, or fly rods prior to her marriage to Don. She proved to be a fast learner and now engages in these activities just as enthusiastically and capably as her husband. She has taken half a dozen big game species with her traditional bow, hunted upland birds and waterfowl every fall, and fly-fished on four continents.

Although she had limited experience behind a camera at the time of their marriage, Don was still doing a lot of outdoor photography then, and Lori learned rapidly. While blessed with a keen eye and a meticulous attention to technique, her enthusiasm and perseverance are the keys to her success. If she must stand in the rain for hours to get the shot, she'll be there long after most photographers would have gone home to dry out. Although their photo credits go to both of them, Don's aging eyes now make it hard for him to manage the controls on a digital camera. While he still offers suggestions about shots, he admits that Lori does most of the actual shooting.

Lori graduated from high school in the same rural Montana community where she and Don now live. After obtaining her nursing degree from Montana State University, she enjoyed a challenging career as a smalltown hospital nurse which continued after her marriage. The decision to retire from medicine was hard for both of them.

Marriage to Don produced a mixed family, with Lori contributing Scott and Nicole and Don bringing along Nick and Genny, obligating them to raise four teenagers under one roof at the same time. All the kids went off to successful careers, and three have managed to return to Montana.

Wife and mother, skilled clinical nurse, all-around outdoorswoman, and capable photographer... Don considers himself a lucky man, because he is.